ERIC VOEGELIN

Twentieth-Century Political Thinkers
Series Editors: Kenneth L. Deutsch and Jean Bethke Elshtain

Raymond Aron: The Recovery of the Political
by Brian C. Anderson, American Enterprise Institute
Jacques Maritain: The Philosopher in Society
by James V. Schall, Georgetown University
Martin Buber: The Hidden Dialogue
by Dan Avnon, Hebrew University of Jerusalem
John Dewey: America's Philosopher of Democracy
by David Fott, University of Nevada
Simone Weil: The Way of Justice as Compassion
by Richard H. Bell, The College of Wooster
Gandhi: Struggling for Autonomy
by Ronald J. Terchek, University of Maryland at College Park
Paul Ricoeur: The Promise and Risk of Politics
by Bernard P. Dauenhauer, University of Georgia
Carl Schmitt: The End of Law
by William E. Scheuerman, University of Pittsburgh
Eric Voegelin: In Quest of Reality
by Thomas W. Heilke, University of Kansas

ERIC VOEGELIN

In Quest of Reality

THOMAS W. HEILKE

ROWMAN & LITTLEFIELD PUBLISHERS, INC.
Lanham • Boulder • New York • Oxford

ROWMAN & LITTLEFIELD PUBLISHERS, INC.

Published in the United States of America
by Rowman & Littlefield Publishers, Inc.
4720 Boston Way, Lanham, Maryland 20706

12 Hid's Copse Road
Cumnor Hill, Oxford OX2 9JJ, England

British Library Cataloguing in Publication Information Available

Library of Congress Cataloging-in-Publication Data
Heilke, Thomas W., 1960–
    Eric Voegelin : in quest of reality / Thomas W. Heilke.
        p.   cm. — (Twentieth-century political thinkers)
    Includes bibliographical references and index.
    ISBN 0-8476-9427-5 (alk. paper). — ISBN 0-8476-9428-3 (pbk. :
alk. paper)
    1. Voegelin, Eric, 1901–   . I. Title. II. Series.
B3354.V884H45   1999
193—dc21   99-19276
                                                            CIP

Printed in the United States of America

♾ ™ The paper used in this publication meets the minimum requirements of
American National Standard for Information Sciences—Permanence of Paper
for Printed Library Materials, ANSI/NISO Z39.48–1992.

For my father, Dietrich Heilke, who taught me the virtue of work well done one stroke at a time, and for my mother, Irma Heilke, who first introduced me to the important questions.

CONTENTS

ACKNOWLEDGMENTS

A volume of this kind can never be everything the author wants it to be: introductions to a corpus of writings from the hand of a prolific and complex philosopher must inevitably simplify, pare away, and leave out. Most especially, one is continually aware of a depth of inquiry and intensity of spirit in a profound thinker's work that can be indicated but not replicated. Accordingly, it is my hope that this slender volume will encourage its readers to return to Voegelin's own words, and beyond those, to the words of his deceased friends in antiquity and modernity with whom he remained in conversation throughout his long life of inquiry and reflection.

Versions of the chapters of this book have been delivered in a variety of settings, including conferences, study sessions, and research presentations. Writing the book was therefore accomplished with the aid of many colleagues, mentors, and friends to whom I owe a great debt of thanks for their encouragement and helpful comments. They include: Paul Carringella, Barry Cooper, Juergen Gebhardt, Gary Glenn, Manfred Henningsen, Thomas Holweck, Murray Jardine, James Old, John Pottenger, Ellis Sandoz, Ruth Shively, Clarence Sills, Peter von Sivers, and Stuart Warner. Their input substantially improved the final version; as always, its many faults remain my own doing. I also wish to thank the students who participated in several honors seminars where we read Voegelin and who alerted me to the pitfalls, traps, and puzzles that his writings pose for the novice reader. Their questions helped me to see again how unfamiliar to modern eyes the topography of Voegelin's concepts and their presentation really can be.

I want to thank the publishers of *The Review of Politics* for allowing me to reprint in somewhat altered form two articles: "Anamnetic Tales:

The Place of Narrative in Voegelin's Account of Consciousness," from *The Review of Politics* 58:4 (fall 1996), 761–92; and "Science, Philosophy, and Resistance: On Eric Voegelin's Practice of Opposition," from *The Review of Politics* 56:4 (fall 1994), 727–52.

Finally, I am especially grateful to Professor Kenneth Deutsch, who encouraged me to develop this introductory map to Voegelin's political thought. I am honored by his invitation to do so.

INTRODUCTION

Well, existence is not a fact.

Eric Voegelin, "The Gospel and Culture"

Recapturing reality in opposition to its contemporary deformation requires a considerable amount of work. One has to reconstruct the fundamental categories of existence, experience, consciousness, and reality. One has at the same time to explore the technique and structure of the deformations that clutter up the daily routine; and one has to develop the concepts by which existential deformation and its symbolic expression can be categorized. This work, then, must be conducted not only in opposition to the deformed ideologies but also to deformations of reality by thinkers who ought to be its preservers.

Eric Voegelin, *Autobiographical Reflections*

During a distinguished academic career, Eric Voegelin was described in numerous ways: as a philosopher of history, a philosopher of consciousness, a foremost political philosopher, and even a theologian. He has also been branded with nearly every ideological label available: fascist and communist, liberal and conservative, existentialist and fideist, socialist and reactionary, Jew, Catholic, and Protestant.[1] His writings have been lauded for the fresh new light they cast on the modern predicament, and they have been castigated for being obscure at best and opaque at worst.[2] The various appellations may all have some vague or even clear reference to fact, and praise and criticism alike of his writings may be deserved. Nevertheless, none of these labels or any other can apprehend the essence of his work: Eric Voegelin was a philosopher in quest of reality. No ideological category can grasp the core of such a quest.

A "quest" implies a journey. An argument embedded in this introduction to Voegelin's thought is that Voegelin's philosophical investigations were, in fact, a kind of journey. The metaphor is particularly apt in Voegelin's case, because it captures Voegelin's own philosophical development and offers a way of tying together the philosophically important turns in his life. The actual *content* of Voegelin's conception of philosophy, moreover, demands such an image. His course of intellectual development is matched in form by his final theory of participating consciousness. If the philosopher's life is a road, we may be inclined to dissect the journey into any number of "topics" that we wish; but to do so would be ultimately to convert the results of a philosophical investigation into a set of doctrines and dogmas. This was an outcome that Voegelin adamantly avoided, because to make such a conversion is to miss seeing the results of a philosophical inquiry as the outcome of an individual participating consciousness in the whole. A lifetime of philosophical investigations leads not to dogma but to a set of principles and statements about the nature of the reality in which and about which the investigations have taken place. Some of the results from the considerable expanse of Voegelin's work are the focus of the present volume.

Several fine introductions to the political thought of Eric Voegelin now exist, and others are in preparation. Taking the fact of that increasing body of secondary literature into account, the present study moves along a different track from much of the introductory work available. It is for that reason both more and less than a general introduction. It is less, because it does not pretend to treat in detail or even in broad strokes the entire expanse of Voegelin's thought; such an effort seems increasingly unsatisfactory to me. It is more, because it takes a somewhat unconventional approach to his corpus: it assembles the treatments of several key problems and episodes in Voegelin's lifework that together frame a picture of his thought as a whole. These are not random topics, however. This study focuses on several themes that can be readily identified as central to Voegelin's thought: the theory of consciousness, the character of political philosophy, the nature of ideology, and the nature of Christianity and its relationship to the political sphere. Accordingly, this introduction to Voegelin's work is by no means exhaustive, but it does seek to provide a window with a full view on Voegelin's thought. Perhaps, in the words of a foremost commentator on Voegelin's work, it may be best thought of as a "probe."[3]

If the notion of a philosophical journey is an apt depiction of Voegelin's life-course, then his political thought is best made intelligible in the context of that course. I begin, therefore, by providing a short biography of Voegelin and an account of the course of his intellectual life. In the light of the burgeoning literature concerned with Voegelin's thought, and with a view to resisting the temptation of reinventing what has already been done, I then offer a review of some of the more prominent introductions to his thought that have become available in the past fifteen years or so. This brief glance at the interpretive literature helps more clearly to situate the present work and the significance of its topic—the political thought of Eric Voegelin. First, then, I turn to a brief overview of Voegelin's life and career.

VOEGELIN'S BIOGRAPHY AND COURSE OF INTELLECTUAL LIFE

Eric Voegelin was born in Cologne, Germany, on January 3, 1901. His father, a civil engineer, moved the family first to Königswinter, also in the Rhineland, and then to Vienna in 1910. There, Voegelin attended a gymnasium and the University of Vienna, where he obtained his doctorate in political science in 1922. Voegelin was by all accounts a brilliant student. He mastered several languages during his years in the gymnasium, where he also received a strong training in mathematics and sciences. Owing to his constrained financial circumstances, and because he did not foresee a career in the civil service, he elected to pursue a doctorate in political science, which required three years for completion, rather than a doctoral degree in law, which required four. His political science training, however, had a heavy legal emphasis: his most important instructor was Hans Kelsen, the leading scholar of legal positivism at the time and the author of the 1920 Austrian constitution.

Voegelin's first publications, beginning at age 22, were on a variety of topics in sociology, philosophy, and legal theory. He and his large circle of friends participated in the intellectual life of a city that was, as Gregor Sebba describes it, a quixotic central European cultural hub:

Vienna in the 1930s was the enormous head of a tiny, mangled country, which did not want to live and was not allowed to die. Impotent
and hypersensitive, Vienna reacted like a seismograph to every political or economic tremor abroad. This shabby, sardonically cheerful city
was an invigorating cultural center of the first order, teeming with
talent, ideas, experiments, hospitable to every kind of intellectual ven-
ture from the stiffly orthodox to the wayward. In 1930–31 I found it
still possible to bring together scholars and politically engaged people
of every persuasion for informal debate on the burning current issues,
probably the last group where Liberal and Marxist, Jew and antisem-
ite, Socialist and Monarchist sat down together until the civil war
ended all that in 1934.[4]

In his circle of friends and interlocutors of the time, Voegelin appears to
have made a strong impression:

Among the scholars, Voegelin had a reputation for fiendish erudition
and for his ability to take off vertically from any question whatever
and to disappear within minutes in the theoretical ionosphere, leaving
only a trail of recondite references behind, a slim young man with
blond hair and sharp eyes behind his glasses, his Pascalian nose jutting
out in a metaphysical curve.[5]

In 1924, Voegelin received a three-year Laura Spellman Rockefeller
Fellowship, which enabled him to spend two years in the United States
and a third in Paris. His abilities had attracted attention, which led to his
nomination for this award. While in the United States, Voegelin attended lectures for a year at Columbia University in New York, and
spent a semester each at Harvard and at the University of Wisconsin. He
also traveled extensively, crossing the entire country from east to west
and north to south during one particularly intense six-week trip.[6] The
two-year stay in America, which led to his first published book in 1928
(*On the Form of the American Mind*), had a profound, lifelong effect on
the shape of his philosophical inquiries. It dispelled for him the parochialism of the central European intellectual, and with it, the general sorts
of parochialism to which learned and unlearned people alike are susceptible. Central European parochialism consisted not only in a cultural
snobbishness against all things American, but also in the notion that specific kinds of philosophical (neo-Kantian) debates about epistemology

and methodology raging in central Europe at the time were the only debates worthy of scholarly attention, and, indeed, that there could be no other set of philosophical problems:[7]

> In brief, there was a world in which this other world in which I had grown up was intellectually, morally, and spiritually irrelevant. That there could be such a plurality of worlds had a devastating effect on me. The experience broke for good (at least I hope it did) my Central European or generally European provincialism without letting me fall into an American provincialism. I gained an understanding in these years of the plurality of human possibilities realized in various civilizations, as an immediate experience. . . . The immediate effect was that upon my return to Europe certain phenomena that were of greatest importance in the intellectual and ideological context of Central Europe . . . no longer had any effect on me. . . . The priorities and relations of importance between various theories had been fundamentally changed, and so far as I can see changed for the better.[8]

On his return to Vienna in 1927, he continued with the academic work that would earn him an appointment at the university. In 1929, he was appointed Privatdozent; he was also an assistant to Hans Kelsen, and he continued to support himself with tutoring and journalism. In 1933, he published a pair of books that analyzed European racism historically and from the perspective of a comprehensive science of man. The arguments in these two books made him a target of the National Socialists; when Germany annexed Austria in 1938, Voegelin was forced to flee for his life. A series of sometimes comical and usually risky adventures, in much the same vein as experienced by other refugees and declared enemies of totalitarian regimes in those years, led to his and his wife's arrival in Cambridge, Massachusetts, in the fall of 1938, where he had been offered a limited-term instructorship at Harvard University.

The first trip to America had been one kind of turning point in Voegelin's life; emigration was another. It was followed by the next intellectual turning point, which was a somewhat more gradual one, lasting through the late 1940s. In February 1939, only a semester after his arrival in the United States, Voegelin contracted with the McGraw-Hill Book Company to write an introductory college textbook in political theory, to be entitled "A History of Political Ideas." The agreement foresaw a manuscript of about two hundred pages, to be delivered to the publisher sometime the following year. Two years later, however, the undelivered manuscript had grown much larger than anticipated, and in 1944 Voegelin reported that his "History" was now a three-volume work. The textbook had become a treatise. A series of editorial decisions as well as the gradual development of Voegelin's thinking on the subject matter of the work led to the eventual publication, not of a "History of Political Ideas," but, in ever-revised form, of *Order and History*, in first three, then four, and eventually five volumes, beginning in 1956 and 1957 with the first three volumes, the fourth appearing in 1974, and the final one appearing posthumously in 1987.

The shift in Voegelin's thinking developed in the 1940s as he was coming to the conclusion that the "History" as he had originally framed it was epistemologically and methodologically untenable. This shift may be indicated by placing beside one another two descriptions of what a "History of Political Ideas" must be. The first is a summary by Hollweck and Sandoz of the 1940 holograph of an Introduction to the "History":

> The focus of this text is on the reality of the "idea" in the formation of political societies. The question posed is whether political societies represent a truth that legitimizes their existence or whether the political is ultimately little more than an imaginative construct that has no ontological foundation.[9]

Second, we have Voegelin's own reflections on his gradual reworking of the notion of a political idea:

> Ideas turned out to be a secondary conceptual development, beginning with the Stoics, intensified in the high Middle Ages, and radically unfolding since the eighteenth century. Ideas transform symbols, which express experiences, into concepts—which are assumed to refer to a reality other than the reality experienced. And this reality other than the reality experienced does not exist. Hence, ideas are liable to deform the truth of the experiences and their symbolization.[10]

So-called "ideas" are the concretized instances of the symbols of order that arise, in turn, out of the immediate experiences of order that men and women have. They use the symbols of order to represent to themselves their experiences and to give meaning to their history. Ideas can be made objects of inquiry in and of themselves, but this is to deform their actual nature as the symbols of lived experiences by means of which human beings express their experience of order, and which they "use" to fashion civilizational order in accordance with those experiences and the symbolizations of them. Consequently, "To set up a government is an essay in world creation," and the "political cosmion" that is created "provides a structure of meaning into which the single human being can fit the results of the biologically and spiritually productive, procreative energies of his personal life, thereby [relieving] his life from the [disordering] aspects of existence that always spring up when the possibility of the utter senselessness of a life ending in annihilation is envisaged."[11] This formulation (written in 1940) was an important breakthrough in the science of politics as Voegelin realized the importance of moving away from the concept of an idea to the concept of a symbol.

He first articulated this move publicly in the Walgreen Lectures in 1951 at the University of Chicago. The text of these lectures was subsequently published as *The New Science of Politics* in 1952, which borrowed materials from the larger project and refined it theoretically.[12] This reformulation, along with Voegelin's growing realization that the materials he had to work through were both massive and historically interconnected, made it clear that a two-hundred-page "introduction" to a history of political ideas, especially one that would be accessible to the average college student, was implausible.[13] The project was not merely reworked into the new *Order and History*, however. Along with these volumes, significant portions of the "History" appeared as separate articles, and John Hallowell edited and published a substantial portion of the later sections under the title *From Enlightenment to Revolution*.[14]

After a short period as an itinerant scholar with postings at Harvard, Bennington College, and the University of Alabama, Voegelin received an appointment as associate professor of political science at the Louisiana State University in 1942. He was eventually named Boyd Professor of Political Science there, but when an invitation came to return to Germany and establish an Institute of Political Science in Munich, he could not resist, leaving in 1958. Voegelin considered his years in Munich "a considerable success," but not without some ambivalence. The library of the institute "became famous and was extensively used by young scholars from other fields because it was the best all-around library for developments in the contemporary sciences of man and society." The students "also did well," publishing a considerable series of monographs that Voegelin praised highly.[15] On the other hand, it remained Voegelin's judgment that the devastation visited upon the German academy by the National Socialists, and by the intellectual corruption that had preceded them, remained widespread and thorough, so that the students of his institute in Munich represented an unfortunately unusual element in the German academy and in German society.[16] During his years in Munich, Voegelin kept up his vigorous scholarly activities. *Anamnesis: Zur Theorie der Geschichte und Politik* appeared in 1966, and the fourth volume of *Order and History* in 1974. Continuing his usual practice, he also published a steady stream of scholarly essays and regularly delivered lectures beyond his teaching obligations.

In 1969, he and his wife Elizabeth ("Lissy") returned to the United States, where he had been named Henry Salvatori Distinguished Scholar at the Hoover Institution on War, Revolution, and Peace at Stanford University. One might have visions of a quiet retirement, but the publications dating from his years at the Institution belie any intimations of a restful withdrawal from the rigors of an active academic life. Voegelin continued his inquiries; indeed, one of his students considers the writings from this period to be among his "finest and most profound."[17] Perhaps the most unusual quality of these writings is the ongoing development and refinement of premises, theories, and insights that continued even during this late period in his life. Eric Voegelin passed away at age 84 on January 19, 1985.

"Neither philosophy nor reality can be reduced to a system." Philosophy is an ongoing quest for understanding about a reality that is always much more than merely an object of scrutiny. Voegelin developed his insights into the structure and dynamics of this quest over a lifetime of philosophical inquiry. A short biography cannot hope to capture the complexities of this inquiry; indeed, an extended introduction to Voegelin's thought can itself only touch on some pieces and aspects. As I turn to a brief review of some of the most important interpretations of Voegelin's thought, I remind myself that "Voegelin's philosophical vision of history and comprehensive reality" was a vision of "an unfinished tale, one told by God in the reflective language of spiritually gifted men and women open to the mystery of truth [made] emergent by [the] divine-human encounter in the In-Between of participatory existence, [which is] human reality par excellence."[18]

MULTIPLE VOEGELINS?

Voegelin the "Revolutionary"

The first major review of Voegelin's work was Ellis Sandoz's *The Voegelinian Revolution: A Biographical Interpretation*, published in 1981. Professor Sandoz is a noted political theorist in his own right, and he was one of a small number of American graduate students at the Institute for Political Science that Voegelin established in Munich. Sandoz's book meets both criteria of its title: it argues "that Voegelin's thought constitutes a revolution in philosophy and political science," and it makes this argument through extensive use of biographical narratives and autobiographical accounts.[19]

But what is revolutionary about Voegelin's thought? According to Professor Sandoz, three features of Voegelin's work give it this character. First, insofar as there can be a comprehensive "science of man," Voegelin's work "effects a radical break with dominant contemporary schools of thought and philosophical movements." This break is on a qualitative level with "the revolutions of Copernicus and Newton in mathematical astronomy, cosmology, and physics." Second, Voegelin's work makes it clear that there can, in fact, be not merely a new science of politics, but a comprehensive science of man, a noetic science. Finally, Voegelin's break with contemporary ways of interpreting human existence and human experience constitutes a radical criticism of current systems of thought in which the "Truth to end the quest for truth in the mysterious process of reality is found or proclaimed," and in which we find expounded a "System to end all systems." It is the second of these three revolutionary characteristics that particularly attracts Sandoz's attention.[20]

Noetic science is a study of human phenomena that rejects the "sciences of the external world as the model of the science of man," proffering instead a "science in a new mode." At the center of this new science

> lies the Question, not as an arbitrary alternative, but as the existentially grounded symbols engendered by the Mystery of Reality and empirically evidenced by every great exploration of the In-Between of reality from prehistorical times into the present. There is no final answer to the Question, other than the Mystery whose meaning becomes more luminous through the process of questioning itself. And the lu-

minosity of the Mystery and depth of its mysteriousness are enhanced
by the process of questioning.[21]

The activity of questioning leads both to a set of "principles of discovery" and a set of results. These "results" include on the one hand a set
of "cautions" about the way in which we should use language to characterize our discoveries and about the nature of the discoveries themselves;
on the other hand they also include a set of methodological, logical,
epistemological, and ontological principles that arise out of the act(s) of
philosophizing.[22] The most important categories of results include an
analysis of the experiences of participation; an examination of the activities of differentiating the components of that participation in the reality
of which we are a part; an analysis of the ways in which experience in
reality is symbolized across cultures, thinkers, and time; and, finally,
Voegelin's rediscovery of reason as "the principle of existence in the
mode of truth" in antiquity and as "*the* principle of science" in any noetic investigation of reality.

Voegelin, then, is not the sort of revolutionary who seeks in a radical way to transform the world into his own image. He is, rather, a revolutionary concerning the science of man: through his "vision of the
whole," he recovers what has been lost to view in modernity, and he
radically critiques that modernity as it is manifested in contemporary culture, politics, and thought. His revolutionary qualities appear both in his
recovery and further development of an ancient mode of inquiry and in
his critique of the contemporary situation based on the inquiry that he
develops.

Voegelin the Philosopher of History

Eugene Webb's study of Voegelin's thought was published in the
same year as that of Sandoz. Webb's approach is more thematic: his focus
is on the unique contributions Voegelin has made to the philosophy of
history. The topic allows a wider window on Voegelin's work than one
might at first anticipate. After all, Voegelin's major works, including the
five-volume *Order and History*, the discarded multivolume *History of Political Ideas*, and several other works are all avowedly historical studies. A
philosophy of history is not for Voegelin an abstruse technical philosoph-

ical topic, nor is the study of historical phenomena a task of dusty archae-
ological excavation in the way that Nietzsche made it out to be. Rather,

> for Voegelin the philosophy of history is the analysis of human life in
> its historical dimension, that is, of human life as a process in which
> choices are made and in which, through the values that are served or
> not served, one may or may not live up to the calling of one's poten-
> tial humanity. History is an enterprise, in other words, in which one
> may succeed or fail, and what the philosophy of history must offer is
> criteria by which that success or failure may be measured.
>   These criteria can be found, Voegelin believes, by the study of
> man and his history.[23]

To uncover the contours of Voegelin's philosophy of history, Webb es-
tablishes a pattern of analysis and presentation that, in its rough outlines,
will become a familiar one in later studies of Voegelin's work. He proceeds to "render explicit the theoretical framework of Voegelin's
thought and then to show his interpretive application of it to the historical data on which it is based."[24]

The components of this theoretical framework include a theory of
consciousness, a theory of experience and symbolization, a theory of experiential knowledge, and a philosophical anthropology. They also include an account of how reality is discovered and how it can be lost. The
presence and absence of reality in the psyche of a particular individual is
expressed in a key symbol in Voegelin's philosophy of history, namely,
the idea of "balance" in the tension of existence:

> Most who begin to reflect on the meaning of history show compara-
> tively little direct awareness of the [experiential tension of existence],
> but tend to objectify its dynamism in an immanentist manner as a
> force moving mankind toward some form of mundane fulfillment.
> The central problem of the philosophy of history is to maintain a sense
> of balance between the transcendental and immanent dimensions of
> man and his life in time. When this balance is lost sight of, then one
> may fail to take seriously the fact that man is essentially incarnate,
> treating him as though he were really a spirit waiting for delivery from
> his fleshly prison so that he may return to his true home in a hyposta-
> tized Beyond. Or one may treat man as though he were an entirely
> natural entity devoid of spirit and essential freedom and governed by

laws that need only be discovered and mastered for an enlightened planner to be able to manipulate him effectively for his own good and for that of society—as defined, of course, by the manipulator.[25]

Webb's intent is to "set forth and explain Voegelin's theoretical principles and to show, at least briefly, how he applies them to the study of historical phenomena." Webb argues that Voegelin develops a theory of man, which he "works out and illustrates with a wealth of historical references," and that, for Voegelin, every theory of history must be founded on such a theory of man, and every properly constituted theory of this type must take into account the full amplitude of human experience. Most especially, it must take into account the fact that human beings are constituted in their humanity by their love of the transcendent.[26] Only with reference to the divine, transcendent pole of existence can a properly formed theory of man, of knowledge, of experience, and of symbolization be articulated. Only with the same reference, therefore, can one develop a properly formed theory of history.

Voegelin the Counter-Ideological Therapist

Professors Sandoz and Webb were the first to write book-length studies of Voegelin's work. Sandoz offered a comprehensive, semibiographical review of the major components of Voegelin's lifework and thought, whereas Webb gave a comprehensive account of Voegelin's work with a view to showing how Voegelin's theories could be applied to the study of historical phenomena. Many of the examinations of Voegelin's thought that came after those of Sandoz and Webb take as their guiding theme some central component of his political thought or his more general philosophy of man. Accordingly, they tend in various ways to cover ground already furrowed by Sandoz and Webb, with greater or lesser success in clarity and comprehensiveness. One notes, however, the frequent reappearance of particular themes and treatments in this secondary literature.

Thus, both Michael Franz and David Walsh have developed analyses of Voegelin's thought that concentrate on Voegelin's response to the perceived disorder of modernity. In particular, both interpret Voegelin's thought as a kind of therapeutic against the ideological politics of modernity. Following one metaphor Voegelin uses, Franz characterizes the politics of modernity as a spiritual revolt; Walsh employs metaphors like "spiritual vacuum," "dead end," and "historical abyss of evil."[27] Franz closely follows Voegelin's own texts, whereas Walsh ranges more broadly in the materials he introduces into his analysis, with Voegelin as only one figure among several—including Fyodor Dostoyevsky, Albert Camus, and Alexander Solzhenitsyn—who write in opposition to modernity.

In Franz's interpretation, Voegelin's "stature as a political philosopher" must be assessed at least in part with a view to his analysis of ideological phenomena, because Voegelin characterized "philosophy itself as 'an act of resistance illuminated by conceptual understanding,'" and because he identified ideologies as a pervasive set of modern spiritual phenomena that deform reality and that are, therefore, to be resisted.[28] Voegelin perceived an intense civilizational crisis in modernity that was signaled in part by the "proliferation of ideological movements." His response to this crisis "can be described as a search for (1) the historical and experiential wellsprings of the crisis, (2) the analytical tools required to render it intelligible, and (3) sources for an appropriate therapy."[29] Franz proceeds with a study of all three aspects of Voegelin's anti-ideological endeavor in a book that is, in summary, "an examination of Eric Voegelin's analysis of the spiritual and historical roots of modern ideological politics."[30]

Ideologies are one manifestation of a disordered consciousness or "pneumopathology." To understand this claim requires a contrasting understanding of what is a well-ordered consciousness or a healthy psyche. Voegelin located the discovery of this distinction between well- and badly-ordered souls in classical Greek philosophy, brought to full articulation in the writings of Plato and Aristotle. Manifestations of pneumopathology and a somewhat compacted articulation of their meaning, however, could be discovered in texts much older than the writings of the Greek philosophers. Out of a comparative analysis of these texts arose one of Voegelin's most important theses:

> [T]hese symbolisms are essentially equivalent, despite their phenotypical differences, in the sense that they refer recognizably to the same structures in reality. There is only one reality; it may be symbolized in a manifold of forms, but no one form is ever fully adequate to or exhaustive of reality's rich and mysterious nature. Myth, philosophy, and revelation are examples of such symbolic forms.[31]

Voegelin's argument concerning equivalences of experience and symbolization "is decisively important," according to Franz,

> for (a) the generic concept of pneumapathological consciousness, (b) the thesis that such consciousness is grounded in the human condition rather than transitory circumstances, and (c) the proposition that the history of such consciousness is characterized by an unbroken continuum of movements.[32]

Voegelin understood "pneumapathological disorientation" to be a spiritual pathology in which dissatisfaction with the human condition as it is given to us leads the dissatisfied one to speculate on the possibility of a radical change. There are at least two broad kinds of pathological response to this experience of dissatisfaction with or anxiety about the contingent nature of existence. First, the anxious and alienated psyche may attempt to escape from the world by disregarding the concrete requirements for living in the world. Such an escape "may be expressed in either a profound disregard for mundane necessities and an all-consuming desire for eternal perfection or a longing for an apocalyptic transformation of the worldly vale of tears."[33] Examples of such millenarian escapism can be found (according to Voegelin) in a few biblical writings, in many of the gnostic writings of antiquity, and in numerous heretical movements of the Middle Ages and the early Reformation.

Second, the escape may take the opposite form of "a turning-away from transcendent reality to live in *this* world alone." In this case, the alienated individual rejects the "transcendent dimension of human experience by establishing man as the measure of all things." A predominant theme in the programs of movements established on the basis of this rejection is an attempt "to usher in an era of human autonomy through a redirection of humanity's energies toward a perfection of the 'estate of man,'" which is in each case, Voegelin argues, "a hubristic revolt against the limitations of the creaturely nature of human beings."[34] Thus, each kind of anxiety is animated in the disordered psyche by a different sort of hope or program for radical change in the basic structures of the world and its transcendent ground. Franz proceeds, then, to show the outlines of Voegelin's historiographically and philosophically complex argument. This argument included for Voegelin the (re)discovery of the classical notion of reason (*nous*) and order and the concomitant discovery of spiritual disease (*nosos*) and disorder in the soul, as well as a (re)discovery of the philosophical categories and analytical tools developed by a series of thinkers to make both kinds of experience intelligible. It also included a close study of how, in fact, such experiences and the symbolization of them over long periods of time are equivalent to each other. Voegelin sought to "draw lines of continuity between patterns of consciousness."[35] Through this analysis of the structures of consciousness and their recurring patterns of experience that are symbolized in a variety of equivalent ways, Voegelin could show how ideologies were, in fact, a particular kind of aberration of consciousness. He could also point, then, to a therapy for such pneumopathologies. At this point, Walsh's analysis becomes particularly helpful for appreciating the direction that such a therapeutic might take.

Franz's close, even if critical, reading of Voegelin's texts tends—no doubt unintentionally—to give his reading of Voegelin's therapeutic a somewhat programmatic quality, but with some doubt in the end that Voegelin managed to articulate a clear therapeutic plan. By casting his net more broadly, Walsh shows how a number of contemporary authors and thinkers have been engaged in the kind of therapeutic Voegelin advocated, even if they have not done so in a specifically "Voegelinian" manner. Similarly, Walsh introduces the reader to a wide cast of characters who speak on behalf of modernity or who criticize it on its own premises. His incorporation of literature and other philosophical analyses helps the reader to imagine more clearly what a counter-ideological therapeutic might look like. Walsh is persuaded by the Voegelinian argument that such a therapeutic "requires a return to the primary experiences and symbols of order" or the basic experiences of order that are available to every open soul.[36] Walsh's use of other literature also directs his account more pointedly to the prescriptive side of the counter-ideological enterprise, to the "ascent from the depths" that is required to heal the pneumopathological condition of modernity.[37] In this regard he emphasizes, as do most of Voegelin's sympathetic interpreters, the importance of a philosophical anthropology and especially a philosophical account of human consciousness, but his literary focus gives this emphasis a more vigorous breadth and, surprisingly, a more immediate political application:

> There is, in other words, a philosophy of consciousness that can articulate the truth of this [rediscovered Christian] existential insight. It

consists in showing how the assertion of a transcendent moral order is an elaboration of the structure of consciousness that is more or less transparent to all human beings. This is not a particular or idiosyncratic point of view; it is an explication of what everyone knows, and can be everywhere verified. Nor does it require special efforts of introspection to identify it, since it can be confirmed in the overt expressions of our world. Even those who deny the reality of good and evil or reject the reality of divine order nevertheless reveal the extent to which "they know that reality moves not only into a future of things but toward their Beyond."[38]

Voegelin the Philosopher of the Good Society

John Ranieri's study of Voegelin's political thought closely resembles the studies of Franz and Walsh in several ways.[39] Like Franz, Ranieri begins with an account of Voegelin's philosophy of consciousness. Also like Franz, he moves to Voegelin's studies of Plato and the Israelites to uncover the important features of this account of human consciousness. Finally, like Franz, he is interested in manifestations of disorder as a contrast with well-ordered souls and societies. In contrast to Franz, however, Ranieri is more strongly interested in the specific contours of Voegelin's Platonic philosophical endeavor of developing a picture of the good society. He is, accordingly, more interested in situating "social reality within the context of reality as a whole" as this reality is depicted in Voegelin's philosophical analysis.[40] Here he resembles Walsh, but with a less pronounced emphasis on Christian forms of symbolism. While Franz's focus is on political ideologies as a manifestation of spiritual disorder, the implications of Ranieri's study are, like Walsh's, more immediately political:

> The crucial issue, then, is the degree to which the discovered truth can be made effective in society. I believe this question to be at the heart of Voegelin's work: Can the truth of order become socially effective? Or, in other words, Is the good society possible?[41]

Ranieri tacitly agrees with Franz that Voegelin's response to this question was generally a Platonic one: the various responses of the psyche to its perceptions of order and disorder can be translated into political symbols and deeds so that the relative states of health or pathology in the psyches of the dominant participants in a regime are reflected in the general character of the regime. In other words, some responses of the psyche to its perceptions of the world are better than others, and this is true at both the individual and the societal levels.

Ranieri is closely guided in his political analysis by Voegelin's philosophy of consciousness, and in particular by Voegelin's insistence that a balance must be maintained in any healthy consciousness between divine reality and concrete human reality. This "balance," as we saw in Webb's analysis, is in fact a kind of tension:

> Every human society bears witness to its preoccupation with existence in the metaxy through the language of "life and death, immortality and mortality, perfection and imperfection, time and timelessness; between order and disorder, truth and untruth; between *amor Dei* and *amor sui*." In coming to understand and live within this tension, that is, in seeking and implementing order, humans give shape to history, society, and polity.[42]

Another way to pose the question of whether the good society is possible, therefore, is to ask, "Can the truth of order be implemented effectively within society?"[43] Through a study of Voegelin's study of Greek and Israelite experiences of order in the first three volumes of *Order and History*, Ranieri concludes that such an implementation is possible, but with two caveats. First, "the gap between the truth of order and society is indeed wide; advances in the order of consciousness can rarely, if ever, be translated into lasting social form. If there was any doubt as to the irresolvability of the tension of existence, it has been dispelled."[44] A modest implementation of the truth of order may be possible; a utopia of perfected men is not.[45] Second, it is also the case that experiences of *disorder* can be equally socially and politically potent.[46] Given this conclusion, Ranieri recalls Dante Germino's assessment that "it is unclear how much room for maneuver political reality affords in Voegelin's philosophy for the creation of a relatively more decent and humane world."[47]

At the root of Voegelin's political philosophy, therefore, Ranieri finds a certain ambiguity:

> Voegelin's views on the possibility of creating a good society escape categorization. . . . his insistence that the structure of reality does not change and the epistemological/ontological framework within which

he operated led him to make certain statements indicating that most attempts to insure a more equitable and just social order are at odds with the "laws of mundane existence" and are therefore a revolt against the order established by God. At the same time, Voegelin clearly believed the state of social disorder in which he found himself to be unacceptable and he strongly desired that it be improved. He was committed to fighting such disorder. A problem arises, however, from within his philosophical perspective, where that dimension of being that is humanly constituted is not always clearly distinguished from human life as conditioned by the operation of lower manifolds. This tension lends to Voegelin's writings on these matters a sense of poignancy, not unlike that found in the later writings of Plato, whom he so admired.[48]

Voegelin's explicit statements on the matter of social and political reform range between "somber pessimism" and "guarded optimism."[49] Part of this ambiguity and caution derives from Voegelin's insistence on maintaining a balance of consciousness between the poles of divine and human, perfectibility and imperfection. To do otherwise would be to suffer the gnostic derailments of ideological utopianism that re-immerse us in the failed political enterprises of modernity.[50] Ranieri offers pertinent criticism of some aspects of Voegelin's caution and helpful insights into the possibilities for renewal that are scattered throughout Voegelin's work.[51] Ultimately, however, Voegelin remains a philosopher for whom political activism is a decidedly secondary concern:

> If he did not deal extensively with the issue as to how such people might act to transform the societies of which they are a part, we might recall that for Voegelin, there could be no more practical contribution than to direct people's attention to that reality which underlies and sustains all knowledge and action. Nor is such an answer evasive, for Voegelin himself was very much aware that his contribution to social change lay not in specific solutions to concrete social and political problems, but in the recovery of those foundational experiences of transcendence that ground authentic humanity. To understand this view of practicality is to understand Voegelin's lifework, and to realize that there is a sense in which to be an authentic political philosopher one must also be a mystic.[52]

Voegelin the Conservative (?)

These cautionary and politically ambiguous features of Voegelin's political philosophy have led more than one reader to brand him a "conservative" of the contemporary stripe. Ted McAllister has taken up this theme in a book-length comparison of Voegelin and Leo Strauss as two of the foremost political theorists to whom contemporary American conservatives have turned for intellectual guidance. Close readers of Voegelin, however, will not be surprised that Professor McAllister's conclusions are decidedly indecisive on the matter of Voegelin's "conservatism."

In the American context, argues McAllister, Voegelin's imputed conservatism arises not simply out of his critique of modernity but out of his specific critique of modernity's most politically potent manifestation in the United States: contemporary liberalism. Just what this liberalism amounts to remains unclear, since it is a political ideology composed of various, sometimes contradictory strains. One summary critique of American liberalism, however, charges that "Americans, dominated by this tradition, [are] unimaginative, narrow, provincial, and self-satisfied yet given to fantasies about idealized human futures based upon naive assumptions regarding human nature and human potential."[53] Liberalism itself seems "directionless and morally empty," ultimately comprised of a kind of utilitarian hedonism, with a nihilistic logic at its core, and a doctrine of perpetual progress as its animating principle. Liberalism is therefore closely related to, and only a half step away from, the totalitarianism that once swept the European continent.[54] Most Americans, these critics seem to warn, are entirely too sanguine about the possible consequences of basing their civil order on such a fragile theoretical foundation.

Since liberalism is a part of modernity, Voegelin's response to it is part of his general critique of modernity. Accordingly, McAllister engages in a summary review of Voegelin's larger critique of modernity as the context for his critique of liberalism. He covers the same ground that most of the other interpreters considered here also review, but in a particularly readable and accessible fashion. In the final chapter of his book, he returns to the question of conservatism, and he concludes that although "Voegelin and Strauss were appropriated, however inaccurately, by conservatives," they are "adopted sons." On the other hand, "conservatives and liberals alike have dealt with little more than caricatures of these philosophers and their works." Although Voegelin shares with Strauss the necessarily reactionary character of all conservatives, their thought cannot be neatly fitted into the categorical boxes of modern ideologies, including conservatism.[55] Voegelin's critique of modernity has a breadth and nuance that politically active citizens may use as a reference point, but that will always supersede the needs of a political program:

> Although most self-proclaimed conservative intellectuals were not philosophers, nor particularly interested in engaging in debates about technical points, they generally recognized that their religious and philosophical inclinations required some systematic defense. In the authors of *The New Science of Politics* and *Natural Right and History* they found, or thought they found, able defenders of the citadel. Voegelin and Strauss exposed the modern philosophical fraud, and moreover, their enterprise—to reawaken the philosophical quest (though not the quest for certainty)—was a necessary part of the larger conservative agenda.[56]

Voegelin was associated from time to time with conservatives and conservative organizations, but his "most important intellectual partners" were not American conservatives. His writings—and not even all of them—served as useful touchstones for many conservatives, but he could not be firmly identified as an unambiguous voice in the choir:

> Strauss and Voegelin provided conservatives with a frightening backdrop against which to view Anglo-American trends. The problems did not concern this or that policy, or even tradition, but emerged from the growing allegiance people were paying to instrumental reason. The belief that humans could control their world and their destiny, Strauss and Voegelin suggested, rested hidden beneath the enormous technical successes of the modern age, and conservatives who believed them could no longer consider technological advances as unqualified improvements. In short, Strauss and Voegelin helped give a historical sweep to the conservative struggle even as they more clearly defined the enemy.[57]

McAllister concludes that Voegelin, along with Strauss, is a compelling figure in his own right and that his desultory alliances with conservative causes are—at best—of secondary importance for appreciating his philosophical enterprise.

Voegelin the Philosopher of Consciousness

The picture of Voegelin that emerges so far, stemming from a variety of interpretations and critiques, is of a thinker whose studies encompassed the magnificent range of, say, an Aristotle or a Thomas Aquinas. He provided broad studies of classical, medieval, and modern European political thought and political culture, of Mongol constitutional theory, of Middle Eastern history and religion, of American political culture, of European racism, of Austrian constitutionalism in the twentieth century, and the list goes on. Several categories of studies, including those of Webb, Franz, and Ranieri, seek to find a broad theme that encompasses as much of this material as possible in a meaningful unity. A group of recent studies that have followed this pattern locate the core of Voegelin's thought in his philosophy of consciousness. I have already noted the importance of this theory in other interpretations, so such an emphasis should not be surprising, nor does it seem out of place.

At least five extant studies of Voegelin's thought take this tack, including a comparative study by Eugene Webb, a brief study by Ronald D. Srigley and a longer one by Michael P. Morrissey, both emphasizing the theological import of Voegelin's theory of consciousness, a study by Kenneth Keulman that begins with Voegelin's theory of consciousness as an entrée into his political theory, and, finally, Glenn Hugh's study of Voegelin's theory of consciousness, emphasizing the role of myth, "mystery," and mythical symbolization in that theory.[58] What do all of these studies have in common? What does it mean to articulate a theory of consciousness as the foundation for a theory of politics, a philosophical theology, or a theory of language? As with other aspects of the works being surveyed in this introduction, these questions will become topics for later chapters, but a preliminary glance is nevertheless in order.

Speaking broadly and crudely, a theory of consciousness is an articulation of what it means to be a perceiving, thinking, participating being in the whole of reality. Such a theory may grow out of a sense of loss. For example, it may be the case, as Glenn Hughes argues, that apperceiving and accepting "elemental mysteries" is a "necessary condition . . . for the proper formation of individual character [and for] the development of adequate social viewpoints and political policies." If an awareness of mystery and the need for it have gradually been lost in the modern period, recovering this awareness may be crucial for recovering from the ills of modernity.[59] Such a convalescence seems to require the development of a theory of consciousness whereby the meaning and function of mystery can be redeemed. In similar fashion, any political theory that seriously proposes to be based on a theory of man will have to confront the problem of consciousness as a constituent part of the creature called "man" and of his doings in the activity called politics.[60] A political theory may also develop out of an immediate experience, not of loss and the questioning it induces, but of absence, namely the absence of order, and it may at the same time be developed out of an intimation of order that infuses itself into the experience of disorder. Aspects of such an intimation include what Voegelin called the "primary experience of the cosmos."[61]

The various accounts of Voegelin's theory of consciousness take into consideration a number of characteristics of this theory. One is the historical character that Voegelin imputes to consciousness. A second is the differentiation of the structure of consciousness into at least three aspects, which include its participatory, reflexive, and intentional dimensions. A third is the primary experience of order and transcendence in consciousness.[62] Another is the symbolic/linguistic expressions of consciousness that make their appearance in human history, and that, in certain respects, constitute that history. How Voegelin presents these sundry characteristics can then be analyzed with a view to understanding his political theory, his theology, his philosophical anthropology, his theory of language, and his philosophy of history.

Voegelin the Political Scientist

For the average reader, a theory of consciousness, a theory of history, even a theory of experience and symbolization each has about it a kind of elusive, evanescent quality, though this impression may not be sustained under serious scrutiny. In the same way, a diagnosis of modernity as a spiritual disorder may give a vague sense of being more theological in tone than of being a properly defined topic of political science. We should therefore be reminded in any introduction to the thought of Eric Voegelin that he was originally trained as a political scientist and that he retained this professional appellation throughout his life. Voegelin's best-known work in the English-speaking world remains *The New Science of Politics*, in which he makes an explicit effort to refound the study of politics on sound principles.[63]

Following this line of interpretation, Barry Cooper has prepared a wideranging study of Voegelin's thought that focuses less immediately on his theories of consciousness, history, or symbolization and more on his inquiry into a series of political problems, past and present.[64] In this and in an earlier study, Professor Cooper emphasizes the foundation of Voegelin's science of politics in "lived experiences," in "self-speaking phenomena" such as literature, poetry, and other symbolic forms of communication, and in empirical evidence generally.[65] Theories of consciousness and of experience and symbolization are ultimately rooted in the everyday experiences and events that confront the political scientist and that are in principle indistinguishable from those of his fellow subjects or citizens. The difference resides in the recipient of those experiences. "Theory," Voegelin reminds us, "is not just any opining about human existence in society; it rather is an attempt at formulating the meaning of existence by explicating the content of a definite class of experiences." The validity of a theoretical argument, moreover, "derives from the aggregate of experiences to which it must permanently refer for empirical control."[66] Accordingly, the soul of the political theorist must be of such a character that his experiences are subject to proper control and interpretation:

> Theoretical experience is a reality in the inner life of a person whose character is formed, precisely, by what is noble and truly eudaimonic. Corresponding to this inner or personal reality is the outer or public exegesis and explication of it.[67]

This reality of the soul notwithstanding, political science begins not in abstraction, but in that which everyone can see, hear, feel, and touch. The problems of politics, which become the topics of a political science, are perennial, being rooted in basic experiences of community that—to reiterate the point—are on their face accessible to everyone at all times.[68]

> A philosophy of politics is empirical—in the pregnant sense of an investigation of experiences which penetrate the whole realm of ordered

> human existence. It requires . . . rigorous reciprocating examination
> of concrete phenomena of order and analysis of consciousness, by
> which means alone the human order in society and history becomes
> understandable. . . . [Since] consciousness is the center from which
> the concrete order of human existence in society and history radiates
> . . . the empirical study of social and historical phenomena of order
> interpenetrates with the empirical study of consciousness and its expe-
> riences of participation.[69]

Thus, the theories of consciousness, of history, of symbolization, and so
on that emerge from Voegelin's inquiries are initiated by the political
situations he confronted, as Voegelin claimed they were. Professor Cooper's particular mode of exegesis of the Voegelinian texts has served,
among other things, to reclarify precisely this point.

Multiple Voegelins Revisited

The preceding interpretations of Voegelin's work are a representative sample of a burgeoning literature. All are reasonable readings. Each
seems to offer an accurate picture of Voegelin's work and intentions.
Given the multiple readings available, such a conclusion leads one to a
further verdict that Voegelin's work is difficult, complex, multifaceted,
and not easily captured within the confines of any particular interpretive
scheme. But this result is what one would expect from a philosopher of
the first rank. In the works of Plato, for example, one also finds considerations of a variety of topics and phenomena, as one does in the works of
Aristotle, Augustine, Aquinas, Hegel, and even the non-philosopher
Karl Marx. Taken side by side, the various accounts of Voegelin's work
confirm rather than deny that his thought comprises a coherent whole;
the sample of interpretations we have glanced at here is an indicator of
that larger whole. Hence, from the perspective of emphasis, or according
to which aspect of human affairs we wish to attend to, there are multiple
Voegelins. In terms of his attempt to give a comprehensive account of
those affairs, however, there is only one Eric Voegelin and one coherent
body of work.

What follows is divided into five chapters. The first chapter begins
with a rehearsal of Voegelin's theory of consciousness and consists of a
consideration of its narrative aspects as a way of making it more accessi-

ble. The second chapter is a study of the public role of political philosophy in circumstances of political disorder. In the third chapter, I examine one of Voegelin's studies of the experiential and historical origins of ideological politics, which shape so much of the modern cultural and political world. The fourth and fifth chapters examine Voegelin's political theology, first against the backdrop of the rise of National Socialism and then with a more general approach to Voegelin's political-philosophical interpretation of Christianity. These five chapters form an introduction to Voegelin's political thought that does not pretend to comprehensiveness, but that offers a window, from the perspective of political theory, on the most important aspects of his deeply penetrating and wideranging studies of human history, political order, and society.

NOTES

1. For examples, see Eugene Webb, *Eric Voegelin: Philosopher of History* (Seattle: University of Washington Press, 1981), 4–5; see also Voegelin's remarks in Eric Voegelin, *Autobiographical Reflections*, ed. Ellis Sandoz (Baton Rouge: Louisiana State University Press, 1989), 46.

2. Even his most sympathetic reader, while defending him, has pointed out the "veil of technical terminology, Greek words, range of strange and familiar sources and documents through which he carefully pursues his anamnestic quest." Ellis Sandoz, *The Voegelinian Revolution: A Biographical Introduction* (Baton Rouge: Louisiana State University Press, 1981), 218.

3. Barry Cooper, *The Political Theory of Eric Voegelin* (Lewiston. N.Y.: The Edwin Mellen Press, 1986), x.

4. Gregor Sebba, "Prelude and Variations on the Theme of Eric Voegelin," in *Eric Voegelin's Thought: A Critical Appraisal*, ed. Ellis Sandoz (Durham, N.C.: Duke University Press, 1982), 7.

5. Sebba, "Prelude and Variations," 8.

6. For details of his stay in America, see Juergen Gebhardt and Barry Cooper, "Editors' Introduction," in Eric Voegelin, *On the Form of the American Mind*, ed. Juergen Gebhardt and Barry Cooper, trans. Ruth Hein, vol. 1 of *The Collected Works of Eric Voegelin* (Baton Rouge: Louisiana State University Press, 1995), xxxv–xli.

7. See Gebhardt and Cooper, "Editors' Introduction," xli, and Voegelin's comments in *Autobiographical Reflections*, 96.

8. Voegelin, *Autobiographical Reflections*, 32–33.

9. Thomas Hollweck and Ellis Sandoz, "General Introduction to the Se-

ries," in Eric Voegelin, *Hellenism, Rome, and Early Christianity,* ed. Athanasios Moulakis, vol. 1 of *History of Political Ideas* (Columbia: University of Missouri Press, 1997), 18. See "Voegelin's Introduction to the 'History of Political Ideas,' " in *Hellenism,* 225–37.

10. Voegelin, *Autobiographical Reflections,* 78.

11. Eric Voegelin, "Introduction to the 'History of Political Ideas,' " *Hellenism,* 225, 226.

12. Eric Voegelin, *The New Science of Politics: An Introduction* (Chicago: The University of Chicago Press, 1952). See especially 27–28 for a restatement of the principles of the earlier "Introduction."

13. See also Voegelin's comments in *Autobiographical Reflections,* 62–64.

14. Eric Voegelin, *From Enlightenment to Revolution,* ed. John Hallowell (Durham, N.C.: Duke University Press, 1975).

15. Voegelin, *Autobiographical Reflections,* 88–89.

16. Voegelin, *Autobiographical Reflections,* 91–92.

17. Ellis Sandoz, "Editor's Introduction," in *Published Essays, 1966–1985,* vol. 12 of *The Collected Works of Eric Voegelin* (Baton Rouge: Louisiana State University Press, 1990), xiii.

18. Ellis Sandoz, "Introduction," in Eric Voegelin, *In Search of Order,* vol. 5 of *Order and History* (Baton Rouge: Louisiana State University Press, 1987), 1.

19. Sandoz, *Voegelinian Revolution,* 2.

20. Sandoz, *Voegelinian Revolution,* 188–89.

21. Sandoz, *Voegelinian Revolution,* 199.

22. Sandoz, *Voegelinian Revolution,* 203ff.

23. Webb, *Philosopher of History,* 10.

24. Webb, *Philosopher of History,* 13.

25. Webb, *Philosopher of History,* 244–45.

26. Webb, *Philosopher of History,* 268.

27. David Walsh, *After Ideology: Recovering the Spiritual Foundations of Freedom* (San Francisco: HarperCollins Publishers, 1990), 3, 9ff.

28. Michael Franz, *Eric Voegelin and the Politics of Spiritual Revolt: The Roots of Modern Ideology* (Baton Rouge: Louisiana State University Press, 1992), 3; Eric Voegelin, *Plato and Aristotle,* vol. 3 of *Order and History* (Baton Rouge: Louisiana State University Press, 1957), 68 (quoted in Franz, *Spiritual Revolt,* 3).

29. Franz, *Spiritual Revolt,* 2.

30. Franz, *Spiritual Revolt,* xi.

31. Franz, *Spiritual Revolt,* 22–23.

32. Franz, *Spiritual Revolt,* 23–24.

33. Franz, *Spiritual Revolt,* 7.

34. Franz, *Spiritual Revolt,* 7.

35. Franz, *Spiritual Revolt,* 105.

36. Walsh, *After Ideology*, 5; for contemporary instances of such experiences and symbolization, see 67, 139, 151.

37. Walsh, *After Ideology*, 130, 137ff.

38. Walsh, *After Ideology*, 221. The quotation in Walsh is from Voegelin, *In Search of Order*, 35.

39. John J. Ranieri, *Eric Voegelin and the Good Society* (Columbia: University of Missouri Press, 1995).

40. Ranieri, *Good Society*, 77.

41. Ranieri, *Good Society*, 102.

42. Ranieri, *Good Society*, 22; the quotation is from Eric Voegelin, "Equivalences and Symbolization in History," in *Published Essays, 1966–1985,* ed. Sandoz, 119.

43. Ranieri, *Good Society*, 103.

44. Ranieri, *Good Society*, 155.

45. "There are certain evils in human existence that are ineradicable; attempts to overcome them by institutional means are doomed to failure, because human nature does not change. Any suggestion to the contrary is utopian at best and at worst can make one an accomplice in totalitarian murder. Liberalism's notion of progress, expressed as a gradual and permanent revolution, is gnostic and at one in essence with totalitarianism. The notion that humanity might move beyond a world order sustained by a balance of military forces toward a more peaceful international order is like a gnostic dream." (Ranieri, *Good Society*, 181).

46. Ranieri, *Good Society*, 103–21.

47. Ranieri, *Good Society*, 181; the quotation is from Dante Germino, "Eric Voegelin's *Anamnesis,*" *Southern Review* 7 (1971): 87–88.

48. Ranieri, *Good Society*, 200–201.

49. Ranieri, *Good Society*, 201.

50. Ranieri, *Good Society*, 214.

51. Ranieri, *Good Society*, 189, 201–13.

52. Ranieri, *Good Society*, 256.

53. Ted. V. McAllister, *Revolt Against Modernity: Leo Strauss, Eric Voegelin, and the Search for a Postliberal Order* (Lawrence: University Press of Kansas, 1996), 53.

54. McAllister, *Revolt Against Modernity*, 66. "Although the political and intellectual current known as liberalism has taken on various forms in the course of its history, most persons would probably agree that one of its characteristics is the expectation that substantial change can be effected in men through institutional arrangements with the result that man and society can be progressively perfected." Webb, *Philosopher of History*, 246.

55. McAllister, *Revolt Against Modernity*, 262.

56. McAllister, *Revolt Against Modernity*, 270–71.

57. McAllister, *Revolt Against Modernity*, 272.

58. Eugene Webb, *Philosophers of Consciousness: Polanyi; Lonergan; Voegelin; Ricoeur; Girard; Kierkegaard* (Seattle: University of Washington Press, 1988); Ronald D. Srigley, *Eric Voegelin's Platonic Theology: Philosophy of Consciousness and Symbolization in a New Perspective* (Lewiston, N.Y.: Edwin Mellen Press, 1991); Michael P. Morrissey, *Consciousness and Transcendence: The Theology of Eric Voegelin* (Notre Dame, Ind.: University of Notre Dame Press, 1994); Kevin Keulmann, *The Balance of Consciousness: Eric Voegelin's Political Theory* (University Park: Pennsylvania State University Press, 1990); Glenn Hughes, *Mystery and Myth in the Philosophy of Eric Voegelin* (Columbia: University of Missouri Press, 1993).

59. Hughes, *Mystery and Myth*, 1 2.

60. Keulmann, *Balance of Consciousness*, xviii–xx.

61. Hughes, *Mystery and Myth*, 43–45.

62. See Hughes, *Mystery and Myth*, 41–69, for a good introduction to this topic.

63. Voegelin, *New Science of Politics*, 22–26.

64. Barry Cooper, *Eric Voegelin and the Foundations of Modern Political Science* (Columbia: University of Missouri Press, 1999) (forthcoming).

65. Cooper, *Political Theory*, 20, 126.

66. Voegelin, *New Science of Politics*, 64: quoted in Cooper, *Political Theory*, 128.

67. Cooper, *Political Theory*, 129.

68. Cooper, *Political Theory*, 16.

69. Eric Voegelin, *Anamnesis: Zur Theorie der Geschichte und Politik* (Munich: R. Piper Verlag, 1966), 8–9, 275–76. This translated quotation is found in Keulmann, *Balance of Consciousness*, xx. I have made minor changes in the translation.

1

ORDER, NARRATIVE, AND CONSCIOUSNESS

To begin with Voegelin's account of consciousness is, in one sense, to begin at the end. Although there are already clear premonitions of his later analyses of consciousness in the introduction to *On the Form of the American Mind*,[1] Voegelin systematically developed his fully articulated theory of consciousness only from 1943 onward, and he had not completely articulated it even in *In Search of Order*, published in 1987, two years after his death. On the other hand, a theory of consciousness stands front and center in any complete account of Voegelin's political thought. Indeed, his lifelong philosophical investigations begin and end with a theory of human consciousness, because such a theory is at the core of a theory of the nature of human existence, which is the beginning of a theory of politics. I have already noted that several recent book-length treatments of his thought either contain the word "consciousness" in the title or are otherwise deeply engaged with its problems,[2] attesting to the unquestionable centrality of problems of consciousness in Voegelin's thought. Voegelin contended that a theory of consciousness was the central constituent of a theory of politics and perhaps its necessary basis.[3] Accordingly, it is at the core of his life-long study of political order, and it was also the center of his critique of modernity, which he viewed largely in terms of parallel crises in intellectual thought and the practice of politics.

Nevertheless, "consciousness" seems an excessively abstract term that is hardly linked in any meaningful way to the everyday problems of politics. More importantly, if Voegelin *ended up* with a theory of consciousness, why should we *begin* there? In answer to the first objection, it was one of the innovations of Voegelin's theory of politics to insist that not only is consciousness linked to everyday political affairs but that the moral and conceptual shape of any political regime is ultimately an expression of the consciousness of those who dwell within it and sustain it. Political order is an expression, according to Voegelin, of a wider conception of order that is given in and through human consciousness of the whole. Without a firm grasp of the spiritual roots and spiritual shape of a specific political regime, the day-to-day events of politics make little sense.[4] "The problems of human order in society and history," Voegelin argued, "originate in the order of consciousness. Hence the philosophy of consciousness is the centerpiece of a philosophy of politics."[5] An analysis of consciousness is therefore an analysis of order, and a political order is a concrete expression of consciousness. In answer to the second objection, let us be reminded that consciousness is embodied. There is no free-floating consciousness, but only physical beings who also happen to be conscious beings. These beings order themselves into communities where consciousness of a reality greater than themselves plays a key role in ordering the community of which they are all a part. In the following three chapters, I will consider three ways in which "deformed" consciousness can have a destructive effect on the proper ordering of a political community. In this chapter, I will consider one of the ways in which Voegelin delivers this theory and the implications of such a delivery for a conception of consciousness.

A theory of consciousness, I have said, emerges out of reflections on the interface between human nature and political activity. But why reflect on human nature? The initiating motivation for such reflection was, for Voegelin, the experience of politics gone bad, which he observed firsthand in Europe in the 1920s and 1930s and from a distance in the 1940s and beyond. In Voegelin's words, "The motivations of my work are simple, they arise from the political situation."[6] This situation included the rise of Bolshevism in Russia, Fascism in Spain and Italy, and National Socialism in Germany. Underlying the emergence of authoritarian and totalitarian regimes were a series of ideologies—Marxism, nationalism, and racism, for example—that were themselves expressions of order, albeit deformed order. The political situation in Germany in the 1920s and early 1930s involved street battles between ideological fanatics of the Left and Right. In Spain, it involved a bloody civil war that attracted the active attention of many foreign nationals for ideological as well as pragmatic reasons. In Russia it involved successive revolutions in

1917, a civil war from 1918 until 1921, and a long-lived murderous regime after that. As I proceed with an analysis of Voegelin's thought, it will become clear that he came to see ideological fanaticism and its practical political manifestations as the outcome of spiritual perversion (pneumopathologies), not merely erroneous thinking or moral turpitude, although it might include these qualities as well. This conclusion was shaped by his gradual development of a theory of consciousness as it relates to the practice of politics.

Voegelin's extensive analysis of consciousness, which ranges in time from the first chapter of his 1928 work, *On the Form of the American Mind*, to the posthumous *In Search of Order*, is cast in philosophical categories and employs critical methods of inquiry. But this analytical way of coming to the problem is only one part of articulating a theory of consciousness, and only one way—even if the most important—in which Voegelin did so. It is what might typically be called the path of metaphysics, and what Voegelin called "noetic" philosophy.[7] By noesis is meant the activity of *nous*; nous, in turn, is "the capacity of seeking [theoretical knowledge] under the guidance of [the seeker's] attraction toward the transcendental" ground of all existence. Noesis is therefore a process of developing or acquiring knowledge. This development is a "reflective understanding involving critical self-awareness on the part of the inquirer based on [an] understanding of the nature of inquiry as such."[8] This form of analysis receives most of the attention of Voegelin's commentators, interpreters, and critics. Their emphasis, however, leaves out the role of narrative in Voegelin's analysis of human consciousness. The reasons for employing it in an introductory work as a way of understanding Voegelin's thought are threefold. First, it is one of the modes of presentation that Voegelin uses. Second, and more importantly, it may well be much more accessible for a first encounter with Voegelin than the more abstract metaphysical terms to which he and his commentators frequently turn. Third, Voegelin's theory of consciousness shows that human existence and consciousness themselves have narrational qualities, and that narrative therefore displays them in a unique manner. It does so even in the philosophical analyses and accounts of human realities. Narrative conveys order, structure, and meaning prior to a philosophical exegesis of either existence or narrative, but it also appears as an ordering feature of such exegesis itself.

In a more general sense, narrative as both a mode and a topic of study has never entirely faded from the scholarly scene, and it has witnessed renewed attention in the past few decades.[9] The studies of Hayden White, Paul Ricoeur, and Hans Kellner, to mention only three, recall for us the centrality of narrative discourse to human understanding. Ricoeur, for example, suggests that the "temporal character" of human experience is a universal feature that is "marked, organized, and clarified" for us "by an act of story-telling in all its forms."[10] Accordingly, the ability to tell and understand stories is central to making sense of our experiences. Ricoeur's argument suggests that we should not be surprised that "story" and "narrative" occur frequently in Voegelin's final, posthumously published volume. The notion of story plays a crucial role in this volume; but neither in this work, which is also his summation of his theory of consciousness,[11] nor elsewhere does Voegelin subject these literary terms to close analysis. Narrative remains a central but largely unexamined element of his theory of consciousness. Similarly, Jürgen Gebhardt draws attention to the importance of the notion of story in Voegelin's understanding of the philosopher's work, but he, too, does not develop the theme.[12] This chapter develops the themes of consciousness and narrative in the following way. First, it rehearses the central metaphors that Voegelin deployed as he articulated a full-blown theory of consciousness for the first time. Then, it briefly summarizes the three dimensions of consciousness that gradually emerged in Voegelin's analysis. Next, it draws an important contrast between exploring and articulating the dimensions of consciousness through a metaphorical analysis on the one hand and a narrative presentation on the other. At that point, it moves to a fuller examination of narrative, including the role of narrative in ethical reflection and in other human practices. Finally, it moves to an examination of Voegelin's use of narrative in his analysis of human consciousness.

THE METAPHORS OF CONSCIOUSNESS

Perhaps the most accessible, yet condensed introduction to Voegelin's theory of consciousness is contained in his metaphors of the "quaternarian" structure of human existence and of the self-reflective actor who finds himself on a known, yet unknown, knowable, yet unknowable, stage. These two well-known metaphors both occur in the "Introduction" to *Israel and Revelation*, the first volume of *Order and History*. They reveal several central themes and regulative principles of Voegelin's analysis of consciousness. Here, Voegelin introduces us to the notion of a structure of consciousness, but also to its ultimately unfathomable quality; to the problem of anxiety, but also to the possibility of enquiry; to the problem of mystery, but also to the possibility of knowledge. The metaphors also contain basic political principles that, Voegelin argues, are uncovered by a proper understanding of human participation in being.

"God and man, world and society," Voegelin begins, "form a primordial community of being." The "quaternarian structure" of this primordial community both is and is not a "datum of human experience." It *is* a datum of our experience insofar as we participate in it, but since it *is not* given to us as though it were an object of sense-experience, external to us, it is "knowable only from the perspective of participation in it."[13] Thus, the first principle: our knowledge of our own existence is structured, but this knowledge is not the knowledge of an object. Since existence is not an object, we cannot readily uncover a morphology of it. At the same time, we and our knowledge of existence are a part of this self-same existence, not in the manner of a free-falling, free-floating, and self-cognizant giddiness, but rather as a structured, yet not fully known, awareness and self-awareness of participation in "something."

Moreover, this "perspective of participation" can be profoundly disturbing, because if existence is not an object, participation in it "does not mean that man, more or less comfortably located in the landscape of being, can look around and take stock of what he sees as far as he can see it." Rather, man is not a "self-contained spectator" but an actor, "playing a part in the drama of being and, through the brute fact of his existence, committed to play[ing] it without knowing what it is." Voegelin continues on a comic note that if one were to find oneself in a "situation of feeling not quite sure what the game is" or how to play it, one could, "with luck and skill," endeavor to extricate oneself from it "and return to the less bewildering routine of [one's] life." But human existence is not a game in this sense: we are not "partially involved" in existence; rather, "participation is existence itself." There is neither an exit from existence nor an Archimedean point above it: "There is no vantage point outside existence from which its meaning can be viewed and a course of action charted according to a plan, nor is there a blessed

island to which man can withdraw in order to recapture his self."[14] Uncertainty and freedom, contingency and necessity, are the contours of
our existence. We find ourselves in a state of determined indeterminacy
and contingent necessity.

The quaternarian structure of existence on a pre-set "stage" is not
created by the bearer of consciousness, but given to him. The "play"—
our existence—has already begun, and our role, at least in its broadest
outlines, is assigned. We neither create nor recreate ourselves. To do so
is like trying, in the absurd Nazi idiom, "to jump over one's own
shadow." It is a magical operation, an illusion induced by resentment
against the givenness of the condition "on-stage." Paradoxically, this resentment—or at least its omnipresent possibility—reveals an indeterminacy at the heart of a seemingly determinate situation: the quaternarian
structure of existence is both given and contingent. The actor on the
stage possesses certain freedoms, among them a transcending ability to
ask questions and the freedom to fashion within wider limits the order
of the God-man-world-society complex. In this sense, then, Nietzsche
was not entirely wrong: we *do*, in many, variously indeterminate respects, fashion our own existence.[15] We cannot quit the play, but we can
move about the stage: "The role of existence must be played in uncertainty of its meaning, as an adventure of decision on the edge of freedom
and necessity."[16]

As these features of our existence become clearer to us, they reveal
a troubling quality at the core of existence, which the metaphors of the
play and of quaternarian structure help to articulate further:

> At the center of his existence man is unknown to himself and must
> remain so, for the part of being that calls itself man could be known
> fully only if the community of being and its drama in time were
> known as a whole. . . . Knowledge of the whole, however, is pre-
> cluded by the identity of the knower with the partner, and ignorance
> of the whole precludes essential knowledge of the part. This situation
> of ignorance with regard to the decisive core of existence is more than
> disconcerting: it is profoundly disturbing, for from the depth of this
> ultimate ignorance wells up the anxiety of existence.[17]

Thus, we neither know completely who we are, what we are, "where"
we are, nor what we are doing. Yet we find ourselves asking questions

about precisely these matters and the questions may make us anxious. Indeed, our experience of the ineffable is often met with precisely the move that Voegelin rejects: we seek to "return to the less bewildering routine of [our lives]." When the anxieties that produce such a "return" in the face of ignorance become extreme, alienation and psychic disruption may result, leading to at least two types of response. First, the anxieties can manifest themselves in the list of symptoms that the Roman orator Cicero catalogued and that point to a disease of the mind: "restless money-making, status-seeking, womanizing, overeating, addiction to delicacies and snacks, wine-tippling, irascibility, anxiety, desire for fame, stubbornness, rigidity of attitude, and such fears of contact with other human beings as misogyny and misanthropy." The pathology that leads to such behaviors is, in Voegelinian vocabulary, the outcome of a "rejection of reason," a rejection of the order of being as it is discerned in consciousness and articulated—among other places—in Voegelin's two metaphors.[18]

There exists, moreover, a second, more powerful and politically destructive possibility. Anxiety and fear over the ineffable, mysterious qualities of human existence may also produce resentment. Coupled with a will to domination, this resentment may, in turn, lead one to speculate on the possibility of performing magical operations from within existence to change its shape, to make the ineffable transparent, the unknowable known, the inscrutable manipulable. This is the dream of millenarian revolutionaries from those of the thirteenth century to the ideological activists of the modern age, whom we will consider more closely in the second and third chapters.

Anxiety and revolt notwithstanding, our participation on the "stage" is "not blind, but illuminated by consciousness." We experience a participation in being that is illuminated by the knowledge of participation itself. And this illumination can be sufficient to produce regulating principles that refuse to allow withdrawal into the self or the expansion of a will to power from the self, as Voegelin carefully conveys:

> There is an experience of participation, a reflective tension in existence, radiating sense over the proposition: Man, in his existence, participates in being. This sense, however, will turn into nonsense if one forgets that subject and predicate in the proposition are terms which explicate a tension of existence, and are not concepts denoting objects.

There is no such thing as a "man" who participates in "being" as if it were an enterprise that he could as well leave alone; there is, rather, a "something," a part of being, capable of experiencing itself as such, and furthermore capable of using language and calling this experiencing consciousness by the name of "man." The calling by a name certainly is a fundamental act of evocation, of calling forth, of constituting that part of being as a distinguishable partner in the community of being. Nevertheless, fundamental as the act of evocation is—for it forms the basis for all that man will learn about himself in the course of history—it is not itself an act of cognition.[19]

The evocation is not an act of cognition, because it calls forth that which remains unknown—the center or essence of man's existence and its place in the whole—but it *is* the manifestation of a discovery:

When man discovers his existence in tension, he becomes conscious of his consciousness as both the site and the sensorium of participation in the divine ground. As far as consciousness is the site of participation, its reality partakes of both the divine and the human without being wholly the one or the other; as far as it is the sensorium of participation, it is definitely man's own, located in his body in spatiotemporal existence. Consciousness, thus, is both the time pole of the tension (sensorium) and the whole tension including its pole of the timeless (site).[20]

Other evocations, or symbols, or expressions of experience may follow as this "sensorium"—consciousness itself—is explored in its depth, height, and breadth. The results of this exploration replicate the intangible mysteriousness of existence between birth and death: "Such terms as *immanent* and *transcendent*, *external* and *internal*, *this world* and *the other world*, and so forth, do not denote objects or their properties, but are the language indices arising from the Metaxy [the In-Between of human existence] in the event of its becoming luminous for the comprehensive reality, its structure and dynamics. The terms are exegetic, not descriptive."[21]

This theoretical observation is an important point. It is what gives Voegelin's theories of both consciousness and politics their seemingly elusive qualities and their novelty. At the pragmatic level, this luminous but non-objective quality of reality is what leads to anxiety, which can, in turn, lead to the spiritual deformation and political excesses of the ideological fanatics. The point is this: reality is not an object to be grasped, nor a "concept" to be defined, but the ineffable "thereness" or the "It"[22] in which we participate and of which we are a part. The language symbols we use to describe our experience of reality cannot, therefore, be tools of dominion but only the means by which we "elucidate our experience of participation."[23]

The exegetical language indices, or evocations, or expressions cast up by the self-exploration of consciousness arise from the self-illuminating event(s) of consciousness itself, appearing in the (narrative) context of the (narrated) experiences of consciousness that every human being "has" or "can have." Thus, they re-evoke the dynamic and structure of consciousness itself. This evocation, moreover, turns out to be susceptible to theoretical refinement, so that "explorations" of consciousness or of human existence can lead to greater critical awareness of its dynamic and structure. In other words, the self-illumination of consciousness is not historically static. On the one hand, it can be progressive, in the sense that its features can be more clearly articulated and differentiated by means of the symbols we generate while exploring them. On the other hand, it can be regressive, in the sense that the exegetical symbols of experience can—for a variety of reasons—be rejected, forgotten, or misused as "concepts" related to objects. Such neglect and misuse once again hide from us the experiences of the structure and dynamic of consciousness that once produced the more-refined symbols. And it is those experiences that the symbols themselves are intended reflexively to (re-)evoke.

Voegelin's work demonstrates the theoretical refinement of such an analysis of consciousness. Beginning with ancient myths and moving through Plato's dialogues and other texts, Voegelin proceeded to "a reflective exegesis of the structures of consciousness" that included "tension," "poles," "intentionality," and "luminosity" as its guiding terms. His results constituted an advance in this field of study. Voegelin's "greater theoretical refinement of analysis," Glenn Hughes rightly suggests, "is due to the *third* structural dimension of consciousness beyond its intentionality and luminosity, its reflective distance to itself, becoming sufficiently recognized, explored, and articulated." In Voegelin's work, the self-analysis of consciousness is further differentiated, so that "reflective distance itself comes into view."[24]

The structural and thespian metaphors in this exploration of human consciousness have so far yielded the following results: (1) consciousness is not an object, yet it is known as a datum of experience in that it is our mode of existence; (2) this mode has the analogical quality of "participation" in "something"; consciousness is not a separate topic of existence but the mode of existence of human beings; (3) there is no escape from this mode, nor an "outside of" this mode that can be known; (4) human participation in existence is both free and determined, uncertain and contained; (5) the mode of existence can be transcended only in the sense of an ability to ask questions about it, but the transcending questions (for example, Leibnitz's "Why is there something rather than nothing?" "Why do things exist as they do, and not otherwise?") are intelligible only as a mode of transcending participation of consciousness in existence; they cannot be given a definitive answer;[25] (6) anxiety and resentment may attend the transcending questions or one of the other of the experiences of conscious participation in an unknowable "something," and these troubling responses may result either in a withdrawal into the material self or in a variety of (magical) exercises designed to make the "something" fully known and manipulable; (7) consciousness appears to itself in more than one mode: three—intention, luminosity, and reflexivity—are evident, and these three may be individually further differentiated; (8) human participation in the reality revealed in consciousness takes on the quality of self-transparent "response" and self-conscious participation in that reality.

INTENTION, LUMINOSITY, AND REFLEXIVITY IN CONSCIOUSNESS

The preceding exercise in metaphorical reflection on consciousness is itself an exercise in the self-illumination of consciousness. Its cursory exploration of the luminosity, intentionality, and self-reflexivity of consciousness serves as a useful anchor for understanding in brief form the three basic "dimensions" of human consciousness as Voegelin gradually articulated them during a lifetime of scholarship. The importance of narrative to the manner in which these three dimensions manifest themselves and, reflexively, the centrality of these three dimensions to any narrative, demands that we give a brief preliminary exegesis of their

structure and dynamic, which will include a few summary lexical definitions. The intentionality of consciousness refers to "the property of
consciousness whereby it is oriented toward cognitive objects."[26] The
luminosity of consciousness refers to the property of consciousness
whereby it is oriented toward itself as a subject, or as a constituent part
of the universe of cognitive objects, or "as an event of participating illumination in the reality that comprehends the partners to the event."[27]
Finally, reflexivity refers, as we have seen, to the quality of consciousness
whereby consciousness becomes cognizant of itself and to itself concerning its own cognitive structures and processes.

The structure of consciousness, made up of these three dimensions,
is paradoxical; it is a sign of clarity, not confusion, to remain cognizant
of this fact. The "equivocation" that constitutes the "paradox of consciousness" is the fact that "we speak of consciousness as something located in human beings in their bodily existence," at the same time that
"we know the bodily located consciousness to be also real" in and of
itself. In the first sense—in bodily located consciousness—reality assumes
for conscious beings "the position of an object intended." Reality is
"external," an object of our consideration and manipulation. In the second sense, the self-same reality in which the "concretely located consciousness" participates is "not an object of consciousness but the something in which consciousness occurs as an event of participation between
partners in the community of being." Thus:

> In the complex experience, presently in process of articulation, reality
> moves from the position of an intended object to that of a subject,
> while the consciousness of the human subject intending objects moves
> to the position of a predicative event in the subject "reality" as it be-
> comes luminous for its truth. Consciousness, thus, has the structural
> aspect not only of intentionality but also of luminosity.[28]

Voegelin borrows from Plato to symbolize this paradox as an existence "in-between" our bodily existence and the comprehending
whole, in which consciousness is "located" on the one hand, and of
which it is a constitutive part on the other. No invention of a system (of
signs or concepts) to overcome this paradox is possible, because there
is no "outside" from which the resolution of the paradox is possible.[29]
Narrative most clearly articulates the paradox without seeking to resolve

it; it reveals the puzzling or aporetic nature of human experience, but it cannot release us from the corresponding tension that results from this insoluble puzzle.[30]

The intentionality and luminosity of consciousness were the two modes of consciousness appearing most clearly in a long line of philosophical texts that Voegelin examined, and beyond them, in a variety of even more ancient religious symbols. Gradually, however, Voegelin also uncovered a third characteristic of consciousness' appearance: it is not only intentional and yet participatory, it is also self-reflexive. Consciousness "knows itself," revealing itself or its processes of discovery to itself. Voegelin symbolized this dimension of consciousness as "the reflective distance of consciousness to its own participation in thing-reality and It-reality." When brought to persistent remembrance, this reflexive quality of consciousness prevents the thinker from being derailed into misconstructions and gnostic or magical speculations. Deliberately to recall one's own experience of the realities revealed in consciousness is to engage in the anamnetic experiments first attempted by Plato and narratively re-enacted by Voegelin.[31]

But what has any of this to do with politics? Surely this highly abstract, slightly mystical description of human experience is far removed from, if connected at all to, the everyday problems of politics. These we usually understand as the problems of "allocating values," of ruling, of coercing, or even of persuading others to join in common projects with us.[32] For Voegelin, however, the leap is not so great. Every society is a "fact, or an event, in the external world" that can be studied like any other natural phenomenon by an external observer. It is not, however, merely that, or even most importantly that. We recall that society was for Voegelin one of the four "poles" of the quaternarian structure in which we find ourselves. Although "it has externality as one of its important components," society

> is as a whole a little world, a cosmion, illuminated with meaning from within by the human beings who continuously create and bear it as the mode and condition of their self-realization. It is illuminated through an elaborate symbolism, in various degrees of compactness and differentiation—from rite, through myth, to theory—and this symbolism illuminates it with meaning in so far as the symbols make the internal structure of such a cosmion, the relations between its

members and groups of members, as well as its existence as a whole, transparent for the mystery of human existence.[33]

Politics is indeed the activity of persuading others to engage in common projects. As an activity of ruling, moreover, it may certainly include co-ercion and authoritative allocations of material and social goods. But such expressions and exercises of power are inevitably located in a variety of social and political institutions ranging from informal and tacit sets of social "norms" to specific constitutional rules to large-scale bureau-cracies. In any case, the exercise of power is interpreted and justified by the meanings that are attributed to power by the human beings who "create and bear" this "little [political] world" as the "mode and condi-tion of their self-realization."[34] To act politically is to speak and act among others with an end in mind, to attempt to share that end with others and hold it in common with them, and also to attribute signifi-cance to it within a wider (shared) context of meaning. This context ranges from a specific tradition of thinking about politics to a crude doc-trine of politics to a scarcely articulated notion of what we are doing in our political activities.

The self-illumination of such a "cosmion," however, raises ques-tions in the mind of the one who reflects on its meaning. We recall that the directedness of political activity toward some notion of what is good leads to a question of the nature of what this good itself might be.[35] The nature of the good is illuminated for society through the symbols it cre-ates in the course of its self-illumination. Indeed, argues Voegelin,

> The self-illumination of society through symbols is an integral part of social reality, and one may even say its essential part, for through such symbolization the members of a society experience it as more than an accident or a convenience; they experience it as of their human es-sence. And, inversely, the symbols express the experience that man is fully man by virtue of his participation in a whole which transcends his particular existence, by virtue of his participation in the *xynon*, the common, as Heraclitus called it, the first Western thinker who differ-entiated this concept.[36]

In other words, the very language we use to order ourselves politically is a language that reflects our experience of order; this experience in turn leads us to reflect on our knowledge of that order through our conscious participation in it. Thus, reflection on the order of things leads to reflection on our consciousness of that order. More important yet, as we shall see, is Voegelin's claim that a badly formed consciousness of order generally leads specifically to a badly formed political order.

NARRATIVE AND METAPHYSICS

The central issue of this chapter concerns the shape of Voegelin's considerations of consciousness. I have suggested that Voegelin's distinctions and the role that his theory of consciousness plays in his overall thought cannot be properly understood in isolation from a consideration of the workings of narrative in his thought, or, more directly, the work that narrative does in the self-understanding of consciousness. This crucial fact, frequently overlooked, may help to remove some of the overly abstract qualities of Voegelin's reflections. Since existence and consciousness are neither categories nor objects but exegetical symbols, how do we "point" to them, as it were? How do we communicate their qualities, their sheer being-there? We do so by means of symbols.[37] But symbols, isolated from a context, are merely the aesthetic decorations of a polite nihilism. The *context*, the connecting fabric, is given by a narrative, and this narrated context encompasses an existential reflection, as William Thompson explains:

> At the very least, narrative brings home the inseparability of form and content, the need to participate in the form to "experience" the content/meaning. The lived, dramatic quality of life (what Voegelin calls the "event" dimension of story), with its "divine-human movements and countermovement," its elements of living activity, tension, struggle, reversal, etc., finds its irreplaceable expression in narrative. But this event dimension of every story involves an attempt to convey "insights into the order of reality."[38]

Thus, Voegelin concludes that "the story is the symbolic form the questioner has to adopt necessarily when he gives an account of his quest as the event of wresting, by the response of his human search to a divine movement, the truth of reality from a reality pregnant with truth yet unrevealed."[39]

To state this conclusion in another way, Voegelin engages in a kind of exegesis of critical exploration that Nicholas Lash describes as the role of theology, philosophy, or "metaphysics" within the Christian tradition. Since this tradition had an integral part in Voegelin's own reflections on the course of Western philosophy and politics, it is clearly appropriate as a source of examples here. According to Lash, Christian practice is a narrative practice. More specifically, it is a practice of autobiographical or "self-involving" narrative, in which the narrator is located within the story she tells. The storyteller articulates the Christian story and its meaning, but she herself is also an integral part of it.[40] In a certain sense, then, it is telling while "on-stage" the story of existence "on-stage." The purpose of theology, "metaphysics," or (noetic) philosophy within this tradition has been to serve as a regulative critique for the stories that are being told. The role of these activities is decidedly *not* to offer determinate "proofs" of God's existence and so forth. Rather, they are activities of ascertaining and testing rigor in logic, conceptual coherence, and terminological consistency when Christians tell their stories or talk about them. They are "non-narrative mode[s] of discourse" that are critical reflections on the story being told.[41]

But what sort of a thing, then, is narrative? First, it is neither precisely a "dimension" of consciousness, nor a "constituent," but rather, like language and temporality, for example, a component of consciousness in and through which consciousness and its objects are reflected to consciousness itself. In simple terms, narrative is the primary mode through and in which the "actor on-stage" reflects on his existence "on-stage." Like consciousness, narrative is itself both intentional (a story told by someone about something) and luminous (a story that "emerges from the It-reality"[42]). The structure of consciousness is thereby replicated along these two dimensions in the structure of narrative.[43]

Second, a narrative is not, strictly speaking, a form of symbolism, but a mode of symbolization. It is an ordering, so to speak, of the symbols of experience into a concrete whole. In Michael Wyschogrod's term, it is a work of "intelligence," which is "a working endowment rather than a theory [that] can be active in the absence of a philosophical theory about the rationality of the universe and the structure of mind that enables it to grasp the rationality inherent in the world." Intelligence is in this sense "a quality of brightness that enables all normal human beings to some extent and some to an extraordinary extent to grasp relations and implications in complex situations." Narrative is the primary, pre-noetic manner in which such relations, implications, and insights are expressed.[44] In Hayden White's terms, following Ricoeur, it is a "'grasping together' of the elements of situations in which 'meaningful action' has occurred," and this grasping is "configured" "through the instrumentality of plot."[45] Narrative thereby becomes the material that noetic philosophy explicates.

By Voegelin's own account—and Lash (in another context) concurs—such a philosophical explication or exegesis can never become an activity of transforming into concepts the symbols that the narrative employs to express the experienced realities of the narrator (or theologian). It can only be a kind of indirect "pointing," a particular use of analogy: "The forms of Christian discourse are set between the poles of metaphor and analogy, of narrative and metaphysics."[46] If it becomes the former, we begin to talk as if—to use our previous metaphors—the "stage" and the "quaternarian structure of consciousness" were objects and topics; the "balance of consciousness" is then lost.[47] (We are reminded again of the need for persistent remembrance of the existential tension between human wisdom and ignorance. The metaphors one weaves into a story to express one's experiences of the Divine or of existence in consciousness are therefore not a conclusion, a result, or a final determination, but a beginning. They are, in Lash's words, a road map, not the countryside. All such metaphors are, like the indices of Voegelin's analyses, exegetical symbols, not determinative concepts. We must not mistake the map for the reality: because our "knowledge of existence is from within, not without," it is limited by the impossibility of a universal and absolute perspective that only an "external" onlooker can supply. Consequently, it must be mediated symbolically, which is to say that it is communicated in tropes.[48] Such tropes, even at the highest levels of differentiation and theorization, remain the constituent linguistic elements of a story that is ultimately and simultaneously the "story told by the It," and "the story [that] emerges from the It-reality." It is a story of which we remain a part and within which we are therefore bounded, even as we seek philosophically to differentiate its components.[49]

The noetic quality even of narrative and the narrational luminosity of consciousness lead Voegelin to reflect that at the deepest participatory (metaleptic) level, "story" itself becomes "the symbolism that will express the awareness of the divine-human movement and counter-move-

ment in the quest for truth.'' This reflection does not, however, reduce
''story'' to merely another exegetical symbol. Rather, as we saw earlier:

> Telling a story in this metaleptic sense of the term is not a matter of
> choice. The story is the symbolic form the questioner has to adopt
> necessarily when he gives an account of his quest as the event of
> wresting, by the response of his human search to a divine movement,
> the truth of reality from a reality pregnant with truth yet unrevealed.
> Moreover, the story remains the constant symbolism of the quest even
> when the tension between divine and human story is reduced to the
> zero of identity as in the dialectical story told by the self-identical *logos*
> of the Hegelian system.[50]

Accordingly, Voegelin's extensive use of concepts, neologisms, and re-
symbolizations, if they remain bereft of contextualizing stories, threatens
to descend once more into a kind of scholasticism, an intentionalist, re-
ificatory ''description'' of consciousness. Its corollary political threat, as
Richard Faber tendentiously but correctly asserts, is a kind of reactionary, conservative authoritarianism.[51] Narrative can, therefore, play a key
role in an exegesis of consciousness, because it provides a context for
the exegetical symbols; this context reduces somewhat the threat of their
scholastic reification, and thereby helps to control the symbols themselves.

On the other hand, using narrative as a way of uncovering Voegelin's theory of consciousness may merely reproduce the existential problem he notes in the matter of mystery, because narrative is itself an attempt to force closure. In a study comparing annals and chronicles as
historical narrative, Hayden White concludes that narrative requires
''the capacity to envision a set of events as belonging to the same order
of meaning,'' which in turn ''requires some metaphysical principle by
which to translate difference into similarity.'' That is to say, ''it requires
a 'subject' common to all of the referents of the various sentences that
register an event as having occurred.''[52] But the introduction of a subject
also introduces a requirement for a meaning, which White, following
Hegel, suggests is always a moral one: ''If every fully realized story, however we define that familiar but conceptually elusive entity . . . points to
a moral or endows events, whether real or imaginary, with a significance
that they do not possess as a mere sequence, then it seems possible to

conclude that every historical narrative has as its latent or manifest purpose the desire to moralize the events of which it treats."[53] Such moralizing binds a narrative, closing off certain possibilities even while it may hold others open; it is a form of signification, hence a closure.

But closures are not all equivalent. Meaning and consequence vary with the signification that the teller of the story intends. Thus, as we will see, Voegelin fought against some closures, as in his attack on modern ideologues who try to force closure on history as a whole. Contrary to the claims of ideologies, we do not know what the ultimate meaning (if there is one) of history *is*, and to purport to do so is to attempt to close the inherent open-endedness of our bounded existence in time.[54] This move closes off the mystery of being, which is to say it rejects the transcendental pole of our existence. It displays ignorance or rejection of the wisdom-ignorance tension that the story of consciousness originally reveals. But other narrative closures—a rejection of ideological systems, for example—uphold the mystery of being, even while they inspire in us hope and trust. Voegelin himself imposes certain forms of this sort of closure, which leads hostile readers to accuse him of right-wing authoritarianism.[55]

One may conclude from the preceding argument that narrative is not merely an appendage to an account of consciousness because of the way it delivers the truths of consciousness, but that it is crucial to any such account. This centrality of the story form is the consequence of the temporality of consciousness: "Everything that is recounted occurs in time, takes time, unfolds temporally; and what unfolds in time can be recounted. Perhaps, indeed, every temporal process is recognized as such only to the extent that it can, in one way or another, be recounted."[56] Indeed, "to experience time as future, past, and present rather than as a series of instants in which every one has the same weight or significance as every other is to experience 'historicality,'" which is to say, meaningful (narrated) existence in time.[57] By this reasoning, to repeat, narrative provides the material that philosophy dissects; it is antecedent to "systematic reflection on consciousness."[58] If consciousness does, in fact, represent itself to itself narratively, then what materials it delivers and how it does so is not merely an issue that is interesting, yet peripheral, to the problem of consciousness, but an integral constituent of it. Narrative does not thereby become a structural dimension of consciousness in the manner of intentionality, luminosity, and reflexivity, because it is not

an aspect of the sheer ontic "whatness" of consciousness as are these pri-
mal components. Rather, to reword Ricoeur, the time dimension of
consciousness makes its mode of self-revelation and self-reflection narrational. Such an account of narrative and consciousness, moreover, makes
philosophy a second-order task, attendant in a critical, regulative manner
on the stories that "consciousness tells." To make this claim is not to lose
sight of the fact that much of philosophy itself is a kind of narrative:
insofar as it is an "exploration," we tell a story of that exploration. But
this latter narrative checks our first-order narrative, which is expressed
not in the analytical, exegetical symbols of philosophy, but in the primary symbols of myth, poetry, and story.[59] The argument suggests, of
course, that even the symbols embedded in fertility idols, ancient friezes,
and paleolithic drawings, for example, are only intelligible because we
can make them a part of a narrative (which may, in this case, be a prior
structure we bring to them or a structure we translate out of them).[60]

THE MODES AND PURPOSES OF NARRATIVE

As I will explore in greater depth in later chapters, Voegelin was
keenly sensitive—along with many of his sympathetic readers[61]—to a
crisis in contemporary thought concerning politics and concerning
human existence more generally. He often used the language of "loss,"
"eclipse," "disorder," or "disturbance" to indicate this crisis.[62] Most of
the terms that he used were not his own, and the texts and historical
episodes from which he drew them indicated that an experience of crisis
in thought or in political order has not been limited to our present era.
His critical analyses of these texts and episodes showed him that such
recurring crises in history have involved a loss of awareness or a rejection
of man's place in the order of being, and that a philosopher's activity
could include the recovery of such awareness. I will consider specific
examples more closely in the following chapters.

Let us at this point consider the following: how does narrative as I
have here described it bring to our awareness the structure and dynamic
of consciousness in such a way that they are made transparent for analysis, in such a way that our understanding of our "place" in the order of
things, as it were, can be either articulated or restored? In other words,

how does narrative function, and what tasks does it perform in regard to consciousness?

At the most basic and obvious level, narrative answers the question: what happened? To speak of consciousness is to fall prey to the danger of treating it as a topic or concept, which may mislead one into forgetting that it is neither of these, but rather that it refers to a continuous event, a dynamic process. Consciousness at one level is a "happening," namely, a process in reality. At another level, it is constituted by a temporal succession of events, which are also processes and events in (and of) reality.[63] And, like any happening, these can only be recalled narratively. This basic fact leads some theologians and ethicists to assert, like Ricoeur, that our lives are essentially narratively formed. As meaningful units, both our lives as a whole and the distinct episodes within them appear to us as narrative constructions, because we are contingent, historically constituted beings who require narrative to make our contingent history intelligible to ourselves.[64]

As a mode of discourse and a topic of study, narrative encompasses much more than can be considered in this chapter: Here I will rehearse only the salient points of its role in relation to uncovering the decisive feature of Voegelin's theory of consciousness. Without excluding other perspectives, I will take my cue primarily from studies of narrative performed in Jewish and Christian theological contexts. This approach is appropriate, I have suggested, because Voegelin's concerns were ultimately either political or placed in the context of a community of scholars, and the practices of narrative in Christian and Jewish traditions are always community affairs.[65] Even though Voegelin preferred Plato's symbolizations and forms of remembrance, Christian narrative studies provide a more accessible deliberation on the role and character of narrative than do Plato's noetic reflections. And since Voegelin did claim to have found particularly well-articulated differentiations of the human experience of existence in the Christian stories, one may expect that an analysis from this narrative perspective will produce immediately pertinent results, not in need of retranslation, for a theory of consciousness seemingly sympathetic to that tradition.[66]

Narratives range from the simple folk tales and fables that seek to teach childhood lessons, to the larger biographies and autobiographies that tell the story of a human life (and perhaps tell it whole), to the grand myths and wider historical narratives of religious and political communities, to the grandest story of the "It-reality" itself.[67] All such narratives have in common a set of functions that are of immediate concern to the problem of consciousness and to Voegelin's analysis of the structure of being. First, a story displays particularities in such a way that it sheds light on the generalities that constitute its particularities or that constitute the "family resemblance" (to use Wittgenstein's phrase) of its particularities in the whole. Accordingly, these "works of intelligence" permit a kind of inductive reasoning. They illuminate particular principles of conduct or consciousness within the context of our consciousness of the whole. Stories become an inductive guide for prudent reasoning, deliberation, action, and reflection on experience.

Second, stories display the essentially contingent character of human existence even as they weave these contingencies into a comprehensible whole. Stories are a way of presenting and illuminating complexity, rendering it at least partially transparent, even for those whose analytical faculties are not of the highest quality: "From the intelligible character of the plot, it follows that the ability to follow a story constitutes a very sophisticated form of understanding."[68] Thus, both in their inductive qualities and in their display of contingencies within a larger context, stories are a kind of illumination. Stories provide a context within which human existence in its particulars and in its general shape can be understood.

Finally, stories perform these two functions by indirection. They do not use analytical categories to "point" to what is being talked about; rather, they use action, plot, and characters to illustrate or illuminate. They are indirect in the treatment of a topic or problem, no matter how intentionalist the author's writing may be. To re-echo Lash, they are metaphorical constructions. How these attributes of narrative operate in practice may be shown, first, in an account of the role of narratives in the more restricted realm of ethical reflection, and then in the broader instance of Voegelin's anamnetic reflections.

SYSTEM AND STORY IN ETHICAL REFLECTION AND CONSCIOUS REFLEXIVITY

Stanley Hauerwas and David Burrell have argued at length that narrative is an important, indeed the central, resource for ethical reflection.

They maintain that "character and moral notions only take on meaning in a narrative," that "narrative and explanation stand in an intimate relationship, and therefore moral disagreements involve rival histories of explanation," and that "narrative functions as a form of rationality" in opposition to the standard, modern account of ethics that calls for a "moral objectivity" in order to secure ethical certainty.[69] In other words, coherent ethical reflection requires not a system but a story.[70] Similarly, moral reflection, in Voegelin's account, requires reflection on who we are and "where" we are, which recurs to reflect on our existence as being "Inbetween" on the quaternarian stage.[71] It seems that reflection on morals or ethics will have a character not dissimilar to reflection on consciousness; in Voegelin's account, at least, the latter subsumes the former. Ethical reflection is a subset of reflections on the order of being. Accordingly, similar arguments can be made on behalf of narrative as a way of illuminating both the intellectual practice of ethical reflection and the deeper Voegelinian question of human consciousness. For Voegelin, narrative conveys the experience and meaning of consciousness beyond the important but—for him—subsidiary role of practical ethical reflection. The deeper role is replicated on the more concrete plane of practical ethical deliberation.

Narrative performs its moral functions in the following ways. First, Hauerwas and Burrell argue that to account for our moral life we cannot take account merely of the decisions we make; we must also have a "narrative that forms us to have one kind of character rather than another." Similarly, an account of existence in consciousness is not merely an account of intentions, which Voegelin sees as the principal shortcoming of the German Idealist reaction to the Enlightenment.[72] Nor are the narratives that form us "arbitrarily acquired," even though "they will embody many factors we might consider 'contingent.'" Such stories are a narrative display of our character, which, in ethical reflection, "provides the context necessary to pose the terms of a decision, or to determine whether a decision should be made at all." Accordingly, "[a]s our stories . . . they will determine what kind of moral considerations—that is, what reasons—will count at all. Hence, these narratives must be included in any account of moral rationality that does not unwarrantedly exclude large aspects of our moral existence, i.e., moral character."[73] In the same way, the structure and dynamics of consciousness are insufficiently accounted for by a series of exegetical symbols that serve as pointers to our experience of them: we require the contextual indirection of a narrative to weave this structure and dynamic into a comprehending and comprehensible whole.

Such considerations are not simply self-authenticating, however, and the language in which they are wrought is not a private code:

> It is exactly the category of narrative that helps us to see that we are not forced to choose between some universal standpoint and the subjectivist appeals to our own experience. For our experiences always come in the form of narratives that can be checked against themselves as well as against others' experiences. I cannot make my behavior mean anything I want it to mean, for I have learned to understand my life from the stories I have learned from others.[74]

In the same way, Voegelin was fond of claiming that the true test of the validity of a philosopher's results is their lack of originality. Insofar as we hear the symbols that express human experience echoed elsewhere, we can be relatively more assured that we are, so to speak, "getting our story straight."[75] Indeed, the solipsism of self-authentication is narratively disciplined and precluded:

> The language the agent uses to describe his behavior, to himself and to others, is not uniquely his; it is *ours*, just as the notions we use have meanings that can be checked for appropriate or inappropriate use. But what allows us to check the truthfulness of these accounts of our behavior are the narratives in which our moral notions gain their paradigm uses. An agent cannot make his behavior mean anything he wants, since at the very least it must make sense within his own story, as well as be compatible with the narrative embodied in the language he uses. All our notions are narrative-dependent, including the notion of rationality.[76]

But the use of narrative in this sense opens up further considerations. Let us consider the problem in this way: How do we ourselves recover a view of our existence that gives us a "history that will 'see life steadily and see it whole,' a view of our past from which good fiction, good philosophy, good theology, good poetry, good art and good deeds can grow," or that "see[s] everything steadily and see[s] it whole,"[77] and how do we make this vision recoverable for anyone else? Voegelin's answer was that the story must speak "with an authority commonly present in everybody's consciousness" and to "what is common (*xynon*) to the order of man's existence as a partner in the comprehending reality."[78] To make this possibility real requires an act of imagination. Narrative engages the faculty of imagination not by delivering an authoritative teaching, but by "disclos[ing] a world in which its readers are invited to dwell, or [by depicting] a character in relation to whom the readers are asked to see themselves."[79] A story consequently has a unique "logic of authorization" that may or may not compel acceptance but that permits our own exploratory gestures:

> The readers are brought into the narratives; it becomes a context for reflection and action. The insights, convictions, dispositions, and so forth that the readers achieve in their interaction with the text are . . . the fruits of a struggle. What is achieved is not simply read off the text and accepted but is rather created through the engagement of the readers—who have their distinctive backgrounds and locations—with the text. It is (or may be) authorized by the text, insofar as it is in keeping with the sense of the story. . . . But what is "in keeping with the sense of the story" cannot be predetermined; it is not latent in the text itself but must be produced through the reader's own engagement with the text. Thus, although the text is normative, . . . its normativeness does not stifle diversity and creativity. Indeed, it positively mandates them.[80]

We now turn to such a text.

"ANAMNETIC EXPERIMENTS"

Ronald Thiemann has spoken of narrative texts as providing "followable world[s]."[81] Such worlds are not offered in doctrinal metaphysics but in stories. Voegelin recorded a brief set of anamnetic experiments that point to such a world through a set of narratives. His lifework might be interpreted as an explication of the meaning of such anamnetic stories. In them, we see the initial, compact representation of a world that Voegelin would then seek noetically to differentiate into its constituent parts. This claim seems to demand that we properly understand not only narrative as such but the specific genre of narrative at hand: what *kind* of story is it that serves as the material, so to speak, for noetic philosophy, and what is the relationship of such stories to the "story of the It" that is in part revealed by the analysis of these smaller stories? Voegelin's "experiments" were the retelling of childhood stories and experiences that seemed to Voegelin either to be pointing to something in (his) consciousness that was beyond the story itself or that seemed to make him aware for the first time of the basic experiential characteristics of human existence, such as the passage of time, the yearning for perfection, the deceptiveness of appearances, and so on.

In the account of narrative that I have offered here, stories are the conveyors of a "structure and an order of meaning" that seems to depend on the story itself for its very existence.[82] For Voegelin we must move one step further (avoiding the nominalism that such an account might imply) and say that narrative is a form of symbolization, referring to and revealing the real, originating experiences of consciousness. Narrative both reveals these experiences and makes their compact revelation in the story open to further noetic analysis—that is, open to analysis that differentiates the elements of the compact experiences themselves. In this way, narrative is, paradoxically, both a symbolization that arises in the "reflective distance" of consciousness and also prior to it in our pre-noetic experiences and the pre-noetic stories of them that we tell. These originating experiences first appear in a narrational mode, because they take place in time. To become intelligible, they must be told to us as stories, because we are time-bound, historical (narratively formed) beings.

The stories of Voegelin's anamnetic experiments are not simply myths, however, because, unlike myth, they are understood from their very origin to be the compact articulation of something to be further differentiated; this is an understanding of itself that human consciousness still bound to mythical narrative does not have. When a person gains such self-understanding, he is on the verge of becoming a philosopher. We recall again that "noesis does not bring knowledge of previously unknown reality, but differentiated insight into hitherto compactly experienced reality."[83]

Moving from "narrativity" and narrative in general to a consideration of specific narratives, we immediately find the plethora of narrative types I spoke of earlier, culminating in the uncompletable story of the "It"—existence and its Beyond—itself. An account of the experience of consciousness within the story of the "It" is a narrative that is the telling of an event, or experience, or a series of them. Voegelin's account of consciousness, in other words, is the telling of the experience(s) of consciousness (and these experiences are made available to us by the luminous quality of consciousness that sheds light on its other qualities) through the events that bring forth the experiences and make them intelligible.

Such an account can be cast in a narrative, then explicated in a noetic analysis (and the account of how we come to the explication is itself a narrative). The initial narrative (the "grasping together" of experiences in time) is, I have argued, prior both chronologically and conceptually to the noetic exegesis. But what, exactly, is "grasped together" in the anamnetic experiments? What, in other words, are the stories, and what are they about? They are, to begin with, a recounting of episodes from childhood memory. Not surprisingly, these episodes are not only recounted in narrative form but the original experiences themselves seem to have been strongly narrativized, even as they made themselves available to Voegelin's childhood consciousness. The importance of most of the episodes, Voegelin states, is clear to him. I take this to mean that he is able without difficulty to read back into these episodes the exegetical indices he developed in his later philosophical analyses. But the experiences and their narration—as Voegelin makes eminently clear—are prior to philosophy. These are the "experiences that have opened sources of excitement," that have "excited consciousness to the 'awe' of existence," and "from which issue the urge to further philosophical reflection."[84]

We are thus confronted with a triple meaning. The narrated experiences of the anamnesis are narrated self-revelations of consciousness in compact form. They are also events that initiate a quest. This quest is an event that is, in turn, "part of a story told by the It, and yet a story to be told by the human questioner, if he wants to articulate the consciousness of his quest as an act of participation in the comprehending story."[85] Third, the narrated experiences are therefore episodes in "an It-story that tells itself through the events of the participatory quests for truth."[86] For the alert questioner, they form—when philosophically differentiated—part of "the consciousness of the quest as an event whose story must be told as part of the story of reality becoming luminous for its truth."[87] Narrative, therefore, cannot be concretely located at a specific level of compactness or philosophical differentiation in the story of consciousness. Rather, it seems to penetrate into every step of the unfolding intentionality, then luminosity, then reflexivity of consciousness itself and, thereby, into every level of the "It-story."

But let us consider for a moment the other narrative qualities of these episodes. Most but not all of the memories are "stories" in the clearest sense of containing a plot, action, and characters. "The Cloud Castle," for example, seems merely a descriptive episode. And yet, the possibility of plot and action lurk in the castle itself: the "Knight of the Wolkenburg" "dwells" there, and he "travels much on mysterious business." Where does he travel? What does he do when he is there? Is the Wolkenburg merely a resting place? Why is he so melancholy?[88]

Beyond these childish queries for elaboration, out of which one can fashion a story (but upon which one can also fashion a noetic reflection), there is the more important fact that at least one implotted character lurks in the deep background of every anamnetic episode, namely the "I" that has the evocative memory. It seems to be for this reason that Voegelin deems it necessary to weave his memories into a wider context, by adding frequent autobiographical-contextual remarks. The story of the person whose memories they are is important to the memories themselves. This larger narrative provides a portion of the reflexivity of the anamnetic event.

The easy narrative structures of the memories pass over nearly unnoticed into their anamnetic and illuminating functions. To speak of "metaxy," "balance of consciousness," and so forth is one thing; childhood memories that excite the imagination are another. Here we have, indeed, the creation of worlds that the reader, too, can imaginatively recreate, enter, and explore. And it is not primarily the childish scenes that are recreated, but rather the puzzles that they evoke. This evocation is part of what Voegelin means when he claims that "the *anamnesis* had to recapture the childhood experiences that let themselves be recaptured because they were living forces in the present constitution of his consciousness."[89] The stories evoke our own memories, and hence our own reflections. But they do so without philosophical vocabulary, without the need for technical expertise. This ease of access renders the stories susceptible, however, to multiple interpretations. One can only grimace, for example, at what a semiliterate and dogmatic "Freudian" might make of some of them. And at this point the regulative language and

practices of the philosopher become a supplement to the anamnetic experiments. The narratives, Voegelin cautions, have to do with "excite-
ments from the experience of a transcendence in space, time, matter,
history, wishful dreams, and wishful times." They serve as indices, not
of sexual repression and Oedipal complexes, but of consciousness becoming aware of the wonder and mystery of existence in space and
time.[90]

These episodes of mystery are fragments, irruptions from a larger
source, namely the consciousness of the participating "I"—in this case
Voegelin and potentially his readers—that recalls them. Although only
fragments, they give hints of a larger whole. They serve as a narrated
lens, so to speak, on a life that we can imagine "steadily and whole."
They do not give us this view, but we can imagine it from them in a
way that we cannot from the analysis of consciousness alone, in the preceding, analytical chapters of Voegelin's *Anamnesis*. The evocations of
wonder recall for us the basic shape of the "stage" on which the drama
(story) of life is acted out. This life becomes visible and intelligible when
we can imagine the whole. Such visibility might *not* occur were we not
forewarned by the prefatory philosophical remarks. But that philosophical caveat (which, we recall, is itself narratively contextualized in a story
of a "quest") does not vitiate the centrality of narrative; it merely suggests the need for a regulative framework to govern such narrative. No
narrative is entirely self-interpreting. Although one may clearly speak of
the "plain sense" of a text or a story, without an exegesis of some kind,
within either a tradition of reading or a tradition of more clearly articulated analytical inquiry, this "plain sense" remains surprisingly elusive.
Texts have a "plain sense" only in a community of consensus. Once
again, we are confronted by the elusive quality of consciousness, whose
characteristics are secured only by a kind of faith complemented by a
community of the faithful. This appears to be the case both within and
outside specifically "religious" contexts, as the notion of a "community
of scholars" attests.[91]

Here again, we are pointed to Voegelin's summation concerning
the authoritativeness of the anamnetic episodes for an account of human
consciousness. Even though these stories have an open-ended quality,
their indeterminacy does not imply that "madness and chaos . . . are
our inevitable fate." As Thiemann has it, madness is inevitable only if
philosophy is construed as a "perfect light that dispels all darkness and

banishes all shadows." But Voegelin does not search for a "true foundation for knowledge [that] needs no external illumination, but glows with the light of self-illumination."[92] He is not an Enlightenment philosophe. "Madness, darkness, and chaos" are not inevitable if the illumination of narrative coupled with philosophical analysis and exegesis is imperfect but accepted in its imperfection. Nor, following Thiemann again, does the fact of interpretive diversity "decide the question of whether texts [or anamnetic episodes and their interpretation] yield followable worlds."[93] Multiple plausible interpretations, "narrative obscurity," and interpretive multiplicity do not vitiate the possibility and necessity of judgment, the possibility of criteria for preferring one reading over another, or the need for exegetical standards. Instead, they challenge us to reflect carefully as we develop such measures. Voegelin used these episodes to reveal the inadequacy of determinate theories of consciousness and to articulate another, more adequate mode of talking about these matters.[94] His anamnetic narratives, set within a philosophically disciplining framework, beckon us to take a look. They cannot do more.

CONCLUSIONS

The philosopher does not puzzle first and foremost over an experience of the "tensional qualities of existence." Rather, he is puzzled, awed, or bemused by the flowing identity of a crowd (*Anamnesis,* 39), by knowing that he does not know (*In Search of Order,* 40), by the awe inspired by the sonority of a vocable (*Anamnesis,* 38), the experience of distance and perspective (*Anamnesis,* 42), the yearning for perfection (*Anamnesis,* 40–41), and so forth. He is engaged by his storied encounter with reality. When this puzzlement, awe, or rapture becomes luminous to itself in consciousness, the story of philosophy begins.

The centrality of narrative to an explication of the dynamics and structures of consciousness implies that one need not be a philosopher or have extraordinary analytical powers to grasp at least the rudiments of the character of one's human existence. Stories deliver up for us a picture of a world. It may be that the dogmatization of such stories means that something of the mystery and depth of being is lost,[95] but such reification is not a necessary outcome of telling stories. Indeed, the anamnetic narratives retain for us a hint of the mystery and tensions of being that a "system" cannot sustain and that a systematic account of consciousness may find more difficult to uphold.[96] It is for this reason, also—since Voegelin's theory of consciousness does not permit us to refer to the "existence" of the "It-reality" (as though it were a "thing")—that Voegelin refers to the "story of the It." Such a story—which contains both the metanarrative or narrative base of the "It-reality," but also the mega-narrative or super-narrative of social and political myth and the personal narratives of biography, along with the anamnetic narration of the self-discoveries of consciousness—keeps in view the entirety of reality from "It" to "I" to "Thou," doing so not blindly but with a view to the whole.

Voegelin's anamnetic episodes bring out from hiding (by an act of remembrance) the originating experiences that potentially bind all narratives together in the meaning given by the whole. They reopen for his readers an exploration of the whole in terms of the fundamental experiences to which all philosophical exploration must return. They are narratives that illuminate in an indirect yet decisive way a true story of the whole, whose authority is "commonly present in [our] consciousness," and whose very presence the stories themselves invoke as they help us imaginatively to drag up into reflecting consciousness the experience and puzzles whereof they speak. The evocation itself is the sign that the stories speak "what is common to the order of man's existence as a partner in the comprehensive reality." We can listen, re-enact, and reflect.

NOTES

1. Eric Voegelin, *Über die Form des amerikanischen Geistes* (Tübingen, Germany: J. C. B. Mohr, 1928), 1ff.

2. Among others, see: Michael Franz, *Eric Voegelin and the Politics of Spiritual Revolt: The Roots of Modern Ideology* (Baton Rouge: Louisiana State University Press, 1992); Glenn Hughes, *Mystery and Myth in the Philosophy of Eric Voegelin* (Columbia: University of Missouri Press, 1993); Kevin Keulmann, *The Balance of Consciousness: Eric Voegelin's Political Theory* (University Park: Pennsylvania State University Press, 1990); Michael P. Morrissey, *Consciousness and Transcendence: The Theology of Eric Voegelin* (Notre Dame, Ind.: University of Notre Dame Press, 1994); Ronald D. Srigley, *Eric Voegelin's Platonic Theology: Philosophy of Consciousness and Symbolization in a New Perspective* (Lewiston, N.Y.: The Edwin Mellen Press, 1991).

3. Eric Voegelin, *The New Science of Politics: An Introduction* (Chicago: University of Chicago Press, 1952), *passim*.

4. Voegelin, *New Science of Politics*, 27–28; Eric Voegelin, *Israel and Revelation*, vol. 1 of *Order and History* (Baton Rouge: Lousiana State University Press, 1956), 3–11.

5. Eric Voegelin, *Anamnesis: Zur Theorie der Geschicht und Politik* (Munich: R. Piper Verlag, 1966), 7; translated in John J. Rainieri, *Eric Voegelin and the Good Society* (Columbia: The University of Missouri Press, 1995), 16.

6. Eric Voegelin, *Autobiographical Reflections*, ed. Ellis Sandoz (Baton Rouge: Louisiana State University Press, 1989), 93.

7. On Voegelin's suspicion of metaphysics, see Eugene Webb, *Philosophers of Consciousness* (Seattle: University of Washington Press, 1988), 128–30.

8. Eugene Webb, *Eric Voegelin: Philosopher of History* (Seattle: University of Washington Press, 1981), 285. Cf. Eric Voegelin, *Anamnesis*, trans. and ed. by Gerhart Niemeyer (Notre Dame, Ind.: University of Notre Dame Press, 1978), 147–63, 89–97.

9. For useful introductions, see Hans Kellner, *Language and Historical Representation: Getting the Story Crooked* (Madison: University of Wisconsin Press, 1989); Wallace Martin, *Recent Theories of Narrative* (Ithaca, N.Y.: Cornell University Press, 1986).

10. Paul Ricoeur, *From Text to Action: Essays in Hermeneutics II*, trans. Kathleen Blamey and John B. Thompson (Evanston, Ill.: Northwestern University Press, 1991), 2.

11. See the "Foreward" by his widow, Lissy Voegelin, in Eric Voegelin, *In Search of Order*, vol. 5 of *Order and History* (Baton Rouge: Louisiana State University Press, 1987).

12. Jürgen Gebhardt, "Epilogue," in Voegelin, *In Search of Order*, 109–18.

13. Voegelin, *Israel and Revelation*, 1.

14. Voegelin, *Israel and Revelation*, 1.

15. Friedrich Nietzsche, *Ecce Homo* ("Why I am so Wise"), ed. and trans. Walter Kaufmann (New York: Random House, 1969), 222.

16. Voegelin, *Israel and Revelation*, 1.

17. Voegelin, *Israel and Revelation*, 2.

18. Voegelin, *Anamnesis*, trans. Niemeyer, 100, 99.

19. Voegelin, *Israel and Revelation*, 2.

20. Eric Voegelin, "Immortality: Experience and Symbol," in *Published Essays: 1966–1985*, ed. Ellis Sandoz, vol. 12 of *The Collected Works of Eric Voegelin* (Baton Rouge: Louisiana State University Press, 1990), 91.

21. Eric Voegelin, "The Beginning and the Beyond," in *What Is History? and Other Late Unpublished Writings*, ed. Ellis Sandoz, vol. 28 of *The Collected Works of Eric Voegelin* (Baton Rouge: Louisiana State University Press, 1990), 185.

22. Voegelin, *In Search of Order*, 20–31.

23. Rainieri, *The Good Society*, 25; for an analysis of Voegelin's understanding of language in the complex of consciousness, see 25–34.

24. Hughes, *Mystery and Myth*, 36.

25. Cf. Hughes, *Mystery and Myth*, 107.

26. Webb, *Philosopher of History*, 283–84.

27. Voegelin, *In Search of Order*, 15–16.

28. Voegelin, *In Search of Order*, 15.

29. Voegelin, *In Search of Order*, 16–18.

30. Cf. Hayden White, *The Content of the Form: Narrative Discourse and Historical Representation* (Baltimore, Md.: Johns Hopkins University Press, 1987), 53.

31. Voegelin, *In Search of Order*, 40–41.

32. For examples, see David Easton, *A Systems Analysis of Political Life* (New York: John Wiley and Sons, 1965), 21; Alan P. Ball, *Modern Politics and Government* (London: Macmillan, 1971), 20; J. B. D. Miller, *The Nature of Politics* (Harmondsworth, U. K.: Penguin, 1965), 14; Bertrand de Jouvenal, *The Pure Theory of Politics* (New Haven, Conn.: Yale University Press, 1963), 30.

33. Voegelin, *New Science of Politics,* 27.

34. Voegelin, *New Science of Politics,* 27.

35. Leo Strauss, *What Is Political Philosophy? and Other Studies* (Chicago: The University of Chicago Press, 1959), 10.

36. Voegelin, *New Science of Politics*, 27–28.

37. Voegelin, *Israel and Revelation*, 3ff. Voegelin, "The Beginning," 185.

38. William Thompson, *Christology and Spirituality* (New York: The Crossroad Publishing Company, 1991), 29–30.

39. Voegelin, *In Search of Order*, 24.

40. Nicholas Lash, "Ideology, Metaphor and Analogy," in *The Philosophical Frontiers of Christian Theology: Essays presented to D. M. MacKinnon*, ed. Brian Hebblethwaite and Stewart Sutherland (Cambridge: Cambridge University Press, 1982), 74. Thompson's interest in Voegelin's pursuit of narrative is purely in the context of his own concern with Christological/experiential dialogue, and not with a view to Voegelin's larger philosophical project (*Christology*, 7–12).

41. Lash, "Ideology," 76ff.; cf. Voegelin, *Anamnesis*, 206. The usage here implies, incidentally, that Voegelin's two metaphors of consciousness with which I began this chapter are, in fact, brief stories. This implication forms a premise of the present chapter.

42. Voegelin, *In Search of Order*, 24.

43. Cf. White, *Content of the Form*, 51–52.

44. Michael Wyschogrod, *The Body of Faith: Judaism as Corporeal Election* (Minneapolis: Winston Press, 1983), 5; cf. Ricoeur, *Text to Action*, 4.

45. White, *Content of the Form*, 50–51. This "grasping together" reminds us

of Voegelin's early statement that "the historical line of meaning stretches like a rope over an abyss into which everything that cannot cling fast falls." (Die Sinn-linie der Geschichte läuft wie ein Seil über einen Abgrund, in den alles was sich auf ihm nicht halten kann, hinabstürtzt.") Voegelin, *Über die Form des Amerikani-schen Geistes*, 14.

46. Lash, "Ideology," 72. Cf. Lash's valuable comments on Thomas Aquinas' philosophical method, 79–85.

47. The term is Voegelin's. It refers to "the precarious awareness of the con-ditions of existence in the *metaxy* ["Plato's symbol representing the experience of human existence as "between" lower and upper poles: man and the divine, imperfection and perfection, ignorance and knowledge, and so on."], easily lost when the experience of being drawn toward the transcendental pole becomes sufficiently vivid to tempt one to expect escape from the *metaxy* and from the existential tension that characterizes it." Webb, *Philosopher of History*, 278, 284.

48. Voegelin, "What Is History," 3–13; *Anamnesis*, 175–82.

49. Kellner, *Historical Representation*, chap. 9; Webb, *Philosopher of History*, 271; Thompson, *Christology*, 28–29; Voegelin, *In Search of Order*, 24, 21, 26.

50. Voegelin, *In Search of Order*, 24.

51. Richard Faber, *Der Prometheus-Komplex: Zur Kritik der Politotheologie Eric Voegelins und Hans Blumenbergs* (Würzburg, Germany: Verlag Dr. Johannes König-shausen and Dr. Thomas Neuberg, 1984), 65–67.

52. White, *Content of the Form*, 16.

53. White, *Content of the Form*, 14.

54. Voegelin, *New Science of Politics*, 118–21.

55. Faber, *Prometheus-Komplex*, 22–25. Eugene Webb has carefully noted some of the problems that Voegelin's language and symbolic closures may pro-duce. *Philosophers of Consciousness*, 119–30.

56. Ricoeur, *Text to Action*, 2.

57. White, *Content of the Form*, 179; Paul Ricoeur, "Narrative Time," in *Crit-ical Inquiry* 7 no. 1 (1980):1, 171.

58 Voegelin, *Anamnesis*, 36–37; Ricoeur suggests such a relationship in *Text to Action*, 9–10.

59. Cf. Voegelin, *Anamnesis*, 36–37; *In Search of Order*, 21; Webb, *Philosophers of Consciousness*, 59–62; and section on "Anamnetic Experiments" below.

60. For an example of such "sense-making," see White, *Content of the Form*, 6–11.

61. Cf. David Walsh, *After Ideology: Recovering the Spiritual Foundations of Free-dom* (San Francisco: HarperCollins Publishers, 1990); and Franz, *Politics of Spiri-tual Revolt, passim*.

62. Voegelin, *In Search of Order*, 45–47.

63. Voegelin, *Anamnesis*, 12–13, 16–17.

64. Stanley Hauerwas, *The Peaceable Kingdom: A Primer in Christian Ethics* (Notre Dame: University of Notre Dame Press, 1983), 24–29. White makes a similar argument in his evaluation and summation of the first two volumes of Ricoeur's *Time and Narrative*. *Content of the Form*, 178–81; cf. Paul Ricoeur, *Time and Narrative,* vol. 1, trans. Kathleen McLaughlin and David Pellauer (Chicago: University of Chicago Press, 1984), 52–87.

65. James Wm. McClendon, *Systematic Theology: Ethics* (Nashville, Tenn.: Abingdon Press, 1986), 170–73, Michael Goldberg, *Theology and Narrative: A Critical Introduction* (Nashville, Tenn.: Abingdon Press, 1982). Hans Kellner, in contrast, seems more skeptical about the possibility of communities built around authoritative narratives (*Historical Representation*, x-xi, 330–33).

66. In the final two chapters, I will consider more closely Voegelin's sympathy for this particular tradition.

67. Voegelin, *In Search of Order*, 13.

68. Ricoeur, *Text to Action*, 4.

69. Stanley Hauerwas and David Burrell, "From System to Story: An Alternative Pattern for Rationality in Ethics," in Stanley Hauerwas, *Truthfulness and Tragedy: Further Investigations into Christian Ethics* (Notre Dame: University of Notre Dame Press, 1977), 15.

70. The strength of this argument is demonstrated, I believe, in the weakness of Kant's examples in his attempt to illustrate how his unstoried ethical system might work. See Immanuel Kant, *Groundwork of the Metaphysics of Morals*, trans. H. J. Paton (New York: Harper and Row, 1964), 89–92.

71. Cf. Voegelin, *Anamnesis*, 97–111.

72. Voegelin, *In Search of Order*, 48–54.

73. Hauerwas and Burrell, "System to Story," 20.

74. Hauerwas and Burrell, "System to Story," 21.

75. Voegelin, *In Search of Order*, 42–47; Michael Goldberg, *Jews and Christians: Getting Our Stories Straight* (Nashville, Tenn.: Abingdon Press, 1985).

76. Hauerwas and Burrell, "System to Story," 21.

77. Joyce Clemmer Munro, "Passing on the Torch," *The Mennonite Quarterly Review,* 60, no. 1 (1986): 10.

78. Voegelin, "The Beginning," 175. "But how does the listener recognize the story to be true, so that by the recognition of its truth he is forced to reorder his existence? Why should he believe the story to be true rather than consider it somebody's private opinion concerning the order of his preference? To questions of this class only one answer is possible: . . . [it] will have no authority of truth unless it speaks with an authority commonly present in everybody's consciousness . . . [unless it] indeed speaks what is common (*xynon*) to the order of man's existence as a partner in the comprehending reality." *In Search of Order*, 25–26.

79. Charles M. Wood, "Hermeneutics and the Authority of Scripture," in *Scriptural Authority and Narrative Interpretation,* ed. Garrett Green (Philadelphia: Fortress Press, 1987), 12.

80. Wood, "Hermeneutics," 13–14.

81. Ronald Thiemann, "Radiance and Obscurity in Biblical Narrative," in *Scriptural Authority and Narrative Interpretation,* ed. Garrett Green (Philadelphia: Fortress Press, 1987), 27.

82. White, *Content of the Form*, 5.

83. Webb, *Philosopher of History*, 285.

84. Voegelin, *Anamnesis*, 36, 37.

85. Voegelin, *In Search of Order*, 24.

86. Voegelin, *In Search of Order*, 29.

87. Voegelin, *In Search of Order*, 24.

88. For an interesting interpretation of this recollection, see Gregor Sebba, "Prelude and Variations on the Theme of Eric Voegelin," in *Eric Voegelin's Thought: A Critical Appraisal*, ed. Ellis Sandoz (Durham, N.C.: Duke University Press, 1982), 51 and 51n75.

89. Voegelin, *Anamnesis*, 13.

90. Voegelin, *Anamnesis*, 37. Webb argues that Voegelin's inclination "to assume that the production of interpretive symbols must be a spontaneous, virtually automatic process" displays the influence on his thought of both Schelling and Schopenhauer, but more especially Kant. Webb's considerations of René Girard's (and Paul Ricoeur's) "hermeneutics of suspicion" adds a useful caveat to Voegelin's rather more optimistic view of what the indices of consciousness provide; myths and symbols can also mislead us by surreptitiously confirming or introducing prejudices, justifications for violence, and other evils. Accordingly, our response to wonder and mystery must be open, yet critical. *Philosophers of Consciousness*, 130ff, 14, 16–18, 206–11.

91. Cf. Hannah Arendt, *The Human Condition* (Chicago: University of Chicago Press, 1958), 50–51, 57–58; Eric Voegelin, *Science, Politics, and Gnosticism* (Chicago: Henry Regnery, 1968), 108–14. A particularly fine example of the role of community in interpretation may be found in the biblical account of the Ethiopian eunuch's conversion to Christianity (Acts 8:16–40). See also Kathryn E. Tanner, "Theology and the Plain Sense," in *Scriptural Authority and Narrative Interpretation*, ed. Garrett Greed, 59–78.

92. Thiemann, "Radiance and Obscurity," 26.

93. Thiemann, "Radiance and Obscurity," 26–27.

94. See especially Webb, *Philosopher of History*, 36–37.

95. Eric Voegelin, *Science, Politics, and Gnosticism*, 108–9.

96. Webb, *Philosopher of History*, 35.

2

CONSCIOUSNESS AND DISORDER: PHILOSOPHY AS RESISTANCE

Voegelin himself identified resistance to the disorders of the modern age as at least one motivating aspect of his work. Indeed, this aspect of his work leads to the interpretation of Voegelin as a conservative thinker. This characterization was one, albeit tentative, possibility that I noted in the introductory chapter. In such an interpretation, Voegelin's philosophical resistance to modernity is a key piece of evidence for his "conservatism." This "resistance" raises two interesting questions for interpreting not only Voegelin's work but the activity of political philosophy in general.

First, I have noted in the previous chapter how philosophy is—in part—an activity of reflecting in a comprehensive way on the "comprehensive reality" of which we are a part and in which we participate. Is it therefore even plausible to speak of philosophy or simply *thinking* as an act of resistance against disorder at all? Second, how shall we understand an activity of "resistance" against disorder within the comprehensive reality? Most particularly, how well articulated must our understanding of that reality be, in order for our resistance to be truly philosophical? After all, existential effectiveness is a separate question from philosophical understanding. What form does such resistance take, and how self-conscious must it be? Let me begin by restricting myself to his considerations on the matter. What follows is divided into four parts.

First, Voegelin's description of his own work can easily lead us to read his texts "backwards," to anachronistically attribute to earlier texts an activity of resistance that is *consciously* present only in his later work. I will therefore begin by turning to Voegelin's later discussion of philosophy and resistance to indicate more clearly what characteristics we must look for in his earlier work if we are to call them works of resistance. This move requires that we remind ourselves of Voegelin's conception of the structure of reality within which philosophy takes place. Second, I turn to his discussion of philosophy as resistance. Third, I review several of Voegelin's later remarks on his earlier work, and I turn to his earlier philosophical texts, including those on European race ideas, to show how his studies indicate the sort of "resistance" he spoke of in his later work. In the concluding section, I suggest how understanding philosophy and social science as an activity of resistance might affect our reading of philosophical and social-scientific texts in general. The underlying philosophical question of this chapter, however, is not merely the matter of interpreting Voegelin's intentions correctly, but of considering the following problem: does the experience of resistance have to be fully articulated and fully conscious in order to be present and existentially effective? If Voegelin's interpretation of politics as in part an activity of ordering a particular "cosmion" is correct, then the level of articulation of that order and the resistance to disorder that may occur within it gain importance for understanding and engaging justly in political activity.

PHILOSOPHICAL RESISTANCE AND THE ORDER OF REALITY

Understanding philosophy as a kind of resistance depends upon a notion that we have already considered and that Voegelin kept foremost in his analyses from *Israel and Revelation* onward: reality has a structure that can be known in part and remains mysteriously obscured in part. Reality remains partially mysterious to us, because we are participants in that which is greater than us and transcends us, and which therefore cannot be fully known to us in the manner of an object of study. On the other hand, the structure of reality and the nature of its parts are accessible to us in some measure. We recall the use of the technical symbol of the quaternarian structure of human existence to describe it. I considered its first appearance in Voegelin's "Introduction" to *Israel and Revelation*; he repeated it in "Equivalences of Experience and Symbolization in History" in 1970:

> The primordial field of reality is the community of God and man, world and society; the exploration of this field is concerned with the

true nature of the partners in the community and of the relations between them; the sequence in time of the verities found is the historical
field of equivalent experiences and symbols.[1]

As we have seen, Voegelin argues that it is within this quaternarian structure that we order our existence, including our political arrangements.

Let us also recall that human experience of this structure and response to it is essentially of two kinds: participation or alienation. Both
kinds of experience and response take place within the given structure
of our existence, and each elicits its own set of responses to that existence. The character of the response is indicated by the linguistic indices
and political propositions that both alienated and participating people
develop in their attempts either to come to terms with, or deny, or re-
shape the nature of reality. Accordingly, each kind of experience produces a corresponding variety of political and philosophical implications.
Voegelin extensively analyzed those arising from experiences of alienation in *Science, Politics, and Gnosticism* and in his various studies of Hegel,
Marx, Nietzsche, Bakunin and others. He analyzed the symbols that
have historically emerged from the experience of participation most extensively in the first four volumes of *Order and History*, but also in *Anamnesis*, and in several articles and essays.[2]

An order is an arrangement of parts into a whole that conforms to a
pattern or a purpose or is oriented toward an end, but that is not deliberately arranged by a specific agent. The available variations in order are
bounded by the intrinsic nature of the components of that order. Social
and political order is, more specifically, the arrangement of the parts of
the social and political fields for the purpose of human well-being,
which includes a properly oriented partnership with other human beings
and with the other parts of being. The possible combinations of the parts
of the quaternarian field of human existence—God, man, world, and
society—within a socio-political order are not infinite, even though the
cultural or artistic expressions of order (and disorder) may take on a variety of forms. Within this four-fold field, experiences and expressions of
participation are experiences and expressions of a right attunement of
the thinker or artist to the order of being. Conversely, experiences of
alienation are experiences of disorder, either in the individual thinker's
soul or in the world around him.[3]

The greatest difficulty with Voegelin's conception of reality and right orientation—and the greatest difficulty with philosophy as an activity—is its apparently paradoxical claim that the structure of reality can be known and analyzed at the same time that its ultimate essence remains a mystery. Recall that the quaternarian field or "community of being" in which we find ourselves is known to us, but it is not experienced as an object: "it is a datum of experience in so far as it is known to man by virtue of his participation in the mystery of its being," yet "it is not a datum of experience in so far as it is not given in the manner of an object of the external world, but is knowable only from the perspective of participation in it."[4]

Two aspects of this paradox are particularly important for our considerations regarding the activity of philosophy. First, Voegelin argued frequently that the orientation of the soul to divine order is the most important element in establishing right order in the quaternarian field. This claim was a constant in his work from 1954 onward.[5] That which transcends us remains beyond us, but its qualities are known in part by the experience we have of being "drawn" to it, of being "infused" by it, of being oriented by it. The paradox in this description is that we are oriented in being by that which we do not know in any full sense of the term, but which we can only sense indeterminately in the psyche. The second aspect of the paradox of recognized orderliness within a reality we know only in part is reflected in Voegelin's observation that we are not participants in reality in the manner of actors in a drama, who can leave the stage or quit the performance if they wish, but in the manner of indentured servants who cannot retire to a restful space away from the stage, and for whom even death is not an assured release from participation.[6] Thus, as we saw chapter 1, not only do we not know where we are, we also do not know what, precisely, we are doing.[7] Our inability to know the what, where, or why of the whole "precludes essential knowledge of the part," which is to say, we do not even know precisely who we are. Ultimately, "this situation of ignorance with regard to the decisive core of existence is more than disconcerting: it is profoundly disturbing, for from the depth of this ultimate ignorance wells up the anxiety of existence."[8]

This quality of paradox and the anxiety it produces, however, is neither a "difficulty" of philosophy nor a "problem" in Voegelin's articulation of reality, but simply a quality of existence that persists whatever our intellectual attempts to overcome it. It is a motivation for philosophy, but also for systematic attempts to overcome anxiety by a variety of ideological "solutions" to the disconcerting aspects of human existence.

Disorder may be found at several levels in the primordial field of existence. It may occur in an inadequate orientation of the self with respect to one or more of the poles of the quaternarian structure. Through a series of speculative psychological operations, for example, we may come to think that we can become gods, or we may claim that the experience of divine transcendence is nothing but a psychological projection.[9] Alternatively, we may reject participation and partnership in the world and seek domination of man, world, or society instead. This is the problem of tyranny in Plato's *Gorgias*, and the problem of the *libido dominandi* of thinkers such as Hegel, Marx, Nietzsche, and Heidegger. Disorder may also arise at the point of understanding or symbolizing the experiences of reality. In this case, we may substitute the linguistic indices of another's experience of reality for the primary experiences "behind" them, treating these indices as objects of veneration, investigation, or rejection, rather than as the symbols of experienced reality that they are.[10] For example, we can make "grace" an object of study, rather than using it as a symbol for the experience in the soul of the force of divine favor. It may thereby become possible, as Nietzsche thought, to bestow grace upon ourselves, since its divine origin was lost to him. Alternatively, we may come to accept only one small range of ordering experiences as legitimate or "real" and reject all others as imaginary or "false." Thus, we may reject any articulation of an experience of divine transcendence that does not conform to a specific religious vocabulary. We may also hold all such attempts at articulation to be essentially "equal," thereby rendering irrelevant the concerted attempts of others either to describe more precisely the reality experienced or to introduce to us new experienced elements of that reality. Both moves are illegitimate in Voegelin's estimation. These forms of dogmatism obscure or limit the reality of our experience, and may alienate the individual who seeks an understanding of order beyond the propositions offered by dogmatizers as the final word on the truth of existence.

Voegelin's analysis and articulation of the structure of human existence give us a framework within which we may judge the varying conceptions of order with respect to their adequacy in reflecting the order of being as it is known and experienced by us. As we have seen, its paradoxical mysteriousness does not keep reality entirely hidden from our sight:

> The ultimate, essential ignorance is not complete ignorance. Man can achieve considerable knowledge about the order of being, and not the least part of that knowledge is the distinction between the knowable and the unknowable. . . . The concern of man about the meaning of his existence in the field of being does not remain pent up in the tortures of anxiety, but can vent itself in the creation of symbols purporting to render intelligible the relations and tensions between the distinguishable terms of the field.[11]

The creation of such symbols, which is the articulation of human experience in reality, is the substance of order in human history.

PHILOSOPHY AND RESISTANCE

If our existence is to remain genuine and whole, we must resist disorder within the quaternarian field in its several dimensions. Voegelin followed Plato in arguing that the human psyche and political institutions are intimately linked. The character of a regime reflects the character of the souls of its ruling class.[12] Accordingly, the disorder of a civilization will be revealed both in its institutions and in the souls of those who rule. Resistance to this disorder, according to Voegelin, initiates philosophy.[13] Resistance is therefore directed both at the abstract level of doctrines (or at the level of the soul), and also at specific socio-political institutions. Institutional malformations may be a more concrete manifestation of psychic disorder, but their concrete appearance—alongside, yet apart from, the psychic deformations that may underlie them—must be resisted in their own right. Philosophy is a resistance to disorder at both the psychic and the institutional levels:

> Philosophy, thus, has its origin in the resistance of the soul to its destruction by society. Philosophy in this sense, as an act of resistance illuminated by conceptual understanding, has two functions for Plato. It is first, and most importantly, an act of salvation for himself and others, in that the evocation of right order and its reconstitution in his own soul becomes the substantive center of a new community which,

by its existence, relieves the pressure of the surrounding corrupt society. Under this aspect Plato is the founder of the community of philosophers that lives through the ages. Philosophy is, second, an act of judgment. . . . Since the order of the soul is recaptured through resistance to the surrounding disorder, the pairs of concepts which illuminate the act of resistance develop into the criteria (in the pregnant sense of instruments or standards of judgment) of social order and disorder. Under this second aspect Plato is the founder of political science.[14]

Through this philosophical act of judgment, spiritual resistance becomes political opposition:

Historically, every position has its counter-positions and . . . these will be characterized as hostile and false according to one's own position. . . . [H]istorically every truth sets itself off against an already existing belief, which the new truth forces into the position of being untrue. . . . [T]his situation—position versus counter-position—is found everywhere. . . . Formally, Socrates is in conflict with Athens; you can set up either side as the position and then call the other side the counter-position. But this, it seems to me, leads to historical relativism. A case like this calls for a decision: Socrates is right, Athens is wrong. (Or the modern liberals' decision: democracy is right, Socrates was a Fascist.) This is the parting of the ways.[15]

The danger of the decision and the consequent parting is that the philosophical act of judgment begins to appear as merely another dogmatic proposition. In his introduction to his analyses of the philosophies of Plato and Aristotle, however, Voegelin warned his readers that "we are not concerned with a 'Platonic philosophy' or 'doctrine,' but with Plato's resistance to the disorder of the surrounding society and his effort to restore the order of Hellenic civilization through love of wisdom."[16] Philosophy is not dogmatics, but a deliberate effort to orient the soul in reality. Philosophy must take into account the entire panoply of reality, and it must differentiate carefully the several dimensions and manifold characteristics of that reality as it is experienced in the soul and in the phenomena of the quaternarian community of being. Such openness, however, eventually entails closure toward conceptual corruptions and disorder.

Voegelin considered resistance to disorder to be the origin of philosophy and the recovery of order to be its purpose. The "act of salvation" that philosophy engenders, moreover, is not a specifically religious experience but the "turning around" that results from an analysis communicated to others. It is an education. Because disorder is first and foremost a problem of the psyche, the education and the philosophical "attack on the corrupt society is not directed against this or that political abuse but against a disease of the soul." Accordingly, the "restoration" that such an education provides "requires a turning-around (*periagoge*) of 'the whole soul': from ignorance to the truth of God, from opinion about uncertainly wavering things to knowledge of being, and from multifarious activity to the justice of tending to one's proper sphere of action."[17]

Education, from the Latin "ex" and "ducere," literally means "to lead out." The analysis of philosophy clears up the disorder, enabling the educator to lead his students out of the spiritual morass and disorientation that intellectual or social and political disorder engender. Such leading out requires careful intellectual discipline and rigor, and its proper result is not merely a new intellectual perspective but a new way of life. What was true for Plato in Athens, moreover, remains true today; the expression of disorder may have changed, but its results and the need for resistance to it remain constant:

> The great representative of modern magical thought [Hegel] cannot be ignored. But since he cannot be ignored, it is not permitted to ignore the manner in which his Magic affects his language and its use. When the thinker breaks through the barrier of reason, he can give to the magical results of his expansion of consciousness an appearance of rationality only by playing magical con-games with the common language. . . . As this type of con-game has become an all-pervasive phenomenon in our "climate of opinion," the analysis of the tricks a magician plays with language is not a wanton "attack" on anybody, but the duty of the philosopher, if he wants to understand the contemporary disorder, and of the educator, if he wants to help the young in the intellectual and spiritual misery caused by their exposure to the formidable pressure of these con-games in their environment.[18]

As each disorder is analyzed to its psychological depths, the "loosening up" of analysis turns into a "clearing up" or catharsis that frees us from the bondage of the darkness.[19] Voegelin's philosophical enterprise is in this sense an attempt at a kind of therapeutic, a healing of spiritual disease.[20] Such a therapeutic demands a judgment, and such a judgment requires a concrete stance on political questions.

Because reality, including the human psyche, has a stable structure (even if its depth keeps this structure partially obscured from us), certain forms of analysis will be more adequate than others; or one form of analysis or articulation of the structure of reality may be more adequate or appropriate in some situations than in others; or some linguistic indices may be more adequate than others.[21] A thinker may, moreover, have overlooked important aspects of reality, or used inadequate or polluted concepts, or misconstructed the analysis in some important way that renders it inadequate. In the same way, some forms of corruption will also require more immediate resistance than others, and some forms of resistance may be more adequate than others. The judgment of philosophy in its resistance to disorder and psychic corruption must take into account these factors.[22] Accordingly, the education and resistance of philosophy is not an education or resistance of dogmatics but of a careful orientation to the known order of reality, and a correspondingly careful rejection of the disordering forces in that reality. Such an orientation requires skill, discipline and a consistent awareness of the reality in which the philosopher finds himself.

RESISTANCE AND SELF-CONSCIOUSNESS

Not everyone is a philosopher. Not every philosophical investigation is equivalent in its breadth of analysis and its depth of results to every other. To what extent, then, are articulation and self-awareness as Voegelin describes them necessary for resistance to disorder to become recognizable and effective? We have seen so far that Voegelin closely linked philosophy and resistance in his later considerations of political phenomena. Philosophy, at least for Voegelin, is motivated by a need to resist social disorder (which may, in turn, be caused by psychic disorder), and it provides the conceptual tools for such psychic and social resistance. The resistance of philosophy, moreover, may have political and social effects that make it the enemy of those whose corruption incites disturbances in the social order. This much is well-known to readers of Voegelin. Voegelin articulated the principle of resistance in his later work. One way to demonstrate the operation of this principle in his work more generally and perhaps to attest to its accuracy beyond Voegelin's own work is to consider the division between his earlier and later work.

This division is located in the 1940s, when Voegelin was in the midst of writing a multi-volume "History of Political Ideas." He gave up this project as he became increasingly convinced that "ideas" cannot have a history of their own, separate and apart from the experiences that underlie them. Thus, as he worked through the materials for his "History," he arrived at a "dead end" in his "attempts to find a theory of man, society, and history that would permit an adequate interpretation of the phenomena in [his] chosen field of studies."[23] Grappling with these phenomena would lead a philosopher to develop a theory of consciousness to account for them; we are now familiar with Voegelin's articulation of such a theory. If we lack such a theory, what is the character of our analysis of the situation in which we find ourselves? Or, to return more pointedly to Voegelin, what of his earlier work? For example, that work is not as closely informed by classical philosophy, nor does it employ the concepts used in his later writings. One may therefore suggest that Voegelin's self-declared philosophical resistance after 1950 is something quite different from the studies he wrote prior to his abandonment of the "History of Ideas" between 1945 and 1950. If that is true, is it not possible that not all political-philosophical activity does, in fact, imply forms of resistance to disorder? To give at least a tentative answer to this question, at least for Voegelin, we need to consider what Voegelin was doing and thought he was doing before 1950, and to compare it with his later studies. If the earlier work appears as a work of "resistance," but less conscious or less well-developed, then Voegelin's claim for the activity of the political philosopher takes on an added credibility.

Reflecting on the period before he finally rejected a history of ideas, Voegelin traced a motive of resistance in his work at least to 1943. He sought a theory of consciousness, he claims, that would "fit the facts of the great stasis that has grown, ever since the eighteenth century, to its present proportions."[24] I examined the outcome and implications of this search in chapter 1. The search took place only after thirty years of investigation into the basic political phenomena in human history. The operative category for these investigations, however, was not philosophy, but science.

Philosophy, speaking literally, is love of wisdom, a desire for knowledge of or within the context of the whole. Since such complete knowledge of the whole is not humanly attainable, philosophy presupposes the hypothetical possibility of such a knowledge but acknowledges its human impossibility. A science, on the other hand, is the systematic and conceptual ordering of a field of phenomena whose boundaries can be more or less well delineated. A science is a confined discourse about reality, in which a conceptual language is developed to describe the structure and dynamics of that portion of reality that is the object of the science in question. The object of a science of politics, we recall, is "the little world of meaning," "illuminated from within by its own interpretation," which we call a society.[25] Science, then, is not philosophy, but its necessary prerequisite, because a hypothetical knowledge of the whole presupposes knowledge of the particulars. A philosopher who makes a claim to be wise concerning human things must have a political science that gives him knowledge of those things.[26]

Voegelin discovered the limits of science between 1945 and 1950, as he began to search more deeply for a theory of consciousness that would give a unified context to his earlier studies and to the work of the great thinkers and philosophers before him. The indices of human experience of reality and the political and social institutions that are constructed in accordance with these indices are empirical phenomena that a science can conceptually order. But science requires philosophy—the systematic investigation of the whole, not merely an empirical part—to give us the existential context within which a science operates. This relationship between science and philosophy, however, is made somewhat more ambiguous in certain of Voegelin's remarks. His evaluation of Max Weber's historical and sociological investigation, for example, seems to indicate that a scientist may be unaware of the existential dimension with which he or she is operating and nonetheless be a scientist.

In Voegelin's estimation, Max Weber's work appeared at the culminating point of the nineteenth-century endeavors to create a "value-free" social science. "Such a science," Voegelin suggested, "would not be in a position to tell anybody whether he should be an economic liberal or a socialist, a democratic constitutionalist or a Marxist revolutionary, but it could tell him what the consequences would be if he tried to translate the values of his preferences into political practice." Voegelin criticized Weber's value-free method of science, because it could not supply Weber with the criteria for selecting the materials to be studied by his science. Since, speaking crudely, politics is an activity of determining and allocating "values" and of building common enterprises around them, Weber's science necessarily fell short of a complete account of the phenomena it purported to study:

> The search for truth, however, was cut short at the level of pragmatic action. In the intellectual climate of the methodological debate the "values" had to be accepted as unquestionable, and the search could not advance to the contemplation of order. The *ratio* of science extended, for Weber, not to the principles but only to the causality of action.[27]

Similarly, Weber's method could not furnish him with the premises of his ethics of responsibility, which were an integral part of his self-conception as a scientist. And yet, Voegelin praised Weber's science and its results, because Weber "knew what was right, without knowing the reasons for it."[28] Weber, in other words, could give no particular reason for what he was doing, but Voegelin thought that Weber's strong ethical character and perhaps his mysticism kept the lack of an existential foundation from irretrievably impairing his work. Weber had both feet planted firmly in reality, but he did not know it, and he was unable to account for his stance; the principles of his science would not permit him to move to a consideration of order as such.[29] In Voegelin's estimation, this unknowing did not generally impair the results of Weber's studies, but it becomes problematic when the scientist tries to persuade others that his science is useful and has integrity: "students, after all, want to know the reasons why they should conduct themselves in a certain manner; and when the reasons—that is, the rational order of existence—are excluded from consideration, emotions are liable to carry you away into all sorts of ideological and idealistic adventures in which the ends become more fascinating than the means."[30] Voegelin, who would spend much of his life filling in the gap in Weber's work by articulating this rational order of existence,[31] could accept the scientific findings of Weber, despite the gap, since these findings, though foundationless within Weber's world, rested on the foundations of the reality that could be recovered by Weber's heirs. The articulation of the rational order of existence requires a science of order, but the articulation itself is the task of philosophy, not science.

In Voegelin's critique of Weber, then, we find the first hint that a scientist does not have to have a fully articulated grasp of reality in the Voegelinian sense in order to furnish us with a science. It is possible for a scientist to proceed with his investigation without being fully aware of the existential dimensions within which he or she is working. Keeping in mind these criticisms of Weber, we can now take a chronological step backward to Voegelin's early work. It seems to me that in certain respects, Voegelin's self-critiques move along lines similar to those of his critique of Weber.

In his autobiographical reflections in 1973, Voegelin saw a clear progress in clarity and conceptual accuracy from his earlier work to his later writings, beginning with *The New Science of Politics* in 1952. We see in his pre-1952 published works an attempt to articulate a science of politics. This attempt was self-conscious, but, as Voegelin later acknowledged, it was defective in several particular ways. For example, Voegelin gave three specific reasons for his hatred of National Socialism. First, he found National Socialism, along with all other ideologies, to be intellectually dishonest.[32] While a scientist "honestly wants to explore the structure of reality," ideologues "indulge in constructions that are intellectually not tenable." They "indulge in intellectual dishonesty" in matters of science.[33] Second, he confessed to an "aversion to killing people for the fun of it." A perverse pleasure in killing people has been an all-too-frequent indulgence of ideology in the twentieth century. Finally, Voegelin was motivated by a desire to "keep his language clean."[34] This reason is closely related to the first: since science is a discourse about reality, the symbols, grammar, and logic of that discourse must be rigorously disciplined to reflect accurately the reality it is about. Insofar as ideologies seek to subvert and obscure reality, their language and concepts will be based on false premises, slogans, and word games.

His motivations concerning his hatred, observed Voegelin, "were perfectly clear to [him] at the time, but clarity about their direction did not mean clarity about the implications in detail."[35] Part of the lack of clarity was scientific, and part, we might say, philosophical. The scientific problem included the absence of an "intellectual apparatus for dealing with the highly complex phenomena of intellectual deformation, perversion, crookedness, and vulgarization." An accurate science first required the necessary social-scientific and historical studies to create such an apparatus.[36] To answer this need in the matter of ideologies, Voegelin developed the concept of a "political religion" to grapple with the deforming qualities of National Socialism. In retrospect, however, *The Political Religions* offered a "stop-gap notion," an "ad-hoc explanation" that was conceptually insufficient for coming to grips with the ideological political phenomena of his time.[37] But Voegelin clearly indicated in his introduction to the second printing of this book the form that a hatred for ideological discourse and killing should take in a scientific (or philosophical) investigation. He also made clear in this introduction the depths at which his resistance (in this case) to National Socialism was rooted.[38] The philosophical lack of clarity of the book resulted from the absence of a theory of consciousness and of a concomitant theory of the structure of the whole. The theory of consciousness—based on "the specifically philosophical realization that the levels of being discernible within the world are surmounted by a transcendent source of being and its order," a realization that "was itself rooted in the real movements of the human spiritual soul toward divine being experienced as transcendent"—would have given Voegelin the "clarity about implications in detail" that he lacked. Voegelin required a theory that would bring into view "the order of being as a whole, unto its origin in transcendent being" before he could hope for a successful scientific analysis, "for only then can current opinions about right order be examined as to their agreement with the order of being."[39]

We see similar attempts to come to grips with the political phenomena of his time, for example, in Voegelin's two earlier books on European race-thinking. In these, he contended with two problems. First, the "knowledge of man," he claimed, had "come to grief." The race theories of the twentieth century reflected an "uncertainty of vision for the essentials," and an inability of the plastic arts to grasp in any meaningful way these essentials concerning human being. His genealogical study of the European ideas of race, he suggested, would help to recover a view of these essentials. The deeper question underlying this study would be: "What significance does the human body and its multitude of forms have for a knowledge of man?"[40] We see here an attempt to link the various realms of human being into a comprehensible whole that illuminates for us the link between our conceptions of human nature and the political formations we construct in response to that nature.[41] Ideas of race were a major formative idea during the early twentieth century, one that had not been closely examined in a rigorous manner. The second book, *Rasse und Staat*, was aimed in part at correcting the theory of politics embodied in Kelsen's positive theory of law. The scientific difficulty concerned Kelsen's neo-Kantian methodology, which excluded from a theory of the state any consideration of political phenomena that could not be treated within the confines of the logic of the legal system itself.[42] Since a state and a legal system are human creations that depend for their legitimacy on the correspondence between their form and the form of human beings, a theory of politics that does not take into account how archetypical perceptions of human nature and human existence are reflected in political institutions is insufficient.[43] If the principal perception of human nature is racial, political institutions (including the legal system) will reflect that prejudice, just as when the principal perception of human beings is one of rational, self-interested actors, political institutions will reflect that (liberal) image of human nature. Again, Voegelin observed that he did not have a "full understanding of the rather primitive semantic games involved" in the methodological misconstructions that would exclude a non-positivist theory of the state, but "at least [he] sensed them."[44] His differences with Kelsen emerged as he became interested in those dimensions of politics that a positive theory of law could not treat,[45] but at the same time, this difference reflected a scientific interest more than an immediate philosophical judgment.

Let us recall Voegelin's analysis of consciousness. His various efforts to come to a better understanding of the sociopolitical and philosophical problems that confronted him in the 1930s and 1940s are captured in his later symbols of "compactness" and "differentiation." If the structure of reality is constant, but our understanding of that reality and our articulation of our understanding—whether in science or philosophy—are not, then there will be more and less accurate understandings and descriptions of what we experience. If the structure of reality, moreover, is complex and "deep," it may be possible to arrive at various articulations that are not so much inaccurate, compared to others, as they are imprecise. These less precise articulations of reality, often rendered in the form of myths, Voegelin called "compact," and the more precise, analytically deeper articulations he called "differentiated." The process of differentiation was, for Voegelin, a process of articulating, ever more precisely, reality as we experience it. This activity may occur in a number of directions at various times in history. In the case of science, Voegelin only slowly came to differentiate between scientific problems and philosophical problems and to distinguish between science and the context in which it is carried out. One such act of differentiation was to realize that one can engage in accurate and useful (social) science without having a full grasp of the wider reality-context within which the activity takes place. Another was to strive to gain a fuller, more conceptually articulate grasp of that context.[46]

It is useful at this point to shift emphasis slightly. The problem of science, philosophy, understanding, and resistance is not confined to Voegelin's own studies. Certainly, he has not been the only thinker ever to grapple with the problems of order and disorder in his time. Indeed, much of Voegelin's work is a conversation with living and dead friends who engaged in similar struggles. His reflections on the "common-sense" philosophy of the American tradition and his later reflections on the shape of intellectual resistance in Germany against the National Socialists will serve as the concluding examples of our considerations. In neither case did resistance to disorder include the full articulation of a political philosophy in the classical sense that Voegelin embraced, but it was a philosophical kind of resistance nevertheless.

The English tradition of "common sense" emerges out of the work of Thomas Reid and other Scottish Enlightenment philosophers. Voegelin described "common sense" as "a philosopher's attitude toward life without the philosopher's technical apparatus." He believed that this attitude incorporated the tradition of classical philosophy, but without retaining "the technical apparatus of an Aristotle."[47] The importance of this common-sense attitude for sustaining the "intellectual climate and cohesion of a society" lay in its "range and existential substance," not its technical articulation. Although it does not contain the technical language of classical philosophy, it is nevertheless sustained and communicated through language—in telling stories, establishing rules and regulations, and articulating and resolving social, political, economic, or administrative problems. The example of "common-sense" philosophy seemed to show that whether or not language is technically precise, it is nevertheless a good indicator of the intellectual and spiritual level at which a society finds itself. For this reason, when Voegelin pursued his political studies, he chose for his object of study the "self-speaking phenomena," that is, those sociopolitical phenomena such as academic theorizing that reflect upon themselves and their own meaning at the same time that they reflect the intellectual order of a society.⁴⁸ The intellectual and spiritual level of American society could therefore be revealed or reflected in the intellectual formulations of men like John R. Commons, Charles Peirce, George Santayana, and Jonathan Edwards, and the same level of German society could be revealed in the critical efforts of Karl Kraus and Robert Musil. Initially, Voegelin seems to have shared with most European intellectuals and scholars a certain disdain for American culture. To his surprise, then, he found that the intellectual level of American society was relatively high, even though it was not infused with the methodological neo-Kantian disputes that animated intellectual debates in central Europe in the 1920s and 1930s. The classical basis of the common-sense tradition made it possible for such disputes to be disregarded or their more reasonable results to be already taken for granted.

In contrast to his generally favorable evaluation of English, and especially, American culture and society, Voegelin argued in his lectures on "Hitler and the Germans" that the intellectual level of German society at the time of the coming of National Socialism was depressingly low. The two specific problems that he analyzed in the lectures were the misuse of language to obscure reality and to create the mirage of another reality, and the loss of a sense of common humanity with one's fellow human beings. The misuse of language included a variety of symptoms and phenomena: the mixing of metaphors into meaningless tropes; the invention of words in order to give trivial statements an aura of profundity; the denial or accurate refutation of lies in order to hide much more savage truths; and the use of clichés to hide one's own intellectual illiteracy or to mask an ideological agenda.⁴⁹ Each of these sorts of demonstrations of intellectual corruption represents what Voegelin called a "loss of reality" (*Realitätsverlust*). His own analysis of this loss and its consequences was based on a full philosophical articulation of the kind that I have outlined in the first two sections of this chapter. But he was also able to point to a list of people who resisted the corruption such misuse of language entails, yet who did not seem to possess the technical vocabulary of classical philosophy. There is no indication, for example, that Karl Kraus, a journalist, was a student of philosophy, but he was firmly in touch with reality: he recognized a lie for a lie, a cliché for a cliché, and the bad grammar that masks the truth as a grammar that reveals stupidity and deception. Similarly, Robert Musil well understood the problem of creating fantastical and libidinous "second realities" within the structure of the first, but he did not have the Aristotelian or Platonic vocabulary to differentiate the elements of this experience in the way that Voegelin later would. This lack did not keep Kraus' and Musil's articulation of the National Socialist corruption of language and society from being psychically effective forms of resistance and reordering. In their case, however, resistance may have been based less on straightforward common sense (Voegelin believed this ordering force to be nearly completely absent in German political culture),[50] than on a notion of *Menschlichkeit* or "common humanity" and "honesty." Once again, such notions could go a long way toward preserving the ethical, intellectual, and spiritual integrity of a society. I will return to this historical episode in chapter 4.

Racism was not restricted to German society. Indeed, modern racism was largely the invention of French and British, not German, writers. Forms of racism similar to those found in Germany also existed in the United States and elsewhere. A combination of historical circumstance and intellectual climate, however, allowed racism to become a national political ideology and public policy in Germany. Voegelin stressed the importance of intellectual climate, observing that the strong tradition of "common sense" in American and British society might be the last bastion against hopeless world-wide ideological corruption.[51]

Ideas of common sense, common humanity, and intellectual honesty indicate that an adequate participation in the order of being need not be self-conscious at the level Voegelin later articulated and that I described at the beginning of this chapter. When this participation does become self-conscious, it results in a noetic exegesis like that of Aristotle. Noetic knowledge is not, according to Voegelin, "abstract knowledge obtained by gathering cases of participation and examining them for general characteristics," but "concrete knowledge of participation in which a man's desire for knowledge is experienced as a movement toward the ground that is being moved by the ground."[52] It is a mystical, self-reflexive, concrete knowledge of human participation in reality, a knowledge that the philosopher seeks, but it is not a requirement for spiritual integrity and resistance against spiritual disorder:

> The desire for knowledge is the reality not only of the noesis, but of every experience of participation, as Aristotle already observed. In every case it engenders symbols that express the truth of the divine, the human, and the world, as well as the relations of the areas of reality

to each other. It is always man's existential transcending toward the ground, even when the ground does not become conscious as the transcendent pole of the desire. Noesis, then, contributes no more than its rendering intelligible the logos of consciousness, which belongs to the reality of participating knowledge even in the absence of noesis.[53]

CONCLUSION: SCIENCE, PHILOSOPHY, AND REALITY

How, then, should we understand the work of a political philosopher? In particular, how should we interpret the development of a philosopher's thought over time? Or, specifically in Voegelin's case, how should we read his earlier work in light of later theoretical developments? I would suggest the following. First, we must evaluate scientific studies and attempts to articulate reality on the basis of our own knowledge of that reality. In Voegelin's case, we can read "History of Political Ideas" with profit only if we keep in mind the fact that he later rejected its fundamental ordering premise, even though he believed its historical studies to be essentially sound.[54] In reading such a work, we must keep in mind the later insights Voegelin and other thinkers had into the structure of consciousness, or else we regress.

Second, reality is reality; human beings cannot transform it at will. At the same time, our apperceptions of that reality can vary—even greatly—and the quality of those apperceptions strongly determines the quality and character of our activities within reality. At the one extreme, we find the murderous activities of Marxists, National Socialists, and other ideologues, whose apperception of reality is obscured or even deliberately and knowingly distorted, whose picture of reality is therefore deeply deformed, and who feel compelled to eliminate those portions of reality that do not fit their deformed image. At the other end, we find the extensive articulation of human experience in reality of Plato, Aristotle, Thomas Aquinas, and others. Even here, however, or perhaps especially here, there exists a constant danger that the symbols of human experience that these thinkers developed in their attempt to grasp and articulate what they experienced will be transformed into dogmatic systems. To mention only one example, the philosophy of Thomas Aquinas is not a "system," even though his intellectual heirs—the Scholastics—

treated his thought as though it were. Having thereby obscured the experiential and existential motivations for Aquinas' investigations, they could proceed with the dogmatics of a pseudo-science that was legitimately open to the benighting attacks of the Enlightenment. The Scholastics would have done well to pay closer attention to the great thinker's remark that he had seen things that made his lifework seem "like straw."[55] In this same way, Voegelin's powerful intellect has left behind a body of investigations that his intellectual heirs will be tempted to transform into a "body of knowledge," or a "system." His recovery of the experiences of reality that underlie the symbols of classical philosophy and the arts should be for his readers not an end, however, but a beginning. We have not "arrived" when we have memorized his philosophy, but merely begun.

Each soul and each generation of souls must recover anew the meaning of order by opening itself to the experiences of being that orient us in the order of being. The task of a science of politics is therefore endless, but it is not a Sisyphean repetition of futility. The "conclusion" of the task, however, stated in either a new or an old set of symbols of order, would be merely a new derailment into dogmatism. One may anticipate, for example, the emergence of "left" and "right" Voegelinians: the left would stress his demand for "openness to being," and the right would stress the conservative strain in his work that made him welcome at the Hoover Institution. With each group disregarding the insights of the other, we would then have two dogmatic camps. One would neglect Voegelin's admonition that the structure of reality imposes on us the existential categories of better and worse: we must make judgments about what we should do, and it is often better to act in one way than another. The other would neglect his repeated denial of belonging to any political–ideological camp and his repeated injunctions that the philosopher must remain open to reality. This openness does not mean that one cannot make judgments or participate in political processes, but it does mean that one never does so with a closed dogma, or simply following a party line.[56]

Third, in between ideology and philosophy, we find various grades of understanding, misunderstanding, and even denial of the primordial structures of the community of being. But the differences between the grades, both in magnitude and quality, can be of the utmost importance. Scholars, social scientists, humanists, and thoughtful people may not be philosophers, yet they may nevertheless be people who seek the truth, the good, and the just, but without the technical apparatus that philosophy provides. Even a science that does not know in the full sense what it is doing is a science worth noting, if it is grounded in reality.

Let me conclude by putting the matter more bluntly: do we need to be the initiates of some inner circle, the disciples of some sage or other who has finally uncovered the truth of the entire matter, in order to be competent social scientists, scholars, or the like, or to resist disorder? In Voegelin's understanding of philosophy and science—no. What he discovered and articulated, he articulated well. Yet he was never entirely satisfied, always seeking further and deeper analyses of reality experienced. His own researches into the order of being and human orientation in being were not, and by the inherent character of our existence could never be, completed. If we accept this notion of incompleteness, we do not forget the problem of dogma and systems that is always at the margins and often at the center of philosophy.

The word "resistance" carries with it a connotation of activism, perhaps derived from the exploits of the French underground, the "Résistance" of World War II. But its Latin root, *resistere,* means more closely "to withstand," not actively to shoot people or to destroy railway bridges and industrial installations. These distinctions in connotation are important in the following way: Voegelin was first and foremost a scientist; resistance in the sense of "withstanding" an existentially corrupting force is a by-product of scientific integrity, at the same time that disorder may be an impetus for science. The existential motivation, namely a feeling of unease or disquiet that underlies the impetus, may be only dimly or partially understood, but this partial clarity does not remove its existential context nor vitiate the imperfect results.[57] The philosophical articulation of our consciousness of reality *clarifies* the activity of resistance, but it does not necessarily *constitute* it. We do not need to be philosophers in order to resist disorder or combat its effects; but as Voegelin's analysis of Robert Musil and Karl Kraus demonstrates, we do need to be intellectually honest and aware of our humanity.

Leo Strauss once remarked that a science of politics that cannot distinguish tyrannical from just government is a kind of madness.[58] This Aristotelian observation is itself an immediate act of distinction between regimes (and between various claims of methods of study to be sciences), and an implicit act of resistance to those who would call themselves political benefactors (or scientists of politics) but are not. Voegelin's writings were from the first to the last such acts of distinction, first as science, later as a combination of science and philosophy. They varied in their success, they may not all have been motivated by an immediate desire to resist some particular form of social disorder (even though they were all endeavors to participate in the ordering enterprise of science), and they shared a gradual, groping progress toward a fuller articulation of the elements of reality. Like any action, they are left for us to use as an illumination of the reality in which they took place. Like any action, we can never be sure beforehand of all their consequences, or of all that they may reveal. I turn now to three episodes of Voegelin's analysis that reveal central elements of reality for political philosophy.

NOTES

1. Eric Voegelin, "Equivalences of Experience and Symbolization in History," in *Published Essays, 1966–1985*, ed. Ellis Sandoz, vol. 12 of *The Collected Works of Eric Voegelin* (Baton Rouge: Louisiana State University Press, 1990), 126.

2. Cf. Eric Voegelin, "Immortality: Experience and Symbol," in *Published Essays, 1966–1985*, ed. Sandoz, 52–94; "On Classical Studies," in ibid, 256–64; "Quod Deus Dicitur," in ibid, 376–94.

3. To prevent a reification of the concept of order, I should add that an order is not an empirical object of study, but a discerned quality of the interrelationship of a set of objects. As such an intellectual abstraction, it is halfway between a concept and an immediate empirical object.

4. Eric Voegelin, *Israel and Revelation*, vol. 1 of *Order and History* (Baton Rouge: Louisiana State University Press, 1956), 1.

5. Eric Voegelin, *Plato and Aristotle*, vol. 3 of *Order and History* (Baton Rouge: Louisiana State University Press, 1957), 68.

6. Voegelin, *Israel and Revelation*, 1–2.

7. Voegelin, *Israel and Revelation*, 1.

8. Voegelin, *Israel and Revelation*, 2.

9. Cf. Eric Voegelin, *Science, Politics, and Gnosticism* (Chicago: Henry Regnery, 1968), 53–73.

10. Voegelin, *Plato and Aristotle*, 2–3.

11. Voegelin, *Plato and Aristotle*, 2–3.

12. Plato, *Republic*, 441c–445e; 544d–e.

13. Thomas Spragens has suggested that nearly all the great political philosophers have begun their inquiries with a perception of crisis. See Thomas A. Spragens, Jr., *Understanding Political Theory* (New York: St. Martin's Press, 1976), 20–45.

14. Voegelin, *Plato and Aristotle*, 68–9.

15. Eric Voegelin, "On Gnosticism," letter to Alfred Schuetz, January 10, 1953, in *The Philosophy of Order*, ed. Peter J. Opitz and Gregor Sebba (Stuttgart: Ernst Klett, 1981), 461.

16. Voegelin, *Plato and Aristotle*, 5.

17. Voegelin, *Plato and Aristotle*, 68.

18. Eric Voegelin, "Response to Professor Altizer's 'A New History and a New But Ancient God?'" in *Published Essays, 1966–1985*, ed. Sandoz, 301–302.

19. For an interpretation of catharsis as a kind of conceptual "clearing up," especially in Aristotle, see Martha Nussbaum, *The Fragility of Goodness* (Cambridge: Harvard University Press, 1986), 388–91.

20. See Michael Franz, *Eric Voegelin and the Politics of Spiritual Revolt* (Baton Rouge: Louisiana State University Press, 1992), 106ff.

21. Voegelin, "Equivalences," 119, 125–26.

22. "It is not immaterial whether an evolution moves from compactness to the differentiation of experiences of transcendence or from differentiated transcendence to immanentizing gnosticism. In the first case, a society of Malaysian natives, for example, living in a complete, harmonic if compact culture, may defend itself against, say, the importation of Western ideas which in themselves can only have a destructive social impact. In the second case, pathologically crippled men try to destroy an existing high culture. It is not one and the same thing for Plato to think beyond a collapsing Athenian city state and for National Socialists and Communists to try to destroy the classical-Christian tradition." Voegelin, "On Gnosticism," 461.

23. Eric Voegelin, *Anamnesis*, trans. and ed. Gerhart Niemeyer (Notre Dame, Ind.: University of Notre Dame Press, 1978), 3; cf. 9–10.

24. Voegelin, *Anamnesis*, 9.

25. Eric Voegelin, *The New Science of Politics* (Chicago: University of Chicago Press, 1952), 52.

26. This foreshortened account cannot do justice either to philosophy or science and the conceptual problems both activities engender. I intend here merely to offer working characterizations of both activities, limited to the purposes of this chapter.

27. Voegelin, *New Science of Politics*, 14.

28. Eric Voegelin, *Autobiographical Reflections*, ed. Ellis Sandoz (Baton Rouge: Louisiana State University Press, 1989), 12; cf. Voegelin, *New Science of Politics*, 13–24.

29. Voegelin, *New Science of Politics*, 17–18.

30. Voegelin, *Autobiographical Reflections*, 12; Voegelin, *New Science of Politics*, 23–26.

31. "Here is the gap in Weber's work constituting the great problem with which I have dealt during the fifty years since I got acquainted with his ideas." Voegelin, *Autobiographical Reflections*, 12.

32. Here again, he attributed his strong inclination for intellectual honesty to the influence of Max Weber. Voegelin, *Autobiographical Reflections*, 45.

33. Voegelin, *Autobiographical Reflections*, 45.

34. Voegelin, *Autobiographical Reflections*, 47. For an early example of Voegelin's contest with intellectual dishonesty, coupled with a quest for precision of language in an effort to resist disorder and ideological corruption, see his "*The Theory of Legal Science*: A Review," in *Louisiana Law Review* 4 (1942), esp. 558–71. Huntington Cairn's reply to Voegelin's review immediately follows. Particularly if this reply is considered in light of Voegelin's critique of Kelsen's pure theory of law, it distressingly illuminates the sorts of phenomena Voegelin was combating.

35. Voegelin, *Autobiographical Reflections*, 50.

36. Voegelin, *Autobiographical Reflections*, 50.

37. Voegelin, *Science, Politics, and Gnosticism*, 5.

38. Cf., Eric Voegelin, *Die Politischen Religionen* (Stockholm: Bermann-Fischer Verlag, A.B., 1939), 7–9.

39. Voegelin, *Science, Politics, and Gnosticism*, 18.

40. Eric Voegelin, *Die Rassenidee in der Geistesgeschichte von Ray bis Carus* (Berlin: Junker und Dünnhaupt, 1933), 1, 5.

41. Cf. Eric Voegelin, "Two Recent Contributions to the Science of Law," in *'The Nature of the Law' and Related Legal Writings*, ed. Robert Anthony Pascal, James Lee Babin, and John William Corrington, vol. 27 of *The Collected Works of Eric Voegelin* (Baton Rouge: Lousiana State University Press, 1990), 87; and Voegelin, "*Theory of Legal Science*," 562.

42. Voegelin, *Autobiographical Reflections*, 21; Eric Voegelin, *Rasse und Staat* (Tübingen, Germany: J. C. B. Mohr, 1933), 6.

43. Voegelin, *Rasse und Staat*, 7.

44. Voegelin, *Autobiographical Reflections*, 21.

45. Voegelin, *Autobiographical Reflections*, 21–22; Voegelin, *Rassenidee*, 6–7. Voegelin never rejected Kelsen's theory of law *per se*, but only restricted its usefulness to a particular realm of law, denying its adequacy as a theory (or science) of politics. Cf. "Two Recent Contributions," 90; and his review of Hans Kelsen, "General Theory of Law and State," in *Louisiana Law Review* 6 (1945): 491. As evidence for the development of Voegelin's own thought during this period, his critique of Kelsen's theory in *Rassenidee* should be compared with his

laudatory and optimistic comments six years earlier in his "Kelsen's Pure Theory of Law," *Political Science Quarterly* 42 (1927): 2, 268–76.

46. Voegelin's concepts of "compactness" and "differentiation" were part of a larger theory of history. Voegelin had found in his historical investigations "epochal, differentiating events, the 'leaps in being,' which engendered the consciousness of a Before and After and, in their respective societies, motivated the symbolisms of a historical 'course' that was meaningfully structured by the event of the leap." Accordingly, "the experiences of a new insight into the truth of existence, accompanied by the consciousness of the event as constituting an epoch in history, were real enough. There was really an advance in time from compact to differentiated experiences of reality, and, correspondingly, an advance from compact to differentiated symbolizations of the order of being." Voegelin, *The Ecumenic Age*, vol. 4 of *Order and History* (Baton Rouge: Louisiana State University Press, 1974), 2. Voegelin's own discoveries concerning his motivations for resistance and the activities of others in this regard were a minor, personal example of such an advance. A clear and useful account of Voegelin's theory of compactness and differentiation may be found in John J. Rainieri, *Eric Voegelin and the Good Society* (Columbia: University of Missouri Press, 1995), 35–38.

47. Voegelin, *Autobiographical Reflections*, 29.

48. Eric Voegelin, *Über die Form des Amerikanischen Geistes* (Tübingen, Germany: J. C. B. Mohr, 1928), 16, 5.

49. Eric Voegelin, "Hitler und die Deutschen" (unpublished transcript, 1964), 93–94, 138, 36, 51 (all translations from this transcript are my own).

50. Voegelin, *Autobiographical Reflections*, 29.

51. Voegelin, *New Science of Politics*, 188–89. Hannah Arendt and Voegelin provided an interesting debate on the relationship and relative importance of ideas and events in historical developments in their 1953 exchange on the occasion of Voegelin's review of Arendt's *The Origins of Totalitarianism*. (Eric Voegelin, Review of *The Origins of Totalitarianism*, by Hannah Arendt, *Review of Politics* 15 (1953); with a reply by Hannah Arendt and a reply by Eric Voegelin, 68–85.

52. Voegelin, *Anamnesis*, 183.

53. Voegelin, *Anamnesis*, 183.

54. Cf. Thomas Hollweck and Ellis Sandoz, "General Introduction to the Series," in Eric Voegelin, *Hellenism, Rome, and Early Christianity*, ed. Athanasios Moulakis, vol. 1 of *History of Political Ideas* (Columbia: University of Missouri Press, 1997), 16–30.

55. G. K. Chesterton, *Saint Thomas Aquinas: "The Dumb Ox"* (Garden City, N.Y.: Image Books, 1956), 141.

56. Voegelin, *Autobiographical Reflections*, 45.

57. "Die geistige Form findet nicht Wahrheiten und stellt nicht Fakten fest,

sondern sie ist auf sich selbst gerichtet und darum haftet ihr immer ein Ungen-
uegen an, das zu neuen Versuchen der Ueberwindung treibt, die notwendig
ebenso unzureichend sein muessen." Voegelin, *Amerikanischen Geistes*, 16.

58. Leo Strauss, *Natural Right and History* (Chicago: University of Chicago
Press, 1953), 4–5. Cf. Leo Strauss, *The Rebirth of Classical Political Rationalism*,
ed. Thomas L. Pangle (Chicago: University of Chicago Press, 1989), 8–12.

3

THE "PEOPLE OF GOD" AND THE RISE OF IDEOLOGICAL POLITICS

It will have become apparent in the first three chapters of this book that Voegelin saw a good part of his scholarly work as an activity of coming to terms with the modern age. This "coming to terms" included a close analysis of ideological politics. Ideological doctrines and the politics they engender are seemingly a modern phenomenon. We may therefore ask: First, what distinguishes ideological politics from other forms of politics? Second, is there a historical "location" where this kind of politics first becomes evident? And third, do such doctrines have clearly discernible experiential roots that can help us to make sense of their appearance?

In this chapter, I will examine Eric Voegelin's first deliberate articulation of an answer to these three questions, which we find in his largely unpublished, multivolume manuscript, "The History of Political Ideas." First, I will say a few words about the work, its origins, and its place in Voegelin's larger corpus, as these are related to the question of ideology. Then, through an explication of Voegelin's "History of Political Ideas" and related texts, I will address in order the three questions listed above. This exercise is partially philological and partially philosophical. On the philological side, I will consider Voegelin's earlier formulations of this problem in light of his later work. Such a move helps to show the unity of Voegelin's enterprise and also to clarify the increasingly abstract terms of his later analysis. On the philosophical side, I am interested in Voegelin's formulations in light of other interpretations of ideological politics.

THE "PEOPLE OF GOD" AND "THE HISTORY
OF POLITICAL IDEAS"

Voegelin wrote about four thousand pages of his "History of Political Ideas" before its theoretical basis became untenable for him. Part 7 of this massive work roughly covers the period 1500 to 1677, beginning with Machiavelli and ending with Spinoza; of this, chapter 4 is concerned with the political program of the "mystical activists," or "People of God," of these two centuries.[1] These activists are for Voegelin the first clear historical exemplar of the politically successful ideological type. The nub of the question as to what motivates "activist mystics" to their revolutionary politics and how these motives are displayed in their political agendas is of philological interest, because it eventually comes to lie at the center of Voegelin's theoretically determined decision to turn from "The History of Political Ideas" to *The New Science of Politics, Science, Politics, and Gnosticism*, and the five-volume *Order and History*; attention to that turn is part of an interpretation of this earlier episode in the "History of Political Ideas." In the historical schema that governs "The History of Political Ideas," this appearance of activist mysticism occurs for Voegelin at the beginning of modernity:

> If we characterize the "modern" period of politics as the age in which the institutions of imperial Christianity experience their definite breakdown and the national states become the centers of Western political order, we may say that this age started twice. Its first start is characterized by [the] person and work of Machiavelli. From the disintegration of medieval institutions emerges the demonic naturalism of power as a formal principle of political order, restricted as to its substance . . . by the idea that the order of power should be the order of a nation. The second start comes with the Reformation."[2]

The "People of God" are for Voegelin the inheritors of both "starts" of modernity.

But what constitutes these beginnings? Part of Voegelin's gradual (and partial) move away from his "History of Political Ideas" consisted in the development of a more adequate vocabulary for explaining the motivation(s) behind the activism of sectarian groups in this and later periods. A reader familiar with Voegelin's later writings, but not this as yet largely unpublished work, will perhaps be surprised to find that the most important categories for understanding the doctrines and motivations of the "People of God" include for Voegelin "experience," "faith," and "realism," all of which appear as central theoretical concepts in the later works, especially *The New Science of Politics* and *Science, Politics, and Gnosticism.*

"Experience," at least of the religious kind, is already in the "History" an important factor for Voegelin in the generation of political ideas.[3] For him, "religious experiences" of a certain type "form the active nucleus" of the movements I will consider here. The "religious cultures that are based on a similar type of experience," including Gnosticism, neo-Platonism, Manicheanism, and Islamic mysticism, are not merely literary forebears of later revolutionary movements; instead, they point to a common set of experiences that inspire "great systems of speculative theology," on the one hand, and similarly structured revolutionary doctrines on the other. "The experiences themselves," Voegelin concludes "are neither Eastern nor Western but fundamentally human. They can spring up anywhere and at any time, though they will neither become socially effective nor blossom out into systems of speculation unless the social environment favors such expansionism."[4] Here we see a clear precursor to the introduction to *Order and History* that we considered in chapter 2.

In the "History of Political Ideas," Voegelin interprets political ideas as the doctrines that emerge from the process of reflecting on experience and seeking to articulate its meaning. What is missing from the ordering of these and related concepts is, as I have already noted, a theory of consciousness by means of which to integrate them into a comprehensive theory of politics. A properly articulated theory of consciousness would provide us with a more precise account of how political symbols are generated and why a common set of experiences can reasonably be argued to be "behind" such engenderings. When such a theory comes to light, "a history of political ideas [is] a senseless undertaking," because

> [i]deas turned out to be a secondary conceptual development, beginning with the Stoics, intensified in the high Middle Ages, and radically unfolding since the eighteenth century. Ideas transform symbols, which express experiences, into concepts—which are assumed to refer

to a reality other than the reality experienced. And this reality other than the reality experienced does not exist. Hence, ideas are liable to deform the truth of the experiences and their symbolization.[5]

Between "The History of Political Ideas" and *Order and History*, Voegelin's "focus of . . . interest thus moved from ideas to the experiences of reality that engendered a variety of symbols for their articulation." "Ideas" remain as the dogmatic markers of the symbols of experiences, but they cannot form the core of a scientific theory of politics understood in the classical sense. Instead, such a theory requires a focus on the "experience of reality—personal, social, historical, cosmic—as the reality to be explored historically."[6] At this earlier stage in his own theoretical development, Voegelin treats ideas as the markers of meaning that establish political order and that clash with one another in the confrontation between meanings. Given the nature of the phenomena, this topical treatment is generally sufficient for an understanding of the workings of political ideas and symbols in the public realm, including those of ideologies, but it largely neglects their origin in basic human experiences.

The missing theoretical components do not keep Voegelin from telling, in "The History of Political Ideas" a story of the movement of the human spirit and its relationship to political order. It is not a Hegelian spirit that "moves" here, but—rightly understood—a Platonic/Christian one. For Voegelin, politics is a spiritual-temporal activity in which the temporal organization of power and the spiritual articulation of the meaning of such power interplay at the mundane-temporal and spiritual-transcendent levels. Spirit may not speak truth to power, but through myth, religious symbols, various arts, and even philosophical discourse, it speaks meaning to it.[7] Consequently, faith is already a guiding category in the "History," even if its experiential and existential roots have not yet been as fully uncovered as in his later writings.

Faith appears in the "History" as a willingness "to orient existence through openness toward transcendent reality." It may be contrasted to the "existential disorientation" that occurs upon a "weakening or loss of faith," in consequence of which human beings seek to find "an absolute orientation of human existence through intramundane experience," thereby lowering the niveau of intellectual culture generally.[8] Such a re-orientation occurs in European civilization with the scientific discoveries of the sixteenth and following centuries that are thought to give new,

liberating insights into the order of existence, so much so that they overcome the limitations of reality experienced and doctrines formulated accordingly in earlier centuries. This reorientation to existence and the
parallel stream of activist mysticism that I will consider here together
form for Voegelin the two tracks of the downward slope of Western civilization, which had reached its spiritual and intellectual height in the
doctrines and insights of the High Middle Ages. Thus, his "History" is
the story of a general rise (with interludes) in civilizational quality and
existential insight from the Greeks through the Romans to the medieval
Europeans and a decline from that civilization into modernity, which is
most strongly characterized for him by extensive existential disorder.[9]

The descent is marked by a process of dissolution of the universal
markers that constitute the spiritual and institutional order of Western
civilization. Primary among these are the notion and political reality of
the Christian imperium, which dissolves through various nationalist and
reformation movements between the fourteenth and sixteenth centuries;
the development of modern science, its emancipation from ecclesiastical
oversight, and its seemingly antibiblical but also philosophically mal-
adroit cosmology; and the development of historical science from the
eighteenth century onward that raises serious doubts about the nature of
the sacred texts and the ecclesiastical interpretation of them.[10] Out of this
dissolution grow new centers of meaning, new forms of political and
social organization (including first and foremost the modern nation-
state), and a gradual dissolution of the spiritual and political authority of
the Roman Catholic Church, which occurs in parallel with the disintegration of the unified *corpus Christianum* that is medieval Europe.[11]

At the end of this process, we find modern men, "spiritual eunuchs" who are philosophically ignorant, with existentially closed souls,
and yet dilettantishly activist and socially successful despite their extensive intellectual and spiritual shortcomings. Modernity is characterized
by the victory of scientism over the spirit; by the success of widespread
existential ignorance against the tradition that keeps alive the intellectual
and spiritual inheritance of the West;[12] and by sectarian movements that
break asunder the unity of Western civilizational experience and reject
its spiritual formations. The "spiritual devastation" of the rational-scien-
tific approach consists in the conviction that such an approach can "substitute for the spiritual integration of personality."[13] The aridity of such a
substitution holds open the possibility of a "re-spiritualization from non-

Christian sources," which includes not only other religions, but, more emphatically, the ideological formations of sectarian groups in the sixteenth century and of revolutionaries in the nineteenth and twentieth.

The life of faith is difficult. It requires strength of spirit to live out faith either politically or intellectually. Faith, Voegelin reminds us, is "the substance of things hoped for," or "an active openness to the transcendental reality." It is active and creative, and the "pneumatic experience of faith . . . constitutes the substance of the Christian community."[14] When internal corruption or a lack of sufficient numbers of faithful to sustain the uncertainty of faith leads to a failure of the institutions that support the life of faith toward the transcendent, the participating members of a civilization may look for meaning elsewhere in less spiritually difficult fields, and this shift will involve the possibility of civilizational disaster, as modernity demonstrates. Ideological warfare is the greatest and most devastating modern example of such a possibility.

Faith is most closely attached to the life of the spirit, but what is meant by "spiritual"? For Voegelin the spiritual [dimension] of human existence provides the "substantial ordering of existence" that gives order and meaning to politics.[15] But the symbols concerning the human soul, the transcendental reality to which it has access, and the relations between the two "are not a body of empirically verifiable propositions to be accepted as true after due examination." Instead, "they receive their meaning as expressions of the spiritual process in which the soul responds with *caritas* to the supernatural aid of the *gratia*; in this response is constituted the *fides caritate formata* which opens the possibilities of reaching out understandingly into the supernatural; it develops the faculties of the *cognitio fidei*, the cognition by faith, concerning matters which are not accessible to natural reason."[16] Such experiences and their symbolization become the meaning-laden core of a civilization, whether it be ordered by Christianity or by some other set of religious symbols and doctrines. Accordingly, the order of modern existence must be understood in terms of spirit:

> [As] a consequence of the interlocking of science and social power, the political tentacles of scientistic civilization reach into every nook and corner of industrialized society, and with increasing effectiveness they stretch over the whole globe. There exist only differences, though very important ones, in the various regions of the global asy-

lum with regard to the possibility of personal escape into the freedom of the spirit. What is left is hope—but hope should not obscure the realist insight that we who are living today shall never experience freedom of the spirit in society.[17]

Such damage to the life of the spirit is made possible when those who carry forward the ordering symbols of a civilization lose the experiential substance of those symbols. In modernity, then, "the active center of intellectual life has shifted to the plane of our knowledge of the external world" from the transcendental plane under which that world exists.[18]

The clash between the scientistic "eunuchs of the spirit" and the philosophers is one conflict in modernity that, according to Voegelin, the philosophers have generally lost and continue to lose. The activist mystics, who form a separate group in the civilizational struggle, are, out of somewhat different motives, the opponents of intellectual high civilization in another way. The history of the sectarian quest for articulation of existential truth in the political realm by such mystics must be understood as a conflict between the "spiritual realist" and the activist mystic. The latter maintains a magical "faith in historical transfiguration" over against the former, who knows full well that mankind will never "through a revolutionary transforming act" change the nature of man "from its present imperfect state to a state of perfection that will make social compulsion unnecessary."[19] This yearning of activist mystics for revolutionary transformation is for Voegelin the core of ideological politics.

The "People of God" is Voegelin's general rubric, taken from radical sectarian tracts and sermons themselves, for a series of sectarian movements arising at a point in European civilization when there was "a growing realization that the institutional unity of Christian mankind had broken down irrevocably and that the plurality of institutions which express the diversified field of intramundane social forces had become an established fact."[20] The "People of God" constituted one of the "social forces" of this field, and they were able to take advantage of the fragmentation of Christendom to become socially active and successful. It was their social success under these conditions, more than their particular aspirations, that was specifically modern for Voegelin:

> [O]ne of the most important components of the "modern" complex of sentiments, the free sectarian spirituality, is not "modern" at all if

by modern we mean an attitude which follows in time the medieval, but is a medieval element which rises from the sub-institutional to the institutional level. Modern is not the anti-ecclesiastical spirituality itself but rather the change of its social relevance. And only when sectarian spirituality becomes socially so effective that it leads to a schism of the Church, do we encounter as a result sentiments and attitudes which can be called modern in the sense that they did not exist before the split in the medieval unit of the Church. The experience of a plurality of Churches, each claiming to represent the true faith, becomes a decisive factor in the growth of such phenomena as mystical religiousness beyond the dogmatic differences, tolerance, scepticism with regard to spiritual authority, religious indifferentism and agnosticism.[21]

I move now from the historical-intellectual background to the specific doctrines of the sectarian groups. Voegelin's claim, which has been noted here without comment, was that the experiential, doctrinal, and organizational bases of these groups paralleled or perhaps anticipated later ideological movements. This claim has had its detractors, and I will consider one such critique at the conclusion of the chapter. But first, let us turn to the movements themselves.

THE HISTORICAL EMERGENCE OF
IDEOLOGICAL POLITICS

"The People of God" are among those "men in communities who go their way through history in partnership with God."[22] It is, however, a different partnership from that conceived of by the Constantinian forms of Christianity, supported by the Roman Catholic Church, that would bear the ordering principles of European civilization for roughly a millennium. The new partnership proposed by the People of God must be understood in light of the Constantinian partnership, because their radicalism is a conscious and intentional counterpoint to the previous forms of partnership. Several unique doctrines comprise the conceptual/doctrinal scaffolding of the new form. Along with this apparatus, there are also recurring sociological traits that define the new movements. The two march hand in hand in Voegelin's analysis; let us first consider the sociological traits.

First, the "People of God" are one strand among many social

movements that embody a set of ideas "in revolt against the institutional superstructure of our civilization."[23] They are political "outsiders," as it were, in revolt against the "establishment" of their day. This type of popular movement is not unique to the Western experience, but all such movements take on forms that vary with the specific spiritual structures and their institutional embodiment in a particular political order. For this reason, the developments in Europe of the fourteenth to seventeenth centuries give rise to a unique form of such popular movements.

Second, the civilization of Western Europe from A.D. 400 to 1600 is informed by a spiritual configuration that takes its direction from a group of canonical texts, namely the Christian Bible. The spiritual meaning of these texts is transcribed politically and embodied civilizationally in a series of institutions. All such institutions, regardless of place and time, must engage in an ongoing process of renovation as they address themselves to the ever-emerging problems of domestic and international change that all political institutions confront. Because the European institutions based their legitimacy on the existential interpretation of a specific set of authoritative texts, an evaluation of how well they embody and live up to the principles articulated in these texts is, on principle, open to anyone who has access to those texts. In other words, "the spiritualism of Christianity, and in particular the spiritualism of the Sermon on the Mount, is a standard that can be invoked against the institution that is supposed to represent it."[24] Accordingly, the spiritual movements of revolt in Europe tended to be not in "generic opposition" to the institutions they opposed, but to see themselves as reformation movements, intending not to destroy but to restore the spirit that had become lost in its institutional representation. Governing institutions are to be reformed, not eliminated.

Third, then, these groups must be understood not only at the level of their intellectual or spiritual engagement, but also at the level of institutional response. Institutions, after all, are imperfect human inventions that "can do no more than stabilize and order the field of social forces which exists at the time of their creation." Accordingly, "there will always be groups and individuals who are dissatisfied with the settlement of the historical moment; and as time goes on and circumstances change, new causes of dissatisfaction will arise." For this reason, any institution must be adaptable, "constantly engaged in the process of re-stabilizing itself through the solution of problems that would destroy its value and

meaning if they remained unsolved." When, due to any number of en-
dogenous or exogenous factors, this activity of adaptation becomes difficult or even impossible, people will become dissatisfied with the institutions, because these no longer effectively represent the existential
truths they are intended to embody. A sufficiently high level of dissatisfaction of a sufficiently large number of people can lead to widespread
political disaffection; with the requisite leadership, such persons may
well "form communities and organize themselves for political action,"
making the "situation . . . ripe for a revolution."[25]

Fourth, an admixture of reformatory zeal and an appeal to central
icons, normally used to establish the legitimacy of "establishment" institutions, but now used to validate their own revolutionary activity, makes
such movements both unique to the Western experience and peculiarly
dangerous to the maintenance of the institutions that they seek to reform
and that are the preservers of high culture. Most popular movements, by
their nature and regardless of time or place, harbor a considerable degree
of "resentment against intellectual and aesthetic values which are realized by the upper class."[26] This resentment often seeks not only to reform the governing institutions so that they conform more closely to the
spiritual standards they claim to represent but also to suppress or even
destroy literary and artistic culture, which is generally perceived to be
the product of a corrupt elite. The danger is that in its efforts to resist
the anti-civilizational aspect of the movements, the elite will miss the
legitimate calls for reform, or simply use the less noble sentiments of the
dissenting groups as a convenient excuse to ignore legitimate grievances.
Such neglect may well result in yet more strident resentment and out-
bursts that "may turn against the spiritual values themselves," so that the
process "which has started with movements for spiritual reform may end
with movements against the spirit." "Spiritually regressive" movements
ironically become the bearers of reform.[27] The difficulty for the political
philosopher or historian evaluating these movements is, therefore, that
they may embody both spiritual and antispiritual tendencies at the same
time.[28]

Fifth, institutional variations over time and from place to place
mean that the social and political effectiveness of such movements is not
uniform; it depends in large part on the ability of ruling institutions to
absorb the reformatory claims without embracing their civilizationally
less edifying aspects. Voegelin argues that the Western Church demon-

strated a considerable ability to absorb reformation movements of various kinds, as is shown in the rise of various monastic orders during the eleventh to thirteenth centuries, which often began as serious, sometimes heretical reformation challenges to the Church hierarchy, but that were integrated into the life of the Church by a prudent elite. As this ability declined in the face of weaknesses in leadership and changes in the political scene, however, the Church hierarchy came to resist reform movements more and more vigorously, which in turn led to increasingly strident calls for reform. By the time of Martin Luther, these calls had often attached themselves to nationalist sentiments, and the Church could no longer deal with them as it had with the Albigensians in a successful unified crusade three centuries earlier.[29] For the most radical of the movements, the demand for reform had changed into a call for revolutionary transformation on a broad scale.

Reform is not equivalent to transformation. The move from the former to the latter is the crucial step that distinguishes spiritual realism—the sober realization that neither humankind nor the world in which we find ourselves is perfectible, but that positive reform is both possible and desirable[30]—from activist mysticism, which is the desire for the total transformation of all social forms into a realm of perfection:

> The symbol of perfection is rooted in the experience of an imperfection that can be overcome only through grace in death. That is the point at which the genuine mystic stops in his speculation; and that is the point from which the activist mystic carries on. The "activist" accepts the dematerialization of the symbol like the genuine mystic; but then he goes one fateful step further: he abolishes the distance between the symbol and the experience, and mistakes the symbol for an experience that can be realized existentially in the life of man in society.[31]

This step into radicalism is the central defining feature of activist doctrine, so that we can say that the yearning for perfectibility transformed into its expectation is the keystone of the conceptual/symbolic apparatus of the "People of God" movements. A waning of the life of faith does not imply that people cease searching for meaning; they are just as likely to redirect the spiritual forces of political life into other—in this case immanent—aspirations. All of the other symbols developed in these movements ultimately flow from the quest for, and belief in, this-worldly perfectibility. Voegelin argues that the same symbols, revealing comparable motives, reappear in similar and even identical form in modern ideological movements. Let us consider several of these symbolic complexes.

The first symbol is the general symbol of the realm of perfection that awaits the this-worldly fulfilling activity of God and His chosen ones. The range of activity on the part of the community of the Chosen ranges from passive waiting to active (and violent) implementation on God's behalf. The more politically relevant examples tend toward the active side of the spectrum, since they seek by a social revolution to bring about the new world order through the human action of spiritual reform coupled with institutional transformation or destruction.[32] The names for the new realm in the People of God movements were generally taken from Christian tradition and included "Jerusalem," "Sion," and "Paradise," among others. These names may indicate a move into a golden future or a return to an idyllic past.[33] The specific contents of the perfect world soon to be realized vary with the particular fantasies or obsessions of the speculative activist who envisions it. In every case, frustration with the defects of the real world of real men and women will soon pass away.[34]

The second symbol is the general symbol, again taken from Christian tradition, for the realm of imperfection, or darkness, or even evil that opposes the People of God. This present world is a "Babylon," informed by the "spirit of Antichrist" that despises the "Saints of God," seeking to persecute and eliminate them so that it may continue its reign of impurity and self-indulgence.[35] A third symbol, one of cosmic struggle between the forces of light and darkness, is a logical extension of the first two.[36] As they become effective as symbols of political enactment, these Manichean oppositional symbols tend to be situated within a wider schema of historical understanding whose prototype was first and most cogently articulated in the theological speculations of Joachim of Fiora in the thirteenth century.

Joachim developed a systematic theology of history, according to which the world is evolving toward an immanent age of perfection, which he symbolized as the "Third Realm," the age of spiritual fulfillment. A Dux, or leader, will appear to establish the era, guided by a prophet who understands the course of history and who therefore understands the (Divine) program for fulfillment in its details.[37] The "community of spiritually autonomous persons," finally, is the collective that is perfected in the new age. These four symbols—the "Third Realm," the "Dux," the prophet, and the "community of spiritually autonomous persons"—have clear potential for revolutionary uses, but Joachim himself was not a revolutionary, nor did he perceive himself to be accomplishing anything more than an orthodox distillation of the Christian tradition. Indeed, his speculations appear to have had the blessing of the ecclesiastical authorities.[38] Clearly, however, the notion of an age of fulfillment beyond this present age implied a critical stance toward the religious institutions of the time. The doctrine of progress, moreover, "applied to the concrete course of world history" was also a decided novelty.[39] The tripartite process of perfection through the three "Ages" of the Father, Son, and Holy Spirit had its source for Joachim in the activity of God, but the door was now opened for understanding the "history of salvation . . . as the process of gradual realization of the freedom of the Holy Spirit," and this process could readily be immanently understood as "the progressive realization of God-given freedom."[40] It is no large step from waiting for God to fulfill His historical purpose to seizing the moment in an immanent revolution directed at the present order; the extinction of the state and other institutions that would be brought about in the Third Age of the Spirit could be a prize to be grasped and not a gift to be received. In this way, realistic attempts at reformation could turn into desires for transformation.[41]

In both complexes of symbols—those of Joachim and the earlier ones taken up by the medieval activist mystics—an immanent form of the Christian idea of perfection holds primacy. Voegelin leaves this symbolic aggregate largely unattended in "The People of God," but in his later *Science, Politics, and Gnosticism* he offers a clear statement of its meaning. The Christian notion of perfection includes both an account of the movement toward the goal and of the nature of the goal itself. These two components of perfectibility are taken up in a variety of ways by those who bring the notion of transcendental perfection down to earth in an act of political transformation. They may emphasize the pathway to perfection, as in various progessivist movements that concern themselves chiefly with the means of reaching a usually somewhat hazy goal. They may emphasize the nature of the goal itself, as in many utopian schemes. And, third, they may combine the two components, giving both an account of the nature of the goal to be reached and the means to get there. This combination is for Voegelin most especially the purview of the activist mystics who seek a revolutionary transformation.[42]

The dream-world of the spiritual activist is not the real world, but a "second reality"[43] inserted over the first, real world in which real human beings with all their limitations and imperfections live, and in which real but imperfect institutions exist, designed to ameliorate the worst deficiencies of the beings who build, sustain, and inhabit them. Thus, a more or less realistic anthropology, reflected in the everyday institutions of power of a society, complete with their shortcomings and continual need for reform, is confronted by the fantasy of historical transfiguration.[44] But since the nature of the world and of the beings that inhabit it are relatively fixed and not open to boundless transfiguration, the revolutionary carries an imagined world around in his head, but he continues to live in the real world with the rest of us. Unfortunately, however, his transformatory activities also occur in the real world, in which real blood is shed and real pain is felt at the hands of the mystical activists. The excesses of the activists are all too familiar to the victims of the various forms of ideological fervor that have swept through the twentieth century.

IDEOLOGICAL POLITICS

"Ideology" (or "ideological") rarely appears in the pages of "The History of Political Ideas."[45] The term, as everyone knows, is itself a piece of modernity that can be traced to the political program of Antoine Louis Claude Destutt de Tracy and the French Ideologues. As founding members of the Institut de France, they sought to develop and disseminate "true knowledge" about how nations are governed. This agenda was based on a "science of ideas" that the Ideologues called "ideology," the object of which was to discover the sources or bases of current ideas about social, economic, and political life. The Ideologues proposed to use the empiricist epistemological premises found in Locke's *Essay on Human Understanding* to examine critically the traditional ideas and institutions of the French Ancien Regime with the intention of developing better, more "rational" ideas on how to govern. The project was a product of Enlightenment sentiments. De Tracy claimed that the political ideas of Europeans prior to the French Revolution were based on the biased perceptions and particular experiences of the privileged classes, not on universal human perceptions and experiences. Consequently, these now antiquated ideas had no universal validity or truth and needed to be replaced with ideas that did. Such ideas could be discovered by de Tracy's new science of ideas, which showed that a properly constituted political regime must be based on the universal need of all human beings to protect their own lives and on the recognition that this need required a liberal-democratic form of government to secure protection for everyone. De Tracy's science appeared essentially to be an apologetic framework for classical liberalism with a practical intent: it was to be the basis of educational and political reform, a science that would understand the practical effects of specific ideas.[46]

When the parochialism of de Tracy's universalism became apparent, the meaning of "ideology" shifted to denote a world-view whose biased perspective was manifest. Marx added to the shift a different usage, dependent on a materialistic account of consciousness, so that the term now enjoys a variety of meanings.[47] All are linked to the notion of a connection between external stimuli and ideas. The causal arrow of this connection can flow in both directions: our environment influences our ideas, but our ideas may also be put to practical effect in the manipulation of the environment. To treat ideologies in this way is, of course, to continue the twin epistemological errors on which de Tracy's science was founded, namely, the notion that we can treat "our ideas—our perceptions, memories, imaginations, and conceptions or thoughts—as objects of which we are directly aware or conscious," and the "mistake of reducing all our cognitive powers to that of our senses and failing to distinguish between the senses and the intellect as quite distinct, though interdependent, ways of apprehending objects."[48] This mistake means that we lose sight of the existential basis (at both the spiritual and the mundane levels) for our political symbols and that a clash of political symbols and ideas is then treated, even by the political theorist, as merely a conflict of dogmas without critical philosophical depth. The science of man indeed comes to grief.[49]

In general, the term ideology is now used sociologically "to refer to a system of ideas or beliefs that the user [of the term] thinks of as in some way limited."[50] This limitation may be one of intellectual scope, of historical breadth, of ethnic range, or of some other kind invariably implying that the "possessor" of the ideology has missed something. Those who use the word tend to presume that ideologies demonstrate partiality and parochialism. Thus, the contemporary usages of the word are generally pejorative, which stands in ironic contrast to its origins as the name for a progressive, demystifying science that was intended to clear up the difficulties of prejudice, parochialism, and self-interest. In a further irony, those who use the term in a pejorative manner frequently seek a "scientific" discourse by means of which to overcome the deleterious qualities of the ideas of almost everyone else.[51] Given the epistemological errors on which such discourses are based, the ironic results are not surprising.

These sociological usages of the term, however, are not quite what the political historian or theorist may have in mind when he uses it. For such scholars, ideologies may be understood as comprehensive and generally coherent sets of doctrines, formulated with the express purpose of guiding political action. An ideology provides a set of answers to basic political, social, and economic questions. In this provision, an ideology is also thought by its adherents to offer a critical framework for evaluating competing ideologies, debunking their myths and falsehoods, and providing sure insights into how political and historical processes really work and might ideally be made to work. Ideologies are systematic accounts of political knowledge; what they may lack in subtlety or philosophical insight they make up for in comprehensiveness.

The contemporary sociological and political-scientific definitions of ideology do not at first glance cohere well with Voegelin's characterization of their existential import. It seems difficult to think of comprehensive and critical systems of thought as the formulations of "second realities" and activist mystical agendas. The answer to the problem appears in attending to Voegelin's theoretical distinctions. There is, for example, a clear distinction for Voegelin between spirit and mind. Spiritual eunuchs, like physical eunuchs, may well have perfectly normally functioning minds. Indeed, Voegelin considers that there must have been first-rate, high-quality religious thinkers, for example, among the Adamite sects of the fifteenth and later centuries, as demonstrated in the complex symbolism they developed to express their thinking.[52] Thus, raw intelligence, comprehensiveness, and even critical insight are not the criteria that help us to distinguish between radicalism and realism. For this reason, too, Voegelin seems increasingly to have rejected the possibility that analytical critiques of ideologies can accomplish much against their proponents, since the issue is not one of intellectual appeal but of spiritual dullness or absence of openness to transcendent realities.[53] The conflict between ideology and philosophy is, therefore, not so much a question of intellectual vigor as of spiritual sensitivity and perhaps common sense.[54]

One may characterize ideologies at the level of meaning in a number of ways. Hayden White describes ideology as "the treatment of the form of a thing as a content or essence."[55] One aspect of the form of human existence, for example, is that it is historical. Progressivist ideologies take this quality of proceeding in time to be the essence of human existence when they develop a progressivist notion of human existence in which perfection occurs as the result of a this-worldly, historical process. Here we might include one aspect of Marxism and the prevailing characteristic of various forms of liberalism. The quality of existential uncertainty is similarly essentialized in Fascism under the symbol of "struggle," which valorizes above all other human concerns the idea of interminable and violent conflict.[56] Similarly, Nazis essentialize the existence of the individual as part of a species into the essence of all political phenomena, identifying all historical events and human characteristics as the efflux of racial characteristics and the competition between races for survival.

Hannah Arendt has characterized ideology using its etymological meaning as the logic of an idea. The pernicious effects of such logic are best described in the implementation of an ideological program in the realm of public policy. The subject matter of an ideology "is history, to which the 'idea' is applied; the result of this application is not a body of statements about something that *is*, but the unfolding of a process which is in constant change."[57] This process, moreover, is not imbued with the mystery of being, which, as Aristotle reminds us, excites wonder in the philosopher; rather, it is entirely accessible to the explanatory force of the ideological program, an object of manipulation rather than a source of awe. Indeed, the logic of the idea is the reality of history that the logic exposes. The essentialization White points to becomes an agenda for intra-historical action: when movements based on such modern ideological notions come to power, the ideas of the ideology itself become the tactical counters of a political program. The programmatic use of ideas leads to a peculiar, immanentist otherworldliness among the active leaders of ideological movements:

> The elite is not composed of ideologists; its members' whole educa-
> tion is aimed at abolishing their capacity for distinguishing between
> truth and falsehood, between reality and fiction. Their superiority
> consists in their ability immediately to dissolve every statement of fact
> into a declaration of purpose. In distinction to the mass membership
> which, for instance, needs some demonstration of the inferiority of
> the Jewish race before it can safely be asked to kill Jews, the elite for-
> mations understand that the statement, all Jews are inferior, means, all
> Jews should be killed; they know that when they are told that only
> Moscow has a subway, the real meaning of the statement is that all
> subways should be destroyed, and are not unduly surprised when they
> discover the subway in Paris.[58]

The second reality of the ideology becomes the policy basis for political action; the fantasy of mystical activism translates into a "supreme con-tempt for all facts and all reality."[59] Destruction and murder are not de-fensive responses to a dangerous situation, but proactive techniques of activist implementation.

Such a description of ideologies is intended particularly to capture the workings of those ideologies—Nazism and various forms of Marx-ism—that led to the formation of totalitarian regimes. Although not all ideologies result in totalitarianism, all display symptoms of totalitarian fantasies, as Voegelin makes clear in his criticisms of progressivist forms of liberalism.[60]

Our discussion to this point has implied a link between the mystical activist movements of the late Middle Ages and Renaissance and the ideological movements of contemporary times. Voegelin's persistent ar-gument in the "History" was that there is no essential difference be-tween modern revolutionaries such as the Marxists, Nazis, and Spanish Fascists (all of whom we conventionally call "ideologues") on the one hand, and the "People of God" on the other. He consistently juxtaposes the two throughout the text as though he were talking about the same phenomenon, with the historical distance between its two instantiations being merely circumstantial.[61] It was Voegelin's contention that the pro-grammatic quality of modern ideologies replicates the programmatic qualities of the aspirations of the mystical activists, the "People of God,"

of the sixteenth century. This claim, which lies at the center of Voegelin's analyses, has, however, been disputed; I now turn to that critique.

THE ORIGINS OF IDEOLOGICAL POLITICS

It would seem from Voegelin's analysis, then, that to find the historical location at which what appears to be ideological politics first
emerges on the political and civilizational scene is to answer the question
of its origins. "It's here"; one points to movements that seem to have a
family resemblance, and that is the end of the matter. There are reasons,
however, to doubt the sufficiency of such an answer. Bernard Yack has
challenged the view proposed by several writers that there is a historical
continuity between movements like the "People of God," and modern
ideologues. Such arguments, Yack contends, amount to little more than
the demonstration of analogies that cannot substitute either for a "genealogy to establish paternity" or for "sufficient evidence of a fundamental
continuity" that is never made apparent. Finding similar characteristics
between religious fanatics on the one hand and ideological movements
on the other does not demonstrate historical continuity. Discontent and
common behaviors, Yack argues, are insufficient evidence either of
shared motivations or especially of historical links,[62] so that religious
analogies alone do not provide sufficient evidence that zealous revolutionary aspirations are "secularized" forms of former religious sentiments
for perfection. J. R. Talmon, Carl Becker, James Billington, Norman
Cohn, and Alexis de Tocqueville are, according to Yack, all representatives of this tradition of arguing from analogy to substantive genealogical
links, as is Eric Voegelin.[63] Modern revolutionary hopes and activities are
not merely the atheistic replicas of previous, religiously expressed hopes
for transformation and fulfillment; the unobjectionable argument that
Christianity is a necessary precursor for the developments of the modern
age is for Yack similarly a non-explanation for the "concrete characteristics" of that modernity.[64]

Yack raises an important question. It is one thing to show that developments within the Christian tradition lead to outcomes in non-
Christian modernity. It is quite another to claim that the precursor is
directly linked in a substantive, genealogical way to the later developments. After all, Marx and other dissatisfied modern thinkers explicitly

deny religious sentiments, and genetic fallacies in historical studies abound: "this is like that," so the scholar erroneously concludes, "this must come from that."[65] The question one must put to Voegelin, then, is: how is "this like that" in such a way that it makes sense to draw genealogical lines? According to Yack, "conceptual innovations" in modernity have "generate[d] new desires and longings by identifying the obstacles to our satisfaction, obstacles which we become aware of in longing for a desired object."[66] Modern dissatisfactions are new dissatisfactions, raising new desires to surmount new obstacles. And many such desires are of a kind that calls for "total revolution" if they are to be fulfilled. Voegelin's answer, as we can discern it in the "History" and later texts, is closely linked to his rejection of a history of ideas.

First, let us consider again what is meant by "modern," in order to pinpoint and characterize specifically "modern" problems as distinct from "premodern" ones. For Voegelin, we recall, the modern period of politics is "the age in which the institutions of imperial Christianity experience their definite breakdown and the national states become the centers of Western political order."[67] As Europe, whose order was represented in Western Christianity, literally disintegrated politically into national communities, these communities consciously emerged as "schismatic, politico-religious bodies." The result for political theory after 1700 symbolizes the core of meaning on the European scene: theory becomes "increasingly parochial in the sense that problems which are specific for the several national communities are misunderstood as problems of universal import, and that the ideas which are advanced for their solution are misunderstood as a political theory of general validity."[68] Voegelin outlines in some detail how this parochialism and existential closure to the realities toward which Christianity pointed, to be superseded by developing a "mystical body of the nation," took place in the English, French, and German cases.[69] According to Voegelin, however, Western Christianity does not disappear without a trace from the cultural and political landscape: rather, its breakdown "means the refraction and gradual transformation of its tradition in the national areas; a substantial stock of ideas remains preserved in this process, particularly at its beginning."[70] Having set the scene, however, I have not yet answered Yack's objection. The "substantial stock" of common ideas, according to Yack, must indicate either a genealogical link between dissatisfactions and their political expression, or a structural continuity. This demand is met, it seems to me, in terms of the categories that govern Voegelin's rejection of the "History of Ideas" in favor of a history of order.

The symbols generated in the search for social order and its meaning express the form and content of experiences of order and searching, thereby depicting and pointing to the reality experienced in these activities.[71] It is at this level of experience that we must argue that family resemblances between phenomena are neither accidental nor peripheral, but essential. The texts and doctrines of ideologists express for Voegelin a deeper reality, not at the level of *noumena*, but at the level of meaning, which is *constant*, and this historical continuity is clarified in a philosophical anthropology that accounts for it. It is at this, the level of spiritual insight and existential motive, and not at the level of consistency, comprehensiveness, or strategic cleverness that one may distinguish between mystical activism and spiritual realism across epochs. To elucidate the nature of the politics of the "People of God" is, therefore, to elucidate the nature of ideological politics in general, because the existential motives that are based on similar experiences of human existence remain constant across time and culture.

In chapter 2 I considered Voegelin's contention that the structure of the world and of human consciousness is relatively constant across time and space.[72] Similar symbols of transformation therefore indicate similar sentiments and similar actions in the real, constant world on behalf of equivalent transformatory fantasies. It makes sense on these grounds to speak, for example, of "gnosticism" as the programmatic expression of a desire that is constant in human affairs from at least the first century b.c.e. onward. Gnosticism here does not indicate a direct *historical* continuity, but a *structural* one. Which is to say, while specific political-philosophical problems may change over time, and even the expression of similar problems may change, the motivations for transformation directed toward such problems indicate a similarity at the level of consciousness on the one hand and the structure of the world on the other, that is more definitive for classifying the motivations and their outcomes together than their dissimilarities are for putting them into different categories of experience and response.[73]

Voegelin was well aware of the problems that Yack raises in this regard:

The selected "models" of Voltaire's, Comte's, etc. histories have, by virtue of the "thesis of generality," the same function in the secularistic context as the "sacred history" in the Christian conception. We have now to show that the parallelism is not accidental, but that a continuity of problems leads from the earlier conception to the later; and we have to inquire particularly into the intellectual operations and the changes of sentiment which result in the "break" of continuity.[74]

Thus:

> If we enumerate the names of Voltaire, Diderot, d'Alembert, Marx and Hitler, and confront them with such names as Ortlieb, Joris, Nicholas, and Bosch, we feel that they do not associate easily; a link is missing in the chain that would lead from the one to the other. With the late medieval mystics we are still in an environment of Christian doctrine; with the Encyclopedists, Positivists, and Materialists we are in a climate of science and world-immanent orientation. The form of speculation is the same, but it expresses itself in a different medium. Hence we can sharpen our question: when and where did the amalgamation occur between the speculation of activist mysticism and the medium of intramundane "intellectualism" and "science"?[75]

Voegelin believed he had located a structural continuity that revealed a constant core of meaning, in the structures of consciousness of these various thinkers, of a kind that superseded the historical contingencies of its various expressions. He claimed for a set of expressions of dissatisfaction and transformation a historical continuity between medieval and modern movements that was more substantive than Löwith's claim of genealogical similarity.[76] This continuity is manifested phenomenally in at least five ways.

First, all of these transformatory expressions of dissatisfaction contained an "idea of universality" or "thesis of generality" that was, curiously enough, often expressed in similar symbolic forms of a Joachite kind.[77] The parallelism is not accidental, because, to repeat the point, "a continuity of problems," namely the meaning of human historical existence in time, "lead from the earlier conception to the later."[78] Second, both the medieval activist mystic and the modern ideologist seek to transfigure the world through political action. The attempt to do so results both in violence and in numerous speculative constructions that are intended to justify that violence.[79] The attempts themselves have a remarkably similar form over time. Third, Voegelin coined the term "eschatological violence" to indicate the occurrence of violence in *this* world as an intended transformatory event, and to indicate its activity in a realm its practitioners hold to be "beyond good and evil" by reason of its intent to effect "the transition from a world of iniquity to a world of light."[80] Both earlier and modern activist mystics indulge in the schema of justification, and for both, the cosmic import of their actions leads to a level of atrocity and murder that "appears as bestiality" to those who still inhabit the real world in which the fantasies are enacted.[81]

Fourth, "since the change of human nature and the transfiguration of history do not come about within the range of human action, such human action as is directed toward this aim cannot operate within the rational relation of means and end."[82] Thus, no transformatory movement of this type actually succeeds, and the mundane results of failure are fairly constant: either the revolution is militarily defeated, or we find that "aggravated forms of centralized, dictatorial power" arise as the transformation that never comes is pressed forward. Voegelin mentions the programs of Cromwell, Robespierre and Napoleon, Lenin, and Stalin. One may also consider Norman Cohn's paradigmatic case of the reign of terror in Münster under John of Leyden in 1534–35,[83] or the bizarre circumstances of 1944, when, in an increasingly losing war effort, train shipments of material to German forces were seriously hampered by the growing shipments of Jews and other "undesirables" to extermination camps, and the prudent, practical political consideration of surrender rather than national annihilation was treated as a treasonable act.

Finally, these political results are accompanied by forms of organization that remain uniform across historical epochs. One can, for example, trace the existence of cell groups from early Gnostics to modern-day revolutionaries. And again, the motivation for the formation of such groups remains constant:

> This peculiar social construction of a nucleus of perfect spirituals, a kind of directorate that through its hierarchy of spiritual degrees reaches into the society of the dominant institutions, is a fundamental form with rich political possibilities. It is the perfect instrument for a secret society for the purpose of honeycombing the existing institutions with a minimum of superficial disturbance, and consequently with a minimum chance of becoming detected.[84]

Whether for purposes of immediate revolutionary transformation, seclusion from authorities, or gradual infiltration, the form remains relatively constant, similarly effective socially and politically, and with structurally equivalent doctrinal content.

All of these phenomenal parallels, however, may still be argued to be merely analogies, as Yack would have it. The search for meaning that becomes an obsessive search for a cure for the ills of the world is, for the political theorist, the constant substantive background to these movements across epochs when it is attached theoretically to a critically differentiated account of human consciousness:

> If we formulate somewhat drastically the deepest sentiment that causes the spiritual tensions of the West, we might say: the bearers of Western Civilization do not want to be a senseless appendix to the history of antiquity. On the contrary, they want to understand their civilizational existence as meaningful. If the church is not able to see the hand of God in the history of mankind, men will not remain peaceable and satisfied but will go out in search of gods who take some interest in their civilizational efforts.[85]

Historically, when (Roman Catholic) Christianity as a source for unification and meaning declined, the search for meaning shifted elsewhere. Eventually, "sacred history . . . [was] discarded altogether, and the meaning of history [was] found in," for example, "the intramundane rise and fall of nations or civilizations," and later in other historical processes.[86] This is not a "secularization thesis" that claims merely a "this-worldly" form of what remains essentially a spiritually desiccated Christianity. Instead, Voegelin argues that the life of the spirit, deprived of a transcendental realm to which to attach its quest for meaning, will look to the intramundane, where it will find new sources of meaning.[87] The "categories of meaning" may often be "Christian analogues," matching earlier Christian forms, but they are not merely "secularized" symbols, borrowed from the Christian tradition, emptied of their religious content, and then redeployed. They are new expressions of intramundane *meaning* whose structure is a closely fitting analogue to earlier Christian forms, because the structure of consciousness and of human existence remains constant, as does the search for a coherent meaning of that existence in time. It is this level of analysis that allows Voegelin to make the following observation:

Voltaire resumed the rearticulation of history at the point where the
thinkers of the thirteenth century had to abandon it in face of the orthodox resistance—with the fundamental change of substance, however, that the spirit of the new Third Realm was not the spirit of the
autonomous Christian personality, but the spirit of the autonomous
intellectual. While Voltaire's construction was not very thoroughly
elaborated, it clearly foreshadows the later constructions of Saint-
Simon and Comte with their "laws" of the three phases: the religious,
the metaphysical, and the positive-scientific. Since the content that
enters the categories is an independent variable, it foreshadows as well
the possibility that new materials may enter the categorical pattern, as
has actually happened in the Marxian and National Socialist constructions.[88]

Such constructions are philosophically inadmissible for reasons I have
already indicated—their claims to "offer a valid interpretation of universal history" or of universal laws of human development or behavior cannot hold,[89] but that should not deflect our attention from their serious
intent to offer a new source of intramundane meaning when the old,
transcendental categories have been lost, and to do so in structurally parallel ways.

    In and of themselves, such new quests for meaning are not necessar-
ily ideological in the programmatic sense of Arendt's account, even
though they are essentializing in the manner of White's characterization.
They become politically programmatic when secular existence in time
gives rise to dissatisfactions that lead to the search for a transformation of
human nature and the nature of the world that we find in the new accounts. Thus, Yack is correct to point out that modern desires and the
obstacles to fulfilling them may have discernibly different qualities from
earlier ones in Christian Europe, but, contra Yack, they express the same
category of human experience with structurally identical symbols and
politically similar outcomes. Michael Franz suggests in a similar manner
that Voegelin's comparative analyses of ancient and medieval movements (including gnosticism, hermeticism, alchemy, and various forms
of religious radicalism) and modern ideological movements are often too
sparse to give definitive answers to questions of their commonality.[90]
Out of these separate, sometimes scraggly trees, however, a forest is visible whose components display a commonality at the level of the structure of consciousness that can certainly be further explored in the details

of its historical instantiations, but whose general form is well-established.[91]

The greatest dangers, it seems to me, in using Voegelin's general categories are twofold. First, they can easily lead to carelessness regarding details. Marxism and progressivist liberalism may both be forms of disordered consciousness, but their concrete actualization in specific regimes has historically been qualitatively different in non-trivial ways. Second, without refinements, the categories of gnosticism, magic, and so forth lend themselves altogether too well to use as the blunt instruments of a reactionary conservatism every bit as ideological as the objects of its scorn. Voegelin himself has been accused of such a stance, along with nearly every other ideological aberration imaginable.[92] Let us recall that Voegelin was a thinker who expressly rejected a school of disciples named after him, asking instead for thoughtful, spiritually sensitive readers and no more. His concepts are not intended as the instruments of a new ideological deformation of a philosophy of history.

On the other hand, a science of politics demands not only that unalike things are recognized for their distinctions, but that like things are treated alike. At the level of consciousness, the drive to the fulfillment of one's yearnings through the radical elimination of obstacles to one's desires displays a constancy of symbolic expression, pragmatic outcomes, and doctrinal/dogmatic coherence that will alert the student of politics to the constants of meaning that inform political actions over time. Only then is the therapeutic power of political science made available against the spiritual diseases of our age.

One way in which spiritual diseases manifest themselves is in their effect on the institutions of a society that are responsible for bearing the civilizational symbols of that society. It is to an episode of the ideological corruption of such institutions that I now turn.

NOTES

1. "The History of Political Ideas" is not strictly chronological in all its portions, so that such a time section must be understood in terms of prevailing themes rather than strict (dogmatic) chronological divisions. A first-rate philological introduction to the entire work may be found in Thomas Hollweck and Ellis Sandoz, "General Introduction to the Series," in Eric Voegelin, *Hellenism,*

Rome, and Early Christianity, ed. Athanasios Moulakis, vol. 1 of *History of Political Ideas* (Columbia: University of Missouri Press, 1997), 3–30.

2. Eric Voegelin, *Renaissance and Reformation*, ed. David Morse and William Thompson, vol. 4 of *History of Political Ideas* (Columbia: University of Missouri Press, 1998), 88.

3. The experiential factor as key in the generation of "political ideas" or symbols of order can be traced to Voegelin's *Über die Form des Amerikanischen Geistes* (Tübingen, Germany: J. C. B. Mohr, 1928), 8–18; *Rasse und Staat* (Tübingen, Germany: J. C. B. Mohr, 1933), 21–36, 122–27; and *Die Rassenidee in der Geistesgeschichte von Ray bis Carus* (Berlin: Junker und Dünnhaupt, 1933), 1–23.

4. Voegelin, *Renaissance and Reformation*, 151–52.

5. Eric Voegelin, *Autobiographical Memoirs*, ed. Ellis Sandoz (Baton Rouge: Louisiana State University Press, 1989), 78.

6. Voegelin, *Autobiographical Memoirs*, 79, 80. Cf. Hollweck and Sandoz, "General Introduction," 15–16, 40–41.

7. Eric Voegelin, *Revolution and the New Science,* ed. Barry Cooper, vol. 6 of *History of Political Ideas* (Columbia: University of Missouri Press, 1998), 71–81.

8. Voegelin, *Revolution and the New Science,* 210.

9. For summary examples of this "story," see Voegelin, *Revolution and the New Science,* 209–215; ibid., 31–34.

10. Voegelin, *Revolution and the New Science,* 52–53.

11. Cf. Voegelin, "The Growth of the Race Idea," in *The Review of Politics* 2 (1940): 289–291. Voegelin blames the Roman Catholic Church itself in part for this dissolution, because of its inability or unwillingness to adapt to the new social and political situations, thereby inducing a much harsher reaction and break between it and its opposing forces than might have been necessary (Voegelin, *Revolution and the New Science,* 52).

12. Voegelin, *Revolution and the New Science,* 212–15.

13. Voegelin, *Revolution and the New Science,* 54.

14. Eric Voegelin, *The Later Middle Ages,* ed. David Walsh, vol. 3 of *History of Political Ideas* (Columbia: University of Missouri Press, 1998), 108. cf. Eric Voegelin, *Science, Politics, and Gnosticism* (Chicago: Henry Regnery, 1968), 108–9; Eric Voegelin, *The New Science of Politics* (Chicago: University of Chicago Press, 1952), 164–65.

15. Voegelin, *Revolution and the New Science,* 211.

16. Voegelin, *Revolution and the New Science,* 59; cf. ibid., 71.

17. Voegelin, *Revolution and the New Science,* 214–15.

18. Voegelin, *Revolution and the New Science,* 59.

19. Voegelin, *Renaissance and Reformation*, 174.

20. Voegelin, *Revolution and the New Science,* 45; cf. ibid., 33.

21. Eric Voegelin, *Religion and the Rise of Modernity*, ed. James Wiser, vol. 5 of *History of Political Ideas* (Columbia: University of Missouri Press, 1998), 134–35.

22. Voegelin, *Renaissance and Reformation*, 131.

23. Voegelin, *Renaissance and Reformation*, 132.

24. Voegelin, *Renaissance and Reformation*, 134.

25. Voegelin, *Renaissance and Reformation*, 133.

26. Voegelin, *Renaissance and Reformation*, 135.

27. Voegelin, *Renaissance and Reformation*, 135

28. Voegelin, *Renaissance and Reformation*, 189–90.

29. Kenneth Scott Latourette, *A History of Christianity: Beginnings to 1500*, vol. 1, rev. ed. (New York: Harper and Row, 1975), 453–58. For an example of the growing nationalist sentiments see Martin Luther, "To the Christian Nobility," in *Three Treatises*, ed. Helmut T. Lehman, trans. Charles M. Jacobs (Philadelphia: Fortress Press, 1970), 28, 30–31, 33ff. Similar nationalist sentiments are already evident in the Hussite wars a century earlier.

30. "From the realist position one might argue that the adjustment of social grievances is most desirable but does not prevent situations in need of adjustment, that social reforms do not change the nature of man or of the world, and that after a reform evil will still be a fundamental problem in human existence. Such arguments are of no avail against the faith in historical transfiguration." *Renaissance and Reformation*, 173.

31. Voegelin, *Renaissance and Reformation*, 166–67.

32. Voegelin, *Renaissance and Reformation*, 166.

33. Voegelin, *Renaissance and Reformation*, 196.

34. Frank E. Manuel and Fritzie P. Manuel present perhaps the most comprehensive account currently available of the history and contents of such utopias in the Western tradition in *Utopian Thought in the Western World* (Cambridge: Belknap Press, 1979).

35. Voegelin, *Renaissance and Reformation*, 145–46, 164–65.

36. Voegelin reproduces several episodes of these symbolisms in *Renaissance and Reformation*, 157–73.

37. Some of the characteristics of these personages are given in Voegelin, *Renaissance and Reformation*, 190–94 under the title, "The Paracletes."

38. Norman Cohn, *The Pursuit of the Millennium: Revolutionary Millenarians and Mystical Anarchists of the Middle Ages*, 2nd ed. (New York: Oxford University Press, 1970), 109.

39. Ernst Benz, *Evolution and Christian Hope: Man's Concept of the Future From the Early Fathers to Teilhard de Chardin*, trans. Heinz G. Frank (New York: Doubleday, 1968), 36, 40.

40. Benz, *Christian Hope*, 42.

41. For Voegelin's more elaborated discussion of Joachim's symbols and theology, see *New Science of Politics*, 110–20.

42. Voegelin, *Science, Politics, and Gnosticism*, 88–92.

43. The term is concisely explained in Voegelin's *Autobiographical Memoirs*, 97ff. "[T]he great Austrian novelists, especially Albert Paris Gütersloh, Robert Musil, and Heimito von Doderer . . . coined the term *second reality* in order to signify the image of reality created by human beings when they exist in a state of alienation. The principal characteristic of this state of alienation, which is supported by the imaginative construction of second realities in opposition to the reality of experience, is what Doderer has called the 'refusal to apperceive' (*Apperzeptionsverweigerung*). The concept appears in his novel *Die Dämonen*, and I always enjoy the fact that he developed it while discussing certain sexual aberrations. The concept of *Apperzeptionsverweigerung* is formally developed in the introductory remarks to the chapter on 'Die dicken Damen'—fat ladies—who are preferred by one of his heroes" (98).

44. Voegelin, *Renaissance and Reformation*, 173–74.

45. Voegelin, *Revolution and the New Science,* 51.

46. H. M. Drucker offers a brief history of the movement in *The Political Uses of Ideology* (London: MacMillan, 1974), 3–12; De Tracy's epistemology and what he intended to accomplish by it is clearly laid out in the beginning of his *Treatise on Political Economy*, trans. Thomas Jefferson and ed. John M. Dorsey (Detroit: Center for Health Education, 1973), 1–31.

47. David McLellan, *Ideology*, 2nd ed. (Minneapolis: University of Minnesota Press, 1995), 9–18.

48. Mortimer Adler, *Ten Philosophical Mistakes* (New York: Macmillan, 1985), 60; cf. Eric Voegelin, *Anamnesis*, trans. and ed. Gerhart Niemeyer (Notre Dame, Ind.: University of Notre Dame Press, 1978), 15–21.

49. Voegelin, *Revolution and the New Science,* 173–83; Voegelin, *Rassenidee*, 1.

50. John Plamenatz, *Ideology* (London: Pall Mall Press, 1970), 27.

51. Cf. McLellan, *Ideology*, esp. chaps. 2 and 5.

52. Voegelin, *Renaissance and Reformation*, 197, 186–87. These qualities are demonstrated in Hieronymus Bosch's misnamed painting, "The Garden of Earthly Delights." *Renaissance and Reformation*, 197–201.

53. Michael Franz, *Eric Voegelin and the Politics of Spiritual Revolt* (Baton Rouge: Louisiana State University Press, 1992), 116.

54. Voegelin, *Autobiographical Memoirs*, 28–30.

55. White, *The Content of the Form*, 30.

56. Benito Mussolini, "The Doctrine of Fascism," in *Readings in Fascism and National Socialism* (Chicago: Swallow Press, 1952 [1925]), 8–9.

57. Hannah Arendt, *The Origins of Totalitarianism*, 2nd ed. (New York: Harcourt Brace Jovanovich, 1973), 469.

58. Arendt, *Totalitarianism*, 385.

59. Arendt, *Totalitarianism*, 385.

60. Voegelin, *New Science of Politics*, 164–65; Voegelin, *Renaissance and Reformation*, 176.

61. See for example, Voegelin, *Renaissance and Reformation*, 173–75, 182, 194–95; Voegelin, *Revolution and the New Science*, 31–2, 43, 45.

62. Bernard Yack, *The Longing for Total Revolution: Philosophic Sources of Social Discontent from Rousseau to Marx and Nietzsche* (Princeton: Princeton University Press, 1986), 14.

63. Yack, *Longing*, 10–18.

64. Yack, *Longing*, 16. His argument here is specifically with Karl Löwith, and on the side of Hans Blumenberg.

65. For an example in historical theology, see John Howard Yoder, *The Politics of Jesus* (Grand Rapids, Mich.: William B. Eerdmans, 1972), 163–83.

66. Yack, *Longing*, 18.

67. Voegelin, *Renaissance and Reformation*, 88. Voegelin traces this breakdown in its broad outlines in *The Later Middle Ages*, chap. 20,"From Imperial to Parochial Christianity" (163–92). This characterization of modernity as the product of an event more than a specifically new mode of thought anticipates Voegelin's later doubt that modernity has a distinct character as such. See Franz, *Politics of Spiritual Revolt*, 87n6.

68. Voegelin, *Revolution and the New Science*, 149.

69. Voegelin, *Revolution and the New Science*, 71–81.

70. Voegelin, *Revolution and the New Science*, 149.

71. Voegelin, *Autobiographical Memoirs*, 78.

72. The most relevant passages include: Eric Voegelin, *Israel and Revelation*, vol. 1 of *Order and History* (Baton Rouge: Louisiana State University Press, 1956), 1–10; "Reason: The Classic Experience," in *Anamnesis*, 89–115; *New Science of Politics*, 165.

73. Gnosticism was Voegelin's chosen term for a category of experiences and responses to them that became, in his evaluation, the regnant ideologies of modernity. "Gnosticism" comes from a Greek word, *gnosis*, meaning "knowledge." It is the form, content, and applicability of a particular kind of knowledge that distinguishes gnostic "knowers" from any other person that would make some sort of knowledge claim.

The most accessible aspect of Voegelin's analysis is his description of the six characteristics of the gnostic experience that together form the gnostic attitude toward the world. First, the gnostic shares with nearly all human beings a dissatisfaction with some aspect of his specific situation. The gnostic, however, comes to believe that "the drawbacks of the situation can be attributed to the fact that the world is intrinsically poorly organized." (*Science, Politics, and Gnosticism*, 83.) As Voegelin points out, it is equally possible that it is not inherently the world that is inadequate in some way, but the human beings who inhabit it. Gnostics reject this alternative. Third, gnostics believe that salvation from the intrinsic problems of the situation they find wanting is possible. Here again, they are not entirely unique: Christians, Muslims, and many others also hope for salvation. It is in the next move that the gnostic attitude begins to take specific shape.

The gnostic confronts us with the imperative that "the order of being will have to be changed in an historical process," and that the evil world we now confront must evolve into a good one historically. Once again, the gnostic rejects a common alternative, namely that "the world throughout history will remain as it is and that man's salvational fulfillment is brought about through grace in death." (*Science, Politics, and Gnosticism*, 84.) In the sixth and final step of the gnostic program we arrive at its namesake:

> If it is possible, however, so to work a structural change in the given order of being that we can be satisfied with it as a perfect one, then it becomes the task of the gnostic to seek out the prescription for such a change. Knowledge—gnosis—of the method of altering being is the central concern of the gnostic. As the sixth feature of the gnostic attitude, therefore, we recognize the construction of a formula for self, and world salvation, as well as the gnostic's readiness to come forward as a prophet who will proclaim his knowledge about the salvation of mankind. (Voegelin, *Science, Politics, and Gnosticism*, 87–88).

We find in this brief description a closely categorized analysis of the experiences of reality that underlie movements typified by the "People of God." Gnostic mass movements included, for Voegelin, "such movements as progressivism, positivism, Marxism, psychoanalysis, communism, fascism, and national socialism" (*Science, Politics, and Gnosticism*, 83); these are not all political mass movements but include "intellectual movements" as well:

> [I]n social reality the two types merge. None of the movements began as a mass movement; all derived from intellectuals and small groups. Some of them, according to the intentions of their founders, should have grown into political mass movements, but did not. Others, such as neo-positivism or psychoanalysis, were meant to be intellectual movements; but they have had, if not the form, at least the success of political mass movements, in that their theories and jargons have shaped the thinking of millions of people in the Western world, very often without their being aware of it. (Voegelin, *Science, Politics, and Gnosticism*, 83–84; cf. *New Science of Politics*, 107–32)

Voegelin suggested later that although the category of "gnosticism" captured much of the modern ideological movements, other factors of experience and response, which I have not explored in this account, had also to be taken into consideration. These included the "metastatic apocalypse," which I will consider in the final chapter of this book, and the historical process of bringing all transcendent experiences into a this-worldly interpretation and framework.

(Voegelin, *Autobiographical Reflections*, 65–67.) Gnosticism, however, remains the core category for distinguishing that set of experiences of reality and responses to it that define the ideological and intellectual mass movements of the modern era.

74. Voegelin, *Revolution and the New Science*, 45. The same methodological and interpretive problems occur in the examination of medieval movements as such.

> "The drawing of this genealogical line immediately suggests the difficulties that must beset a closer investigation of the process, particularly in its early phases. The movement, up to the sixteenth century, is an undercurrent in civilizational history. It is essentially a movement in the strict sense of a religious movement in the souls of single individuals and of such followers as they may be able to gather. These movements do not easily crystallize into a rational system of ideas that could be transmitted as a body of doctrine, in the manner in which a body of Aristotelian writings could be transmitted to the Arabs and Western Scholastics. It is very difficult, therefore, to establish whether one can speak of a "history" of the movements in a more rigorous sense at all. They are clearly related with each other through the centuries by the general structure of their sentiments and attitudes; but whether this affinity is always due to an actual historical influence from one wave of the movement to the next, or whether the experiences that supply the drive of the movements spring up anew every time, without close determination by preceding similar movements, is largely an open question. (Voegelin, *Renaissance and Reformation*, 139)

75. Voegelin, *Renaissance and Reformation*, 202.

76. Yack, *Longing*, 17; cf. Karl Löwith, *Meaning in History* (Chicago: University of Chicago Press, 1949), esp. 11–19, 191–213.

77. Voegelin, *Renaissance and Reformation*, 203ff; *Revolution and the New Science*, 44–45. These theses of generality or universality have "the same function in the secularistic context as the 'sacred history' in the Christian conception."

78. Voegelin, *Revolution and the New Science*, 45.

79. Voegelin, *Renaissance and Reformation*, 173–74.

80. Voegelin, *Renaissance and Reformation*, 174.

81. Voegelin, *Renaissance and Reformation*, 175.

82. Voegelin, *Renaissance and Reformation*, 175.

83. Cohn, *Pursuit of the Millennium*, 261–80.

84. Voegelin, *Renaissance and Reformation*, 182.

85. Voegelin, *Revolution and the New Science*, 56.

86. Voegelin, *Revolution and the New Science*, 120.

87. Voegelin, *Revolution and the New Science,* 42–3.

88. Voegelin, *Revolution and the New Science,* 43.

89. Voegelin, *Revolution and the New Science,* 43.

90. Franz, *Spiritual Revolt,* 105.

91. The issues at stake are well delineated in Eric Voegelin, "The Origins of Totalitarianism," in *The Review of Politics* 15, no. 1(January 1953): 68–76 and Hannah Arendt's "Reply," Ibidem, 76–84.

92. Richard Faber, *Der Prometheus-Komplex: Zur Kritik der Politotheologie Eric Voegelins und Hans Blumenbergs* (Würzburg, Germany: Verlag Dr. Johannes König-shausen und Dr. Thomas Neuberg, 1984); Voegelin, *Autobiographical Memoirs,* 46.

4

WHO IS GOD'S SERVANT?
POLITICAL THEOLOGY IN
VOEGELIN'S POLITICAL
PHILOSOPHY

In the first four chapters of this book, I have considered Voegelin's theory of consciousness, his argument for the political role of a critical philosophy in a well-ordered society, and his critique of ideological politics. In the present and the next, concluding chapter, I will consider his political theology, which is revealed in his critique of yet another civilizational episode—the rise of National Socialism in post-World War One Germany. Voegelin's analysis of this episode displays once again the substance of his political analysis; it also reveals his political theology.

The complicity of the German Roman Catholic and Lutheran churches in the activities of the National Socialist regime from 1933 to 1945 is a matter of historical record.[1] Indeed, the more general complicity of Christian churches with their "home" cultures and the seemingly persistent inability of Christians to engage their cultures critically has become a question of some import not only for Christians on the left wing of the political and/or theological spectrum, but over a wide range.[2] The "causes" given for this failure vary widely; they include suggestions that Christians who integrate too closely the substance of Christianity and their surrounding culture have an insufficient grasp of their (Christian) story, that they have a defective conception of the church, or that theirs is a philosophically poorly grounded theology.

In a series of lectures delivered in Munich in 1964, entitled "Hitler und die Deutschen" (Hitler and the Germans), Eric Voegelin briefly and without intending a full-fledged participation in all the details, added his voice to this debate in terms of the failures of German Christendom in the twentieth century. He argued that the intellectual corruption of German society in the decades before and after the First World War allowed Hitler to come to power with little opposition in 1933 and that the German churches shared in this corruption. Diagnosing the weakness of postwar German critiques of the Nazi period, he suggested that the same intellectual corruption evident in the Nazi era continued to plague the German polity (and the German churches) decades after the Second World War. Voegelin's examination of intellectual corruption calls forth the themes of the present study: consciousness, resistance, ideological warfare. Nazi Germany is a civilizational episode in which the imperatives of a healthy polity are—largely by negative contrast—made clear for Voegelin and his listeners.

The "intellectual niveau" of a polity is determined not by any single one of its institutions but by the integrity of its most important institutions in concert. In Western European society, this set includes the Christian churches. Voegelin argued, however, that in Germany the churches had, for the most part, clearly failed in their cultural and political role as champions of the life of the spirit. In this chapter, I will examine Voegelin's treatment of this ecclesiastical failure. The textual focus of Voegelin's critique was the interpretation of Romans 13, combined with selected passages in Genesis. By means of these Biblical excerpts, many Lutheran and Catholic clergy taught "Christian submission" to the Nazi government. Voegelin's own interpretation of these passages and his strong criticisms of the failure of the majority of German Christians, especially among the senior clergy, to resist the Nazi regime illuminate the perplexities and responsibilities of the Constantinian church in the modern, post-Constantinian world. ("Constantinian" refers to that historical point from which Christianity in Europe becomes officially sanctioned as the politically representative religion of the political community.) Voegelin's critique is shaped by his political philosophy and particularly by his understanding of the relationship between Pauline Christianity and Platonic/Aristotelian political philosophy. The specific content of his critique of German Christendom, therefore, is to be understood in the context of his general critique, in these lectures, of German intellectual and spiritual elites.

In this chapter, I will introduce the substance of Voegelin's lectures, *"Hitler und die Deutschen."* One central motif in this interpretation is the proper metaphor to be used in describing both the role of the state in human affairs and the proper forms of resistance available to the citizens of states that abuse this role. The second part of the chapter is an examination of the relationship Voegelin saw between a philosophically responsible interpretation of Romans 13 (a text that serves as the theological counterpoint of Voegelin's critique, but also of the German political-theological discussion regarding the relationship of the citizen to the state) and the ability rationally to resist, both theologically and politically, the claims of Nazi ideology. Voegelin's interpretation of Romans 13 is set within a wider understanding of the meaning and civilizational role of Christianity. Accordingly, his appraisal of the Roman Catholic and Protestant churches in Nazi Germany provides a concrete example of how Voegelin thought this civilizational role should operate. Second, it offers a window into Voegelin's political theology. Third, it thereby illuminates for us Voegelin's interpretation of Christianity. I will take these in turn, leaving the third aspect of Voegelin's analysis for the final chapter, in which I will consider Voegelin's understanding of Pauline political theology, and his historical interpretation of the role of Paul's doctrines in the political and intellectual history of Western Europe. This interpretation of Pauline theology serves as the wider philosophical context for Voegelin's interpretation of Romans 13.

GERMAN CORRUPTION

The German churches' miscarriage of responsibility was one of a series of such failures in German society to resist the claims and deeds of the Nazis. It rested, according to Voegelin, on a deep-seated corruption in the intellectual and spiritual life of German society and especially among the German elite. Looking at Voegelin's analysis of this problem will enable us to develop a closer understanding of how his political theology worked together with his theory of politics to illuminate the problems of the modern age.

"Corruption" has had two meanings in Western political thought, emerging from two separate political traditions. For classical liberals, it describes a condition of arbitrariness in the allocation of political resources. Liberalism may be characterized as a political doctrine asserting that all human beings possess a set of inalienable natural rights, and that all individuals in a society should as a result of these rights share equally in extensive economic, political, and social freedoms. These liberties are secured to citizens of the liberal regime by means of an array of political arrangements consisting of a bundle of fundamental constitutional guarantees and a set of institutions for assuring these guarantees. Accordingly, liberal regimes are generally characterized by representative government, extensive civil liberties for their citizens, and a market or quasi-market economy. Liberals seek through universal laws to protect the individual as far as possible from the intrusions of other individuals and of government in his pursuit of private, self-interested activities. This protection is formally secured through an assumption of legal equality—the same rules apply equally to all—and through the careful delimitation of governmental power. Corruption is said to occur when these rules are not universally enforced or when they are applied unequally, either on the basis of idiosyncratically arbitrary criteria, or on the basis of ascriptive criteria not permitted under the universal rules embodied in liberal law.

In premodern classical thought, on the other hand, corruption describes the destruction of the social fabric through the corrosion of community interest. Corruption occurs especially when those who are responsible for the integrity of the community no longer, either through deliberate unwillingness or inability, fulfill their prescribed leadership roles, but turn instead to private pursuits at the expense of the public interest.[3] This understanding of corruption is still evident in Machiavelli, perhaps the first "modern" political philosopher, and yet a thinker intensely interested in politics above all as an activity of glory, rather than administration, economic regulation, or the public securing of peace for private ends.[4] Seen through classical eyes, a liberal regime may itself seem to be a species of political corruption.

Although institutions and the ends of political action were of central concern to him, Voegelin was interested, in his analysis of interwar German politics, first and foremost in *intellectual* and *spiritual* corruption, which, when widespread among intellectual, religious, and political elites, is in its form and effect closely related to the classical notion of political corruption. No institution, moreover, can withstand for long the thoroughgoing spiritual corruption of those who inhabit and are supposed to sustain it.[5] Intellectual corruption may be described as a loss of contact with reality, which Voegelin describes as a form of "stupidity" (*Dummheit*). He locates examples of this conception of intellectual corruption as a diagnostic tool in Plato's concept of *amathes*, in the Israelite notion of the *nabal*, and in Thomas Aquinas's concept of the *stultus*.[6] This form of stupidity occurs when "a human being, because of his loss of reality (*Realitätsverlust*), is incapable of properly orienting his actions in the world in which he happens actually to live."[7] Its linguistic correlate, and perhaps the most immediate indicator of its presence, is the loss of a mastery of the language used in the sector of reality with which the intellectually corrupt individual or cohort has lost contact. Voegelin called this loss"spiritual illiteracy." The linguistic indicators of a loss of reality can be manifested in a variety of ways: the mixing of metaphors into meaningless tropes; the invention of words in order to give one's trivial statements an aura of profundity; the denial and accurate refutation of lies in order to hide much more savage truths; and the use of clichés to hide one's own intellectual illiteracy or to mask an ideological agenda.[8] German public discourse was, in Voegelin's estimation, corrupted, filled with sloganeering and clichés, but evidencing no firm grasp of the real. The attempts of men like Karl Kraus and Robert Musil to expose this linguistic corruption in the German-speaking realm and to restore language to its role as a reflection of reality drew Voegelin's recognition.[9]

One may differentiate, along with Robert Musil, between various forms of stupidity. The "honest stupidity" of an inability to perform mentally must be contrasted with the "higher" or "intelligent stupidity" of the ideologue, who displays not a mental handicap but a pneumopathology.[10] The latter may be the product of a failure in education or of a deliberate will to reject reality as it is given to us and a desire to replace it with a "second reality," a private thought-world in which one has arranged the world as one sees fit or as one arbitrarily "intuits" that it should be. The upshot of Voegelin's analysis of the German case of intellectual corruption and the widespread diffusion of second realities was that Hitler's rise to power could not be understood merely by considering his personality:

> His success must be understood in the context of an intellectually or morally ruined society in which personalities who otherwise would be grotesque, marginal figures can come to public power because they superbly represent the people who admire them.[11]

Hitler's successful appearance on the German political scene, therefore, was not only the result of political cleverness on Hitler's part; it was also the result and the manifestation of a deep-seated corruption among the Germans, particularly in the ruling elites.

The premises of Voegelin's analysis are those that I have already explored: reality has a structure, conscious human beings are consciously and firmly part of that reality—however indeterminate at the margins— and not only can they know something about the structures of reality, but they must know about them to participate with integrity in the life of the community of human beings that is part of that reality.[12] "Pneumopathological" responses to the anxieties of being that may arise from this condition of human existence are a matter of historical record, and we have seen that they were a central subject of Voegelin's lifelong philosophical investigations. His primary focus in "Hitler and the Germans" was the inability or unwillingness of German intellectual elites to come to terms with a variety of such aberrations. These failures are themselves the "pneumopathological phenomena of a social rot."[13]

Voegelin began his concrete investigation of the phenomena of intellectual and spiritual stupidity in German society with an analysis of Percy Schramm's study of Hitler's regime, "The Anatomy of a Dictator."[14] By beginning with this thoroughly inadequate work, Voegelin illustrated in detail the problems of intellectual illiteracy, the loss of reality, the pervasive use of clichés in academic studies, poor methods of scholarly investigation, the ideological corruption of social-science terminology, and the inability conceptually to come to grips with the National Socialist rise to power, this last problem being in part the result of the other problems that continued in German intellectual circles even after the Second World War. At the conclusion of his searing critique of German intellectual life, Voegelin turned to the role of the German Protestant and Catholic churches in the Nazi regime. Here we find an unexpected account of the role of religious faith and institutions, even in a modern political community, and a rare articulation of Voegelin's political theology.

ROMANS 13

Voegelin's analysis of German Christendom consciously hinges on a dispute concerning the meaning of a section of the Apostle Paul's letter to the Christians in Rome, in which he explains to this fledgling congregation the relationship of the Christian to the ruling authorities. Voegelin begins his interpretation with the "fact" of a national Christendom. This fact itself poses problems, both for a critique of Christian behavior and for an interpretation of the Apostle Paul's exhortation to the Christians in Rome three hundred years before the invention of "Christendom" and roughly fifteen hundred years before the segregation of Western European Christendom into national churches. "Everyone," writes Paul, "must submit himself to the governing authorities, for there is no authority except that which God has established." The church to which Paul was writing was a minority group of believers, politically disestablished, and living under a regime that was intermittently hostile even to the existence of such a community of believers. These historical factors give a central importance to the shape of the presentation in a modern interpretation of this passage. What did Paul's instructions to this group of Christians originally *mean*? What is a post-Pauline, *establishment* church to take as its meaning out of the Pauline texts? What does the National-Socialist regime in a modern nation-state have to do with the emperor and his governors in the Roman *ecumene*? What did the Christians in Rome hear in the word "submission" (*hypotassesthein*) that modern Germans (and others) might hear differently after the writings of Kant[15] or the experience of the Prussian bureaucratic state (or, in regimes outside the German sphere, for example, after the English, French, or American revolutions)?

Untangling this nest of questions will accomplish two ends. First, it will show Voegelin "in action," so to speak, unraveling the various threads of a specific and perplexing political problem in modern politics. His analysis is a demonstration, in this case, of the viability of his categories for understanding political phenomena. Second, it will also begin to uncover for us the features of Voegelin's understanding of Christianity, which has itself become a major point of contention among his interpreters. First, I move to a consideration of Voegelin's interpretation of Romans 13 as against its use by the German churches. Then, in the final chapter, I will consider Voegelin's account of the advent of Christendom and its meaning for Christianity. This account leads to an examination of Voegelin's political theology as it emerges from his view of Christendom.

Let us recall first principles. A society or political community is for

Voegelin a "cosmion," a unit of meaning that is constituted both symbolically and concretely and "illuminated with meaning from within by the human beings who continuously create and bear it as the mode and condition of their self-realization."[16] The order of a political community is given in the symbols of human self-understanding that emerge from human experience of self, world, and transcendence. The spiritual aspect of human existence provides the "substantial ordering of existence" that gives order and meaning to politics.[17] But these symbols concerning the human soul, the transcendental reality to which it has experiential access, and the relations between the two "are not a body of empirically verifiable propositions to be accepted as true after due examination." Instead, "they receive their meaning as expressions of the spiritual process in which the soul responds with *caritas* to the supernatural aid of the *gratia*. The *fides caritate formata* is constituted in this response, which opens the possibilities of reaching out understandingly into the supernatural. The soul develops the faculties of the *cognitio fidei*, the cognition by faith, concerning matters that are not accessible to natural reason."[18] Voegelin expresses such experiences here in Christian symbols, but the experiences are not specifically Christian, and their particular symbolization can become the spiritually meaning-laden core of any civilization, Christian or otherwise.

Concretely, the order of a political community is established through the set of institutions that orders a society and whose meaning is illuminated in the symbols of human self-understanding that emerge from human experience. From the later Roman Empire onward, according to Voegelin, the basic ordering symbols of civilization in Europe derived from Christianity, amended by local considerations and Greek philosophy. It became the civilizational and political function of the Christian church to serve as the institution that transmitted the spiritual substance of Jesus' teachings into the surrounding society, thereby playing the role of a civilizing force. As a result, the church became the primary locus of resistance to anti-civilizational disorder in imperial Roman society from the fourth century onward. At the other end of this story, the ordering symbols and the civilizational powers of the Christian (Roman Catholic) Church eroded during the late medieval and Renaissance periods as the *corpus Christianum* that was Europe during the Middle Ages broke up into individual national units, and this erosion produced severe civilizational strains and spiritual disasters on the European scene. Nazi Germany was in at least one sense an instantiation of such a disaster.

Let us return to the problem of Paul's "original" meaning in Romans 13. The difficulty for a political-theological interpretation of a New Testament text is that while Christianity may have been the civilizing force, via Greek philosophy, for the European world, this role was not tailor-made for the Christian Church; the administration of the spiritual substance of Christ required some emendations if it was to serve its civilizational role. Thus, "[t]he Church has become the great civilizing influence in the Western world because it was able to compromise the strict teachings of the Sermon on the Mount with the weakness of human nature, with the existence of governmental power, and with the historical content of pre-Christian civilization."[19] In other words, the ethic of a minority community of believers had to be transformed into the ethic of an imperial, establishment religion. There were three key compromises, according to Voegelin, that were essential if the civilizational role of Christianity was to be realized. First, the rites of (infant) baptism and communion were made to establish membership in the Christian Church by means of "sacramental reception," and not through some guaranty that the receiving individual was necessarily "a member of the invisible Church." Accordingly, one's salvational status was known to God alone, and it was not open to communal judgement as it had been, on the basis of one's actions, in the early, non-establishment Church. Second, when Christianity came to accept governmental power "as a part of the 'world,'" willed by God, the Church was able not only to sustain itself through the "difficulties of the early centuries," but also, by the ninth century, to integrate the functions of royalty into the panoply of spiritual gifts, each manifested by an individual member, that together comprised the activities of the church. The royal power of the secular realm, in other words, had become a spiritual function of the church when the two realms permeated one another.[20]

Finally, and for Voegelin perhaps most importantly, there is the accommodation he attributes to no less an ecclesiastical luminary than Paul of Tarsus himself. This accommodation is "the compromise with history through the recognition that God revealed himself to the pagans through the law of nature and to the Hebrews through the Old Law before he revealed Himself to the world at large through the Logos that had become flesh."[21] According to Voegelin, this compromising move made it possible "for the early patres to absorb the Stoic natural law into Christian doctrine, and by virtue of this absorption to create for Christianity a system of ethics that was applicable to the relations between men who live in the world."[22] This initiative is especially crucial for Voegelin, and I will consider it in detail for its apparent philosophical-political consequences.

The necessary material agent for the effective mediation of these compromises into the social realm was for Voegelin the "sacramental organization" of the medieval church:

> The mediation of grace through the sacraments makes grace objective. The state of grace cannot be obtained through religious enthusiasm or through the efforts of heroic saintliness; it must be obtained through sacramental incorporation into the mystical body of Christ. The development of the sacerdotal office with its administration of Grace through the sacraments and the objectivity of the priest's administration that makes the sacrament effective independently of his personal worthiness are the decisive organizational steps without which the compromises with the natural and historical order of society could not have fully unfolded their potentialities.[23]

With these adjustments, Christianity became a civilizational achievement of the first order. In the next chapter, I will consider more closely the contours of this achievement and Voegelin's interpretation of it.

Voegelin's exegesis of Romans 13 in "Hitler und die Deutschen" assumes this historical context of accommodation, and it is therefore brief. He focuses most of his attention instead on the activities and public pronouncements of members of the Protestant and Catholic clergy. From these he draws a behavioral profile whose shape can then be analyzed for its existential content. The Christianity-as-establishment perspective of Voegelin's philosophical analysis is clear:

> The German people (*Volk*), not understood in a folkish sense, but, let us say, the German society within the Reich boundaries of 1937, was at the same time essentially a church-folk (*Kirchenvolk*). There was a small percentage of non-confessional respondents, and one percent was Jewish. Church-folk and German folk are therefore identical, and their identity is once again hidden from view—and here again the insistence on institutional cliches—when we speak of church and state,

then we hide the human and political fact that the church represents the spiritual ordering of man toward God.

That is to say, the German people in politics and the German people in the church are one and the same, and, as people, it is part of their constitution to be oriented transcendentally. The churches are nothing but the representation of the spiritual transcendence of man."[24]

Accordingly, our clichéd classical liberal language of "church and state" (which occurs as readily in Germany as in America) gives the impression of "two separate communities that stand over against one another," but this is not the case. It is the same society, "with separate temporal and spiritual representatives."[25] Both sets of representatives in Germany were deeply corrupted, however, so that the latter fully participated in the general existential rot of German society.[26] With the destruction of the Weimar Republic through the ideological conflicts of left and right, the churches remained the sole representative of human order in the face of National Socialism, but they failed for the most part to protest or to represent the interests and dignity of humankind, precisely because the same existential disorientation was evident among the leaders of the churches as present in the remainder of German society.[27]

Voegelin's three lectures on the problem of the loss of reality among the leaders of the German churches mostly take the shape of examining particular instances of failure. Underlying these instances, however, Voegelin points to trends in the specific development of German theology that made a well-grounded resistance to the anti-human claims of the National Socialists less likely. The philosophical anthropology (*Menschenbild*) of the German churches remained poorly developed due to a lack of substantive contact with classical philosophy (especially Plato and Aristotle), due to the unhappily strong influence of German Romanticism, especially as this was transmitted in the nationalist "folkish" doctrines of Friedrich ("*Turnvater*") Jahn,[28] to a lack of substantive philosophical knowledge among the clergy concerning modern ideological movements, and even to a lack of historically oriented theological training. In consequence, the German clergy focused not on the wider questions of humanity and the role of the churches in representing humanity in its transcendent orientation toward God, but remained narrowly self-interested and focused on intra-church issues until the National Socialists threatened their interests.[29] The German clergy, in other words, saw for the churches no function as social or political critics in their role as the representatives of universal human interests. Governmental malfeasance—the building and populating of concentration camps, the mistreatment of citizens, the establishment of legalized racism—was of no concern if it did not affect the institutional interests of the churches.[30] Out of this milieu would come the astonishing statement that it was the duty of [Catholic] Christians "to whom the voice of their church is holy," to remain "loyal to the legitimate authorities [*Obrigkeit*] and conscientiously to fulfill their duties of citizenship with a fundamental rejection of all illegal or seditious activities."[31]

Paul's text in Romans 13 was used to bolster this position, in what Voegelin called a "brazen textual falsification." Voegelin begins with the observation that Luther's translation "everyone is [to be] subject to the authorities," is a mistranslation of Romans 13:1. Rather, it should read, "Let every soul be in subjection to the governing powers." The language of Paul, Voegelin claims, is taken from "conventional Stoic political philosophy" (again the "compromise" with pagan language that Voegelin here extends to Paul himself). The assumption of the Stoic notion of a hierarchy of being into which human beings are ordered is that the political hierarchy is ordered in accordance with the moral law; accordingly, Paul's words, understood in this perspective, do not imply "that we should be subject to any authority one pleases and certainly not . . . that one is to be subject to the authorities when they do evil."[32] In Voegelin's reading, this passage is situated within the tradition of classical political philosophy: ethical conduct is oriented through the life of the spirit and the practice of virtue, and the corrective in the face of human failings is administered by the political authorities, who punish wrongdoing with a view to justice and restoring the moral order. Paul's injunction, moreover, is directed at those who have misunderstood the nature of Christian freedom to mean that submission to political authority is no longer necessary.[33] Rather, in view of "the time" (*kairos*), Christians are to subject themselves to the authorities as a part of the love that is to form their existential perspective in all their actions. In no way, however, does the text therefore imply obedience to simply any authority, and especially not to the laws of the National-Socialist regime.

Throughout his critique, Voegelin refers for his interpretation of Christianity and particularly of Christian political ethics to the standards of human conduct and decency unveiled in the Stoic and classical political philosophies that the church took over as part of its civilizational role. The standards of conduct are found in one's existential orientation, which is communicated through "common sense," through classical philosophy, or, in the case of the churches, through a historically refined theology.[34] When through ignorance, incompetence, or deliberate intellectual malfeasance these standards are missing even among the elites of ecclesiastical (or other civilizational) institutions, we witness a phenomenon of dehumanization (*Entmenschung*), in which organizational interests supersede one's concern for the neighbor so that the crimes committed against him or her by an evil regime are disregarded.[35] Indeed, rather than leading to protest, the dehumanizing of the German churches led to their nazification.[36] Having forgotten their role as heralds and instruments of universally available salvation, or as stewards of a universal grace, the German churches found the transition to the racist, xenophobic, and ultra-nationalistic vocabulary of the National Socialists easy. It was a "decay of the spirit in the church" itself.[37]

THE CHURCH AS REPRESENTATIVE
OF EXISTENTIAL TRUTH

For Voegelin, then, the Christian story is overlaid with the symbols of the experiences revealed in the symbols and myths of Platonic/Aristotelian philosophy. This philosophical assertion is made publicly authoritative by the philosopher's call to pay attention to what is present in consciousness, and nothing more: "Man must play his part in the drama of history, responsive to the pull of the golden cord of divine love yet ever conscious of his essential ignorance concerning both the nature of the Whole and his own role in it. All that the philosopher can do is to bring this ineluctable condition to our attention."[38]

If the church's role is to be described as Voegelin describes it, why, in these terms, was the church such a spectacular failure in Nazi Germany? Voegelin's answer falls into two parts, and it focuses on the fact that the German churches either forsook or allowed to lapse into forgetfulness that aspect of doctrine which upholds the universal role of the church. The core problem, for Voegelin, is the tension that exists between the Church as the universal, mystical body of Christ whose

head—Christ—is the head of all mankind and the church as the concrete, culturally located organization in the world with material interests
and local problems to solve. This tension became especially acute in the
West with the development of national churches during the disintegration of European Roman Catholic Christendom in the sixteenth and
seventeenth centuries. In this tension, we have, on the one hand, the
doctrine of the sovereignty of Christ, which is a universalist claim with
a perspective toward all humankind, as Thomas Aquinas explains:

> This is the difference between the natural body of man and the
> Church's mystical body, that the members of the natural body are all
> together, and the members of the mystical are not all together—
> neither as regards their natural being, since the body of the Church is
> made up of the men who have been from the beginning of the world
> until its end—nor as regards their supernatural being, since, of those
> who are at any one time, some there are who are without grace, yet
> will afterwards obtain it, and some have it already. We must therefore
> consider the members of the mystical body not only as they are in act,
> but as they are in potentiality. Nevertheless, some are in potentiality
> who will never be reduced to act, and some are reduced at some time
> to act; and this according to the triple class, of which the first is by
> faith, the second by the charity of this life, the third by the fruition of
> the life to come. Hence we must say that if we take the whole time of
> the world in general, Christ is the Head of all men, but diversely. For,
> first and principally, He is the Head of such as are united to Him by
> glory; secondly, of those who are actually united to Him by charity;
> thirdly, of those who are actually united to Him by faith; fourthly, of
> those who are united to Him merely in potentiality, which is not yet
> reduced to act, yet will be reduced to act according to Divine predes-
> tination; fifthly, of those who are united to Him in potentiality, which
> will never be reduced to act; such are those men existing in the world,
> who are not predestined, who, however, on their departure from this
> world, wholly cease to be members of Christ, as being no longer in
> potentiality to be united to Christ.[39]

This doctrine of the sovereignty of Christ provides the church with a
universal perspective and with the possibility of concretely representing
the human orientation toward the transcendent. Christ's headship *in po-
tentia* over all mankind gives the church, as the representative of that
transcendent headship, a (humanitarian) interest in all mankind. Here we

have for Voegelin the most philosophically articulate expression of the human orientation the church must assume in its mundane activities.[40]

On the other hand, the Constantinian church, as the representative of the universal lordship of Christ, of the universal grace of God, and of the good news to all men, is also the *nationally localized* representative of man's transcendence toward God. It is possible, therefore, for the church to misunderstand itself as holding a "special position over against the rest of mankind, as though the rest of mankind did not belong to mankind and humanity is a privilege of a (particular) church membership."[41] One may observe a similar move in the gnostic movements of the Middle Ages and in the dehumanization of the "other" (through categories of class, race, or gender, for example) in modern ideological movements. This tension between "church as establishment institution" and Church in the "Thomistic sense of *ecclesia* as *corpus mysticum*" is the tension that must be properly resolved for Romans 13 to be adequately understood, not as a nationalistic call to muddle-headed obedience to whatever authority might be in office, but as a philosophically rooted injunction to responsible submission. The church exists as a concrete entity in the world, but with specific claims regarding the rule of God over the rule of secular powers and their truth-claims. It is therefore a *necessarily* political entity, as part of its specific civilizational function, because it occupies a concrete space in the world, but with a universal claim. Its role, however, is not to transform the world, but to witness to it, not with political might, but by the power of the Spirit.[42]

Intellectual and spiritual corruption is not mere forgetfulness. It is the refusal to consider carefully the premises of one's actions, the place one occupies in the world, and what it means to be human. It is the phenomenon of Robert Musil's second reality, in which the world we make up in our imagination is taken to be the true one, justifying stupidity and criminality even among those who should most closely represent the universal orientation of all mankind toward the transcendent as against the particularist claims of nationalists, classists, racists, sexists, and the like.

The mediating role of the Constantinian church compels it to reckon with the consequences of intellectual and spiritual corruption, not in terms of the restoration of a vision lodged in a kind of "original form" of the church, but in the restoration of a philosophical tradition to its

proper place. Thus, Voegelin does not, for example, advocate a return
to the staples of the American revivalist model—"primitivism" and
"biblicism"—nor does he see possibilities in a parallel German tradition.[43] Instead, he calls for a reorientation in the quadri-polar or quaternarian space of existence that I explored in the second chapter. This reorientation will be based on the recovery of a *philosophical* vision. The
question of political authority is guided here not by a tradition of interpretation *within* the church but by a philosophical tradition that guides
specific ecclesial concerns.[44] It remains, however, to judge the adequacy
of that response, both on its own terms, and within the context of an
increasingly post-Constantinian, and even post-Christian, world. Perhaps such a question of adequacy could be raised in a context that does
not dispute the basic philosophical anthropology that shapes Voegelin's
interpretation of Pauline Christianity. We would, however, have to ask,
for example, what difference a locally church-centered hermeneutic of
Paul's texts would make to Voegelin's vision of a civilizing mission
(would these texts become merely the curious writings of an insignifi-
cant sect?), or if the interpolation of Stoicism into Paul's thought is sustained by a careful textual-critical examination, or what difference the
(new) minority and quasi-disestablished status of Christian churches in
the West would make to their purported civilizational mission. In this
chapter, I have examined Voegelin's interpretation of a Pauline text, the
principles of which interpretation are located within the horizons of an
Augustinian-Thomistic Christendom (supplemented by a closely argued
philosophical anthropology that moves somewhat beyond the text itself), and the context of which is the breakdown of a civilizational order
whose original core of meaning appears to have been located in this text
and others like it. We are left with the question, does the disintegration
of that Christendom and many of its civilizational achievements still
leave open a space for appropriating the political text at hand (Romans
13)? Equally open is the question, for whom would such an appropria-
tion be possible, credible, and worth the trouble? Voegelin's exegesis
might suggest that we focus our attention elsewhere, leaving Romans 13
to the "sectarians," whose care for Western civilization is incidental to
their reading of a non-civilizational, God-given mission for the assembly
of believers, to the principles of which they extend a higher loyalty.[45]
For Voegelin, it seems clear that a proper understanding of political authority and the principled relationship of moral human agents to such

authority begins not with Jesus the Messiah or the Apostle Paul, but with Voegelin and his dead friends, the philosophers. Voegelin's politically oriented interpretation of Christianity and its civilizational role therefore adds to Christian theology, and at the same time omits from it a sufficient number of characteristics, doctrines, and perspectives that it behooves his sympathetic Christian readers—of which there are many—to reflect both on what he does and what he does not do in his interpretation. It is to these questions concerning the meaning of Christianity in Voegelin's political philosophy that I now turn.

NOTES

1. See, for example, Richard Gutteridge's thorough study, *Open Thy Mouth for the Dumb! The German Evangelical Church and the Jews, 1879–1950* (Oxford: Basil Blackwell, 1976); see also several of the essays in Otto Dov Kulka and Paul R. Mendes-Flohr, eds., *Judaism and Christianity under the Impact of National Socialism* (Jerusalem: The Historical Society of Israel and the Zalman Shazar Center for Jewish History, 1987).

2. Miroslav Volf, *Exclusion and Embrace: A Theological Exploration of Identity, Otherness, and Reconciliation* (Nashville, Tenn.: Abingdon Press, 1996), 35–37.

3. For an example of public interest overcoming private (commercial) interests among political and commercial elites in early modernity, see the account of Robert Duplessis and Martha C. Howell concerning the economic elites at Leiden in the sixteenth century: "Reconsidering the Early Modern Urban Economy: The Cases of Leiden and Lille," *Past and Present* 94 (February 1982): 49–84). Machiavelli's appeal to the Italian princes is a similar echo against the intrusion of private interests that corrupt the common weal. *The Prince*, chaps. 14 and 26).

4. See Machiavelli, *The Prince,* chaps. 8 and 26; for a political evaluation of Machiavelli along these lines, see Hannah Arendt, *The Human Condition* (Chicago: University of Chicago Press, 1958), 77.

5. For an analysis of this problem from the perspective of classical conceptions of the virtues, see Alasdair MacIntyre, *After Virtue* (Notre Dame, Ind.: University of Notre Dame Press, 1984), 194–96.

6. Eric Voegelin, "Hitler und die Deutschen" (unpublished transcript, 1964), 60–61 (all translations from this transcript are my own).

7. Voegelin, "Hitler und die Deutschen," 60.

8. Voegelin, "Hitler und die Deutschen," 36, 51, 93–94, 138.

9. Eric Voegelin, *Autobiographical Reflections*, ed. Ellis Sandoz (Baton Rouge: Louisiana State University Press, 1989), 16–19.

10. See Eric Voegelin, *Science, Politics, and Gnosticism* (Chicago: Henry Regnery, 1968), 36; "Hitler und die Deutschen," 159.

11. Voegelin, *Autobiographical Reflections*, 18.

12. Voegelin, *Science, Politics, and Gnosticism*, 17–18.

13. Voegelin, "Hitler und die Deutschen," 159.

14. Percy Ernst Schramm, "The Anatomy of a Dictator," in Percy Ernst Schramm, *Hitler: The Man and the Military Leader*, trans. and ed. Donald S. Detwiler (Chicago: Quadrangle Books, 1971), 17–133.

15. See Immanuel Kant, "An Answer to the Question: 'What is Enlightenment?'" in *Kant's Political Writings* , ed. Hans Reiss (Cambridge: Cambridge University Press, 1970), 54–60; and Kant, "Perpetual Peace: A Philosophical Sketch," in Reiss, *Kant's Political Writings*, 126–7.

16. Eric Voegelin, *The New Science of Politics* (Chicago: University of Chicago Press, 1952), 27.

17. Eric Voegelin, *Revolution and the New Science,* ed. Barry Cooper, vol. 6 of *History of Political Ideas* (Columbia: University of Missouri Press, 1998), 211.

18. Voegelin, *Revolution and the New Science,* 59; cf. ibid., 71.

19. Eric Voegelin, *Renaissance and Reformation*, ed. David Morse and William Thompson, vol. 4 of *History of Political Ideas* (Columbia: University of Missouri Press, 1998), 140.

20. A well-known Christian expression of this melding may be found in Thomas Aquinas' advice to the monarchical ruler that he look to the moral, not merely material, good of his people (*De Regimine Principium*: I.2.10), but this spiritual function can also be seen in Protestantism. J. S. Bach's well-known aria, "Schaffe koennen sicher weiden," from the cantata "Was mir behagt," for example, illustrates this same role: "Flocks and herds may safely pasture, when their shepherd guards them well. They whose monarch loves them truly, knows their needs and fills them duly, will in peace and comfort dwell." Trans. Henry S. Drinker (Celle, Germany: Hermann Moeck Verlag, 1963). The function of "shepherd," understood in the Christian texts as the function of Jesus, and mediated by him through the leaders in the Christian churches is here taken over by the secular ruler, whose function as guardian for the physical and spiritual well-being of his people replicates the earlier function of the spiritual overseer. The difference between "station" as Luther, for example, conceived it and the *charismata* of the early Christian conception is, of course, glossed over, and it is not surprising that Aquinas relies (as did Augustine) chiefly on Old Testament texts for his particular use of "shepherd."

21. Voegelin, *Renaissance and Reformation*, 141.

22. Voegelin, *Renaissance and Reformation*, 141. A pertinent example of such

absorption may be found in St. Ambrose, "On The Duties of the Clergy," in *St. Ambrose: Select Works and Letters*, trans. H. de Romestin, vol. 10 in *A Select Library of Nicene and Post-Nicene Fathers*, ed. Philip Schaff and Henry Wace (Grand Rapids, Mich.: Wm. B. Eerdmans, 1955) 1–89, which Roland Bainton has aptly described as a "free re-working of Cicero's *De Officiis*." (Bainton, *Christian Attitudes Toward War and Peace: A Historical Survey and Critical Re-evaluation* [Nashville, Tenn.: Abingdon Press, 1960], 90. As John Howard Yoder points out, there is nothing new in Voegelin's assertion, it being a prevalent interpretive principle in twentieth-century biblical scholarship, but one containing doubtful premises when applied specifically to the New Testament texts of Paul. Yoder, *The Politics of Jesus* [Grand Rapids, Mich.: Wm. B. Eerdmans, 1972]. 166–92).

23. Voegelin, *Renaissance and Reformation*, 141.

24. Voegelin, "Hitler und die Deutschen," 162.

25. Voegelin, "Hitler und die Deutschen," 162.

26. Voegelin, "Hitler und die Deutschen," 162.

27. Voegelin, "Hitler und die Deutschen," 163.

28. Voegelin, "Hitler und die Deutschen," 181.

29. Voegelin, "Hitler und die Deutschen," 163–64.

30. Voegelin, "Hitler und die Deutschen," 164.

31. Voegelin, "Hitler und die Deutschen," 185–86.

32. Voegelin, "Hitler und die Deutschen," 194.

33. Voegelin, "Hitler und die Deutschen," 194–95, 197.

34. Voegelin, "Hitler und die Deutschen," 220.

35. Voegelin, "Hitler und die Deutschen," 206.

36. Voegelin, "Hitler und die Deutschen," 207ff.

37. Voegelin, "Hitler und die Deutschen," 221.

38. Walsh, "Voegelin's Response," 278.

39. Thomas Aquinas, *Summa Theologica*, Pt. III, Qu. 8, art. 3, trans. the Fathers of the English Dominican Province (Benzinger Brothers, 1947). Hypertext Version (New Advent Inc., 1996).

40. Voegelin, "Hitler und die Deutschen," 226–28.

41. Voegelin, "Hitler und die Deutschen," 229.

42. For a contemporary exposition of this role, see Dietrich Bonhoeffer, *Ethics*, ed. Eberhardt Bethge, trans. Neville H. Smith from the 6th German edition (New York: Macmillan, 1965); for the debilitation of this idea in Bonhoeffer's own activity, see James Wm. McClendon, Jr., *Systematic Theology: Ethics*, vol. 1 (Nashville, Tenn.: Abingdon Press, 1986), 187–208. The most cogent biblical statements of these ideas may be found in the "Letter to the Ephesians," whose authorship and intended recipients are disputed in contemporary scholarship, but whose "heritage," at least, is clearly Pauline. Cf. Marion L. Soards, *The Apostle Paul: An Introduction to His Writings and Teachings* (New York: Paulist Press, 1987), 150–52.

43. George M. Marsden, *Fundamentalism and American Culture: The Shaping of Twentieth-Century Evangelicalism, 1870–1925* (New York: Oxford University Press, 1980), 223–24; Franklin H. Littell, *The Anabaptist View of the Church: A Study in the Origins of Sectarian Protestantism* (Boston: Beacon Press, Inc., 1958), 46–108.

44. For a "revivalist" criticism of this approach, see Richard F. Lovelace, *Dynamics of Spiritual Life: An Evangelical Theology of Renewal* (Downers Grove, Ill.: Inter-Varsity Press, 1979), 172–84.

45. For an example of such a mission and its incidental but constructive civilizational effects, see Philip Hallie, *Lest Innocent Blood be Shed: The Story of the Village of Le Chambon, and How Goodness Happened There* (New York: Harper and Row, 1979).

5

CHRISTOLOGY AND THE PROBLEM OF DOCTRINAL/POLITICAL AUTHORITY

VOEGELIN AND CHRISTIAN INTERPRETATION

Given his interpretation of the civilizational role of Christianity in the West, we should not be surprised that Eric Voegelin occupies a somewhat ambiguous position among Christian thinkers. On the one hand, some political theorists in recent years have hailed him as a philosophical friend of the Roman Catholic Christian tradition in political thought, and they have appropriated his work accordingly.[1] On the other hand, some of these same writers, and others perhaps less sympathetic to Voegelin's efforts, are critical of his conception of the meaning and content of the Christian gospel. In a recent article, Murray Jardine has once again raised this question, suggesting that a perception of Voegelin's friendliness toward Christianity may be based on an overly sympathetic reading of his work from that perspective.[2] As we saw in the previous chapter, the political question at issue in this debate concerns the source of moral and even institutional and civilizational authority for political regimes.

Claims on the story of Jesus and tamings of it are a constant feature of Christendom in the so-called medieval period of Western civilization, and they are not a new phenomenon to modernity either. The analyses of both Joshua Mitchell and W. A. Waterman have shown that until the early modern period, at least, Western political thought attached itself to some form of the Christian tradition or its stories as a means of establishing its own identity. That is to say, attention to Christology remains important for understanding what certain political philosophers in the recent Western tradition are trying to do.[3] Mitchell has suggested that how

145

we conceive of (or ignore) Jesus is important to what kind of a political identity we give ourselves in the context of that tradition. He shows how this is the case for Locke, Hobbes, Luther, and Rousseau; it may also be true even of the "late-modern" Nietzsche, whose *Genealogy of Morals* has been aptly described as Augustine's *City of God* written in reverse.[4]

Two discussions prior to Jardine's on the specific matter of Voegelin's orientation to this question are the critiques of David Walsh and Bruce Douglass. In the customary manner, Walsh briefly recounts Voegelin's critique of modernity and the roles Voegelin sees Christianity as having played in the development of modernity, along with its potential as a source for a therapeutic against that same modernity. His review of Voegelin's view of Christianity concludes that it is not only philosophically astute, but comprehensive and traditionally orthodox, "with the single exception of what is most important: the story of Christ's representative suffering and death to redeem fallen humanity."[5] More concretely, Voegelin does not pay attention to "the liberating new vision of man's relationship to God within the Gospel experience," or the "real life change of perspective effected by the experience of faith in Christ."[6] Douglass comes to a similar conclusion, but with a stronger emphasis on Voegelin's critique of the Protestant Reformation. What is missing in Voegelin's understanding of Christianity, Douglass suggests, is "the sense of the Gospel as salvation *in the specifically Christian sense.*"[7] For Voegelin, no sort of salvation can transcend the "tension of existence" but must reflect it in a manner that ultimately echoes Plato's treatment. For the Christian, however, salvation means, in Douglass' Protestant vocabulary, "the restoration of a broken relationship with God or the creation of a 'new man.'"[8]

The reasons for Voegelin's oversight—if that is what it is—are perhaps as nuanced and complex as Walsh suggests, but both he and Douglass are agreed that at least one crucial reason for Voegelin's selective interpretation and acceptance of the Christian gospel rests in his abiding effort to avoid and, indeed, to overcome gnosticism in its ancient, medieval, and modern variants. We have seen Voegelin's work on this problem in chapter 3. Its outcome in regard to Christianity is best demonstrated, I believe, in his treatment of Paul, and I will take this up presently. Jardine's considerations of Voegelin's treatment of Christianity move on somewhat different ground from those of Walsh and Douglass. Jardine has less concern for Voegelin's interpretation of Christianity *per se,* and more interest in his reading of the role of Christianity in the genesis of modernity, but he comes to a conclusion similar to those of Walsh and Douglass.

Jardine begins with the broadly accepted premise that the core activity of Voegelin's work is to analyze the meaning of modernity and thereby intellectually and spiritually to overcome its shortcomings. He argues that Voegelin offered at least four accounts of how the modern world came into being. The importance of Christianity to this account is that, for Voegelin, modernity is "essentially the declining stage of Christian civilization."[9] Without dissecting this admittedly complex, perhaps debatable, and certainly broad claim, Jardine poses the clear question that arises from it for the political theorist: if we accept Voegelin's claim, "What is the fatal flaw in Christianity, or at least in the conventional interpretation of orthodox Christian symbols, which led to the decay of the Christian symbolic order?"[10] In Jardine's interpretation, Voegelin implies that a renewal of human spiritual and intellectual life beyond postmodernity would require either a replacement for Christianity or a "significant reworking of Christian theology"; either of these two possibilities would firmly expel Voegelin from the "conservative" camp as defined by Christian political theologians.[11]

The first three Voegelinian accounts of modernity's genealogy interpret modernity as in some way the result of a response to inadequacies in Christianity, and all three establish the gnostic character of modern thought.[12] Thus, either "the gnostic symbols of modernity are a response to the vacuum created by the inadequacies of Augustine's philosophy of history," or "modern gnosticism is a response to the general uncertainty created by Christianity," or "the disintegration of Christianity is the result of literalist deformation of Christian symbols, resulting in their destruction as ordering forces for Western humanity."[13] The fourth and, for Jardine, most radical interpretation of modernity that emerges from Voegelin's writings is that "certain essential features in the structure of Christianity . . . *necessarily* [lead] to the derangements of modernity." Specifically, it may be that a "central feature of Christian theology," according to Voegelin, "is an attempt to abolish the structure of reality" by mistakenly identifying "the theophanic event of Christ's resurrection as the *beginning* of the transfiguration of reality rather than as the most fully differentiated theophanic event *pointing toward* that transfiguration."[14] In this reading, as in those of Walsh and Douglass, we find once again that a preoccupation with gnosticism controls Voegelin's interpretation of Christianity.

My purpose in this final chapter is to consider anew Voegelin's interpretation of the Christian "theophanic event" and to show that his analysis results in a problematic understanding both of the politics of Jesus (and Paul) and of the nature of the Christian church. Given the centrality of Christianity—and, by implication, the life of Jesus—to the cultural and intellectual history of Europe, and therefore to Voegelin's own thought, which is rooted in that heritage, the problems of this interpretation are not peripheral to Voegelin's enterprise.[15] While Jardine's commitments are less clear, Walsh and Douglass seem, respectively, to defend a Roman Catholic and a Protestant position against Voegelin's reading of the Christian gospel. In this chapter, I wish to consider Voegelin's work—in whatever limited way this may be possible—from yet a third position. The intent is not merely to offer yet another "perspective," but to raise the possibility of an inherent inadequacy in Walsh's and Douglass' rejoinders along with Voegelin's analysis. I will argue that the critiques of Walsh and Douglass share with the Voegelinian analysis an insufficient consideration of Jesus' political teaching, and that all three too readily treat the Church only in its post-Constantinian manifestation as a civilizational force, reading backward from that point to its earlier, non-Constantinian status. We have seen that Voegelin accepted this reading in full awareness of the crucial distinction between the Christian experience before and after the birth of "Christendom," a birth that came with the gradual institutionalization of Christianity as the official religion of the late Roman Empire during the fourth century. My rejoinder to Voegelin's historically accurate "civilizational" account is intended to take up Jardine's suggestion that Voegelin's analysis of Western civilization should perhaps prompt Christians to rethink the relationship of Christianity and classical Greek philosophy as the two prime constituents of the Western tradition, conventionally understood.[16] I intend here to pursue that suggestion through an examination of Voegelin's Christology and ecclesiology, not so much with the intention of criticizing Voegelin's *historical* account, which I hold to be accurate, but with the purpose of reconsidering the "civilizational" possibilities of Christianity. Such a reconsideration is intended, among other things, to highlight Voegelin's unique interpretation of the meaning of Christianity and to show the close integration of this interpretation into his wider thought. In so doing, it calls into question the affinity some of his Christian readers perceive between his thought and the general Christian tradition.

Let me pose the question concerning the meaning of Christianity more bluntly. In his lectures at the Divinity School of the University of Chicago in 1963 on modern Protestant theology, Paul Tillich rejected Friedrich Schleiermacher's implicit contention that Christianity is the "religion among religions," and the "highest" or the "absolute" of these.[17] Christianity, Tillich contended, is not "the true religion over against the false religions which have distorted divine revelation." Rather, Tillich saw in the writings of the Apostle Paul a rejection of "religion" altogether.

> Paul in Romans did not speak of the Christian religion. He spoke of Christ. He would not say that the Christian religion is the decisive thing. . . . he attacked the Christian religion as it existed in his time. He attacked the Jewish-Christian (legalism) as well as the Gnostic distortions (lawlessness). This means that while Paul criticized all religions, he does not exempt Christianity from criticism. He does not put Christianity against the other religions. Rather, he puts Christ against every religion, even against the actual Christian religion as this was expressed in the congregations which he founded.[18]

It is this contrast between Christ and Christianity that I wish to pursue here in the Voegelinian context of a spiritual therapeutic. First, I will review the Voegelinian problematic as I have pursued it throughout this study. Second, I will review the path Voegelin traced from the roots of the problem to its full blooming in modernity. Third, I will turn more specifically to Voegelin's consideration of Christianity in this context, and then offer a counter-interpretation of Christianity to Voegelin's. Finally, I will contrast these two narratives of Christianity in terms of the *political* implications each presents.

CHRISTIANITY AND HUMAN ORDER

Voegelin's philosophical anthropology is crucial to an understanding of his theology. Voegelin's analysis of European racism, a three-part, two-volume genealogical and political-theoretical study published in 1933 in Germany, begins with the sentence: "The knowledge of man has come to grief." Pursuing this knowledge would eventually put Voegelin's name on the Nazi enemies' list in Austria and lead to his flight to the United States with the coming of the Anschluß in 1938. What is this knowledge of whose integrity Voegelin despaired? It is the knowledge whose exploration I have pursued in this study. At the time he wrote the sentence, it was for him the ability to see in a clear, theoretically cogent manner the components of human nature and experience, and their relationships to one another and to the political community that bases its symbols and institutions of order on an understanding of them. It was, in other words, precisely that knowledge that was generally missing from the German society of the early and middle twentieth century. In political science, as we have seen, a proper "knowledge of man" includes a theory of meaning that recognizes the roles that human self-understanding plays in the symbolic and concrete constitution of a political community. Race is only one of many such symbols, resting on a particular conception of human nature and used in a historically particular manner as a way of constituting a community on its basis.

In Voegelin's view, a proper understanding of science and the knowledge of man that it gives for political-symbolic purposes had gradually been lost through the various reductionistic and scientistic endeavors of the Renaissance and Enlightenment to overcome the dogmas of Scholasticism and through the deformation of the related ideological discourse from the seventeenth century onward.[19] Having devoted his life's work to the task of re-establishing a science of man, Voegelin came to the conclusion that the political science of Plato and Aristotle, complemented by the differentiating insights of Christianity, was the most theoretically developed political science historically available. In a letter in 1942 to Leo Strauss, he summarized this conclusion:

> [A]t the center of Platonic *political* thinking stand the *fundamental experiences,* which are tied together with the person and death of Socrates—catharsis through consciousness of death and the enthusiasm of eros both pave the way for the right ordering of the soul (*Dike*). The *theoretical* political-ethical achievement seems secondary to these fundamental experiences. Only when the fundamental order of the soul is defined, can the field of social relations determined by it be system-

atically ordered. . . . The "scientific" treatment of political and ethical problems seems to me to be possible since and because of Plato, because a myth of man (Socrates-Plato) has become the stable point for the choice of the relevant materials. . . . Only from the Aristotelian position is the completely scientific-theoretical treatment of the political possible; but it is possible because the Platonic form, grown from the myth, can now be assumed as a datum and thus without the existential participation [of the philosopher] in the myth. . . . Christianity and historical consciousness seem rather to be steps in the direction of the universalization of the image of man, than steps that lead away from it. In my opinion that is the decisive reason for the superiority of the Christian anthropology over the Hellenic.[20]

In Voegelin's critical characterization of modernity, this elevated science of Plato and Aristotle had degenerated in the Western tradition into a series of dogmas and pseudo-sciences that now informed the order of society to the detriment of a properly human life. Combined with the power of the technology spawned by the steadily advancing natural sciences, the civilizational outcome, as I noted in chapter 3, looked grim to Voegelin: the "political tentacles of scientistic civilization" could be felt everywhere, and "freedom of the spirit in society" in this "global asylum was hardly likely.[21] As we have seen in the previous chapter and in Jardine's apt summary, Christianity is implicated in this development, because the basic ordering symbols of Western civilization derive from Christianity, amended by local considerations and Greek philosophy. These ordering symbols and the civilizational powers of the Christian (Roman Catholic) church eroded during the late medieval and Renaissance periods as the *corpus Christianum* that was Europe during the Middle Ages broke up into individual national units, and this erosion produced severe civilizational and spiritual disasters in Europe.

The history of this breakdown is complex, and I have indicated Voegelin's detailed tracing of it, both in his discarded "History of Political Ideas" and in various other writings. Its central political feature is the transfer of unifying power from the symbol of the body of Christ over all (European) Christendom into the symbols of particularistic national units from the fifteenth century onward. This development entailed a gradual break with the "idea of the unity of mankind in the spirit of Christ."[22] The central existential feature of this breakdown may be essentially described in terms of a reorientation that is made possible by the experiences and symbols of Christianity itself.[23]

The ongoing implication of our study is that the order of modern existence must be understood not only in terms of institutions but in terms of spirit. Let us recall that existence in the global asylum of which Voegelin speaks comes into being when the experiential substance of the ordering symbols that are carried and sustained by Christianity is lost, so that in modernity, as we recall from chapter 3, "the active center of intellectual life has shifted to the plane of our knowledge of the external world" from the transcendental plane under which that world exists.[24] This primary characterization of modernity, whose essential roots can be found in gnostic motives awakened by Christianity itself, seems for Voegelin to govern any possibly responsible philosophical interpretation of Christianity.

For Voegelin, to reiterate the point, the Christian church had a civilizational function, at least in Europe and those portions of the globe colonized by the European powers: it was to serve as a civilizing force by institutionally transmitting the spiritual substance of Jesus' teachings into the surrounding society. When the ecclesiastical order began to break down toward the end of the Renaissance, however, Christianity did not disappear as a source for symbols of meaning. Rather, Christian symbols were interpreted in accordance with the new experiences of the secular, non-Christian order. Thus, "the 'breakdown' of Western Christianity does not mean its disappearance without traces from the scene; it rather means the refraction and gradual transformation of its tradition in the national arenas; a substantial common stock of ideas remains preserved in this process, particularly in its beginning."[25] We recall that, at the concrete level of experience and political symbolization, the reordering is a new search for meaning in which "the [new] bearers of western Civilization" seek to interpret their "civilizational existence as meaningful," and not as a mere "appendix" to antiquity. To do so, they seek out new gods, who, unlike the medieval church, "take some interest in their civilizational efforts."[26] The reordering is, for Voegelin, often a crude, immanentistic derivative of Christianity and often gnostic, but it is a reordering nevertheless, and one that shapes the modern world.

THE CONSTANTINIAN TURN

At the end of this story of the decline of Christendom, we return to the beginning. Let us recall that the new role of "civilizing force" requires alteration and compromise in the Christian tradition. The changes that Christianity endured on its way to becoming the source of civilizational order are, however, no small matter for the shape and meaning of Christianity itself. In the ethical stance of the Christian churches, for example, several key changes take place in the fourth century as Christianity moves from its status as a minority faith to its new standing as the imperial religion. In the clearest sign of the new Christian ethical attachment to the empire, Christianity moves from pacifism to just-war doctrines:

> The pre-Constantinian Christians had been pacifists, rejecting the violence of army and empire not only because they had no share of power, but because they considered it morally wrong; the post-Constantinian Christians considered imperial violence to be not only morally tolerable but a positive good and a Christian duty.[27]

Among the many disputes between Christians, "war alone was repudiated until the time of Constantine, for until then no extant Christian writing countenanced Christian participation in warfare."[28] Constantine, who accepted Christianity in 312 A.D., is therefore a useful marker as the turning point in the gradual process of Christianity moving from a minority religion to the imperial religion that serves as the civilizational force that Voegelin describes.[29]

This turn from pacifism to just war doctrines is indicative of the much wider transformation of Christian ethics, ecclesiologically and eschatologically, that makes up the compromise that allows Christianity to play its civilizational role in the late Roman imperium and in medieval Europe. Several features of this transformation are especially prominent, and they indicate the ethical changes that the integration of Christianity into the life of the imperium requires. As Jardine has pointed out, as Yoder shows, and as Voegelin's own analysis of the "compromises" Christians must make to enter this life implies, the achievement of integration is not without its difficulties.[30] In the first place, the pre-Constantinian Church is a minority whose single set of ethical claims is addressed to all its members, but not necessarily to the surrounding society. The post-Constantinian Church, however, is made up of everyone. This sociological fact means, second, that the ethical claims of the church must be distinguished into an upper level addressed only to the (professional) religious class and a lower level addressed to the laity, which is everyone else.[31] The highest ethical claims of the church, in other words, cannot be directed to the entire Christian community, since this community cannot be distinguished from society at large. Third then, while the pre-Constantinian Church is a visible, concrete entity—a minority community in a larger, sometimes hostile society—the "true believers" of the Constantinian church are an "invisible" church, no longer visible in their minority status, since they are no longer apparent in their voluntary membership and concrete practice. Closely related to this development, pre-Constantinian Christianity is outward behavior, whereas post-Constantinian Christianity turns inward. Fourth, and again closely related, pre-Constantinian belief is based on individual assent and commitment, whereas post-Constantinian Christianity is sociological and politic. In its political outlook, pre-Constantinian Christianity views God's rule in history as invisible—no civil authority can legitimately claim to speak and act for God in a trans-historical way. In the post-Constantinian view, however, God's rule in history is actualized in the reigning authority, so that the civil (Christian) sovereign becomes God's privileged agent. Finally, pre-Constantinian Christianity is at its core counter-cultural: the content of ethical guidance is the teaching of Jesus, and the criteria for ethical judgement are based on faithfulness to the teachings of Jesus. In the post-Constantinian world, Christianity *is* culture and the universal source of ethical authority. Accordingly, the content of ethical guidance becomes "station," "office," or "vocation." Ethical criteria are based much more on questions of effectiveness (utility), and much less on obedience to ethical injunctions or examples.[32] Here we see most clearly the compromise with pagan ethics. In particular, (Christian) moral deliberation becomes defined by utilitarian considerations:

> But once the evident course of history is held to be empirically discernible, and the prosperity of our regime is the measure of good, all morality boils down to efficacy. Right action is what works; what does not promise results can hardly be right.[33]

The sum of these changes, as Yoder argues, is that the ethical stance of Christians changed radically from one epoch to the other, and that this ethical turn was a reflection of other, deeper changes in the Christian conception of the order of things. Voegelin minimizes these differences between the two ecclesiastical eras with the terse observation that, had "the community of the gospel . . . not entered the culture of the time by entering its life of reason, it would have remained an obscure sect and probably disappeared from history; we know the fate of Judaeo-Christianity."[34] But what does the life of reason, represented by imperial civilization, demand? More directly, how is Paul's injunction of submission—a pivotal text in Voegelin's critique of late German Christendom—to be understood under this rubric and in this new vision of the church as compared with the previous one? Since the role and mission of the church appears to have changed radically between the time of Paul's writing and Constantine's acceptance of the Christian faith, and especially since this change has been in the direction of affiliation with political power, these interpretive questions are much more than doctrinal niceties.

PAULINE ESCHATOLOGY

In Voegelin's view, the compromise between the substantive claims to truth of the church and the truth-telling of the pre-Christian, pagan world is the most important of the three "compromises" Christianity makes with the "world." This accommodation between two worldviews and their attendant vocabulary enables Christianity to speak to the world in the world's own language with a view to the world's own interests. The compatibility of Christian and pagan thought-forms, however, does not end in the doctrinal accommodations the former makes to the latter. Indeed, the novelty of Voegelin's historical analysis is to show that Pauline Christianity and Platonic/Aristotelian political science/philosophy are at their deepest level complementary and fully compatible. This compatibility is ultimately the bridge between Voegelin's philosophical critique of intellectual corruption and his critical analysis of the failures of the Christian churches in Germany. More generally, it is for Voegelin the bridge between Christianity as a particularistic sect of the Roman Empire and Christianity as the spiritually ordering force of a civilization.

Philosophy penetrated and permeated the gospel message at an early stage, according to Voegelin, thereby making it a socially ordering force. Its merger with Greek philosophy allowed Christianity to move from an non-inquiring doctrine to a magnet for inquiring minds that would shape the gospel message philosophically into a civilizational force. In Voegelin's interpretation of the early history of the Christian message, the radically different languages of experience that arise from Platonic and Aristotelian philosophical investigation on the one hand and the gospel message or biblical language on the other can be integrated.[35] While this move might give some interpreters pause, Voegelin explicitly affirms it as the proper hermeneutic principle to use in a serious reading of Paul: "The Pauline analysis of existential order closely parallels the Platonic-Aristotelian. That is to be expected, since both the saint and the philosophers articulate the order constituted by man's response to a theophany."[36]

"The differences between prophecy, classic philosophy and the gospel must be sought in the degrees of differentiation of existential truth," argues Voegelin, but the key difference between the visionary experiences of Paul and his exegesis of them on the one hand and the philosophical experiences of Plato and Aristotle and their exegeses of these on the other is Paul's shift in emphasis from "the divinely noetic order incarnate in the world to the divinely pneumatic salvation from its disorder, from the paradox of reality to the abolition of the paradox, from the experience of the directional movement to its consummation."[37] Accordingly, "the noetic core . . . is the same in both classic philosophy and the gospel movement," but the pressure of Christianity toward the abolition of existential tension and the consummation of the perfection that constitutes one pole of that tension makes it permanently susceptible to derailment into gnostic or millenarian movements.[38] Paul's vision of the Resurrected is not merely "a theophanic event in the Metaxy," but "the beginning of the transfiguration itself" to the point of obsession.[39]

Both Douglass and Walsh have objected to Voegelin's description of Paul's eschatological consciousness as "obsession," with the rejoinder that Voegelin's emphasis on an inherent gnosticizing tendency in Christianity and his thorough rejection of it in fact alters "the *substance* of the meaning the symbols [of Christianity] originally conveyed" to the point of making the Christianity of Paul and the teachings of Jesus unrecognizable.[40] Voegelin had himself diagnosed the fragility of the life of faith, with the conclusion that human existence in the In-Between of birth and death, of knowledge and ignorance, is at all times a tenuous affair, not for the spiritually timid, and that it may all too easily degenerate into an ideological/gnostic quest for certainty.[41] It would seem, this being the case, that he should be hesitant to so thoroughly control, if not root out, the Christian expression of the experience of eschatological tension, since it is but a symbolization of human experience under historical consciousness that attests to the tension and depends, not on human action for its alleviation, but on the activity of God in a hoped-for future. It seems, however, that he found the pull to be too strong in Paul's writings. Nevertheless, if we find that "in the pneumatic theophany of Paul with divine creativity differentiated, an eschatology is required to complete the meaning of the movement," we may ask if there is a possible *practical content* for this eschatology that does not imply imminent derailment into gnostic forms. The question then becomes, are there other aspects of the experience of theophany for Paul that temper or regulate his eschatological fervor?

Voegelin, as David Walsh points out, "wishes to uncover the universal order of mankind in history and not the order of a particular confessional church."[42] Corresponding to this consistent effort at universalism is his rejection of specific doctrinal formulations and of the institutionalization of the life of the spirit into representative communities as inevitable distortions into "pseudo-objectivist dogmas" of that life and of openness to the divine transcendent ground.[43] "To follow Christ means," for Voegelin, "to continue the event of divine presence in society and history: 'as you have sent me into the world, so I have sent them into the world' ([John] 17:18)."[44]

For Voegelin, the authority of Jesus that underwrites Paul's injunction to submission is a civilizational authority in which the redeeming power of Jesus' resurrection is mediated through the lens of pagan philosophy and the proper institutions. But for a Christian, this description pointedly raises the question, if, indeed, it does not beg it, what the specific *content* of this "divine presence" is to be. What will its concrete characteristics and its regulating features be? For Voegelin, this is to ask the wrong question, because revelation is its own content, as in Socratic-Platonic philosophy with its "movement in the In-Between of existence." This conception of revelation minimizes the more strongly experienced pull in Paul's writings of the *eschaton,* and this minimization shapes Voegelin's reading of Romans 13, for example, in a specific direction. Since, for Voegelin, "there is no doctrine to be taught but only the story to be told of God's pull becoming effective in the world through Christ, the Saving Tale that answers the question of life and death can be reduced to the brief statement: And this is life eternal: To know you, the only true God, and Jesus Christ whom you have sent [John 17:3]."[45]

It is no small matter in this context that Voegelin prefers to render the Pauline term *theotes* as "divine reality," because, in contrast to "*godhead, divinity, or deity,* which carry the implication of a personal God," Voegelin's term "renders best the author's intention to denote a nonpersonal reality which allows for degrees of participation in its fullness while remaining the God beyond the In-Between of existence."[46] This usage, it seems to me, raises the question yet again whether Voegelin's stance keeps him from recognizing a non-gnostic *practical* content in Paul's vision and the vision of those in Paul's tradition, without the need for depersonalizing a deity that Paul generally describes in personal terms. For Voegelin, "The classic meaning *in* history [for Plato and Aristotle] can be opposed by Paul with a meaning *of* history, because he knows the end of the story in the transfiguration that begins with the Resurrection."[47] The "central issue" for Paul is, therefore, "not a doctrine, but the assurance of immortalizing transfiguration through the vision of the Resurrected." Although Voegelin notes that "transfiguration is experienced as an 'historical' event that has begun with the Passion and Resurrection of Christ," he puts "historical" in quotes to indicate its tenuous status at the level of mundane occurrence.[48] This tenuousness is linked to the problem of a dogmatism that obscures, if it does not hide altogether, the fundamental experiences that are the essence of the theophany of the Resurrected, in the life both of Paul and of other Christian thinkers. It also, however, leaves open the question whether or not a substantive ethic is *inherently* a part of this experience as it seemed to be for Paul.[49] In contemporary Christian experience, the "Unknown God whose *theotes* was present in the existence of Jesus has been eclipsed by the revealed God of Christian doctrine," which, because of the countermeasures of the Enlightenment to the dogmas of Scholasticism, is "one of the great causes of the modern spiritual crisis,"[50] but this circumstance does not preclude a different non-dogmatic but ethically substantive alternative.

To identify a Christian radicalism that is eschatologically temperate means first, then, to extricate it from the Western problem by questioning the direct line of the Voegelinian genealogy, according to which the modern, gnostic revolt against the truth of existence is essentially a long-developed "deformation of the theophanic events in which the dynam-

ics of transfiguration was revealed to Jesus and the Apostles."[51] Paul's
eschatological myth of transfiguration is retold in modern revolutionary,
millenarian "philosophies of history," whose conception of beginning
and end are a deformed version of Paul's mythical tale of Beginning and
End.[52] Philosophical control is reasserted over this myth, as we have
seen, with the recovery of the experiences revealed in the symbols and
myths of Platonic/Aristotelian philosophy. This philosophical reassertion
is made publicly authoritative by the philosopher's call to pay attention
to what is present in consciousness, and nothing more: "Man must play
his part in the drama of history, responsive to the pull of the golden cord
of divine love yet ever conscious of his essential ignorance concerning
both the nature of the Whole and his own role in it. All that the philosopher can do is to bring this ineluctable condition to our attention."[53]

Voegelin's analysis of Paul's language and the experiences behind it
point, as Yoder's exposition shows, to a multitude of questions concerning the status of Christendom (the "civilizational" form of Christianity).
The two chinks in Christendom's walls that I will explore here are the
questions of the Christian language of experience and of its links to eschatology and political-historical representation.

ESCHATOLOGY AND REALISM (A)

The question Voegelin poses for the Christian concerning eschatology is similarly posed by John Milbank in his magisterial survey of the
ontic premises of modern Western philosophy: Is a Christian eschatological consciousness possible that neither derails into millenarian activism
nor relinquishes its first principles in the Augustinian manner of Niebuhrian realism?[54] Let me ask the question in a more decisively Voegelinian
mode: is a Christian eschatological consciousness possible that does not
shrink the "horizon of openness" to transcendental experience in the
soul or in consciousness, and that remains open to the "illuminative experiences of truth" from which the symbols of order historically
emerge,[55] but, I will add, without reverting to an Augustinian surrender
to political realism?

From a Voegelinian standpoint, putting the question this way is crucial, because the final task of the philosopher, after having cleared away
the ideological language of modern politics and having restored the

"formative experiences of order that can replace the ideological 'eclipse of reality,'"[56] is to resolve "those unbalancing difficulties which, having been present from the start, contributed so extensively to the decline into untruth."[57] Voegelin argues that Christianity is itself a significant source of such imbalance, and I have noted the existential conditions that a restoration would require. How would the attention the philosopher draws to the need for restoration be practically—socially and ethically—satisfied? Stated in the extreme, it seems that Voegelin presents us with two alternatives: a "balance of consciousness" preserved by philosophy or a millenarian revolution. But is there a way to be Christian that lies between Voegelin's call to philosophy and the historical problem of millenarian revolution, but that retains existential integrity while so doing? If we were to take up the possibility of an eschatological ethic that is neither revolutionary nor consciously a compromise with Platonic philosophy, what would it look like? What would be its social and political form? It seems to me that we are confronted in late modernity with two serious possibilities. The first is the Christian realism of Reinhold Niebuhr, and the second is the radical ethic of Anabaptism, as expressed in the writings of theologians like Yoder and McClendon. It is doubtful that any other stance, from a Christian point of view, is consistently tenable.

In Niebuhr's Christian realism, we find first of all a decisive rejection of any practical instantiation of the metanarrative that a radical ethic of peaceableness might imply. For example, Niebuhr reduces the tension between the Christian story of God's peace and the world's story of the fratricide that is necessary for political foundings[58] to a tragedy within the Christian story, not between God's story and man's. Accordingly, he would decisively reject the possibility of living in accordance with the early Christian ethic of peace that we saw in Yoder's dichotomy between pre- and post-Constantinian Christian ethics. The Christian, Niebuhr maintains, must be active in the world, taking responsibility for the neighbor within the secular political life of the nation as well as in other spheres. To do so, he must give up pretensions to peaceableness, since they can result only in secular defeat, which would in practice be an irresponsible resignationism. Niebuhr echoes Machiavelli: "anyone who determines to act in all circumstances the part of a good man must come to ruin among so many who are not good."[59] This stance, it seems to me, is consistent with Voegelin's civilizational reading of the role of

Christianity. Any other option seems a stance of millenarian optimism or revolutionary politics that has lost any sense of the balance of consciousness required for a sane politics. But is this the case? What are the premises of sanity here?

We may make an intermediate step with an oft-recited reading of Augustine's conception of history: the argument that for Augustine the Christian *eschaton* described in the final three chapters of the canonical *Apocalypse of John* is not a future realm of perfection but a picture of the church in its present form. The end of the reign of the church will be brought about by God Himself in His own time, and the task of Christians is to wait faithfully until that time comes. There is no further meaning in/of history than this.[60] Christians are on a pilgrimage, not toward a specific goal that lies *within* the historical stream, but to one that lies outside it, in God's ultimate fulfillment.

Two consequences flow from Augustine's exposition. First, this conception of history seems to indicate an intra-worldly adjustment of the early Christians, who had strong expectations of the return of the Messiah that were not fulfilled. Augustine's exposition is the final outcome of a reinterpretation of the eschatological message of Jesus, according to which his disciples could expect his imminent return and a concomitant completion of all things in the judgment of God over the deeds of all men. This reinterpretation may be seen as the great shift in Christian consciousness from its earliest to its later phases.[61] The shift, as Ernst Benz describes it, is from the future to the present.[62] The "Kingdom," understood as God's transformation of all things into a realm of perfection, fades from view and is replaced with "the necessity of orienting and establishing the Church in this world," which in turn requires a reinterpretation of the canonical texts.[63] The final result of this process of reinterpretation, argues Benz, may be found in the writings of Augustine, and so we have arrived by a different path at Voegelin's same "compromises": Augustine replaces "the original expectation of the imminent return of Christ" with a "doctrine of the institutional Church as the present Kingdom of God" that will stand for one thousand years. And the basic characterization of this Kingdom, at least in its external, institutional form, is given in Yoder's summary that we have charted.[64]

Second, however, such a reassessment of Christian millennial expectation does not require an *eidos* of history, and, as Gerhart Niemeyer has lucidly shown, it did not for Augustine. In Niemeyer's reading, Augustine did not have a philosophy of history in the sense of an "attempt to make history intelligible by means of judgments couched in terms of universal concepts."[65] It may be that Augustine opens up such a possibility by positing a God-ordained End of history that is then made the object of speculation of a philosophy that employs universal concepts in its consideration either of the stream of particulars that terminate at the end of history or of that End itself. To be coherent, Niemeyer argues, such an activity of speculation would require "the invention of the 'age' or 'phase' of history as the apparent 'intelligible unit' of historical understanding," and such a notion did not appear until Joachim of Fiora, eight hundred years after Augustine, from which point it gathered momentum into the modern era of so-called philosophies of history that include the speculations of Hegel, the French positivists, and Marx.[66] For Augustine, however, the "intelligible unit" in history is, on the one hand (as for Aristotle), the "noble" or "conspicuous" deed, and, on the other hand, a "vision of God" that is "the highest good both within history and as completed in the eschaton."[67]

If the specifically Christian eschatology does not, in fact, demand or even imply an *eidos* of history, and if it does not demand an immediate appearance of a Messiah to provide a coherent account of the "gap" between the first and second theophanies of Christ, then we have opened up a space for the appearance of a Christian eschatology that meets Voegelin's demands for existential balance, that is not millenarian in the revolutionary sense, that does not necessarily imply Niebuhrian realism, but that remains true to the Christian consciousness of transformation both in the future and also in the here and now as Walsh and Douglass seem to demand. We have also introduced an additional caveat as to tying too closely the gnosticism of modernity to "Christianity" as such.

Let us, therefore, take a second intermediate step. The question I am posing in this chapter regarding the place of Christology is not whether Jesus will be accorded authority or not, but of what kind this authority will be. For Voegelin, it is a civilizational authority in which the redeeming power of Jesus' resurrection is mediated through the lens of pagan philosophy and the proper institutions. Walsh, who is one of Voegelin's ablest contemporary commentators, shows how this authority can be effected with an existential balance, but with more attention to the transforming power of the Christian message in the here and now.

Walsh begins with the experience of love and forgiveness that is made available in the Christian vision of reality. While the experience of love and the forgiveness that is part of it may have implications rippling into wider society, its enactment is first, for Walsh, deeply inner and private:

> Dimitri's willingness to sacrifice himself not for what he is accused of, but to atone for the evil he has actually done, makes little sense from a pragmatically rational point of view. Even less does the belief that his sacrifice will somehow make the world better for all the poor babes who are crying within it. But it has the ring of a profound truth about it. In a world where all things are connected, where the good or evil done in one part can have consequences elsewhere, it is not so irrational. The suffering willingly undergone by one person can have wider effect on all others. Representative suffering begins to appear as the most definitive victory over disorder.[68]

But the "fullness of divine presence" within individuals that "transformed their lives" does not, as it did for Paul, immediately translate them into a like-minded community of believers who practice the results of transformation together and without any necessary recourse to the language of the pagan world. Clearly, Walsh sees that in Christ, "the nihilistic lust for domination" can be overcome,[69] but the practical ethical result of this overcoming remains Constantinian:

> The problems that press upon any conscientious observer of our situation today . . . can no longer be ignored. It is imperative that the existential rediscovery of philosophic-Christian truth be unfolded into the order of human existence within society and history. Having struggled and emerged victorious over its inverted opposite, Christianity can once again provide the authoritative public foundation of order. If the existential resolution we have followed is representative, then it must be capable of demonstrating this broader significance. The bearers of the philosophic-Christian illumination must be able to show how their experience provides the most profound realization of our humanity. Even further, they must be able to make transparent the philosophic-Christian significance of the movement of civilizational progress as well.[70]

For Walsh, human beings "by opening toward Christ are . . . drawn by the divine reality that has fully absorbed humanity into itself in Jesus," but this understanding leads to a civilizational, not an ecclesiastical, response:

> Beyond this core attunement to transcendent order is the extrapolation toward the order of the whole. The victory in Christ over evil, through his loving self-sacrifice on the cross, is experienced as the effective means of creating order in history.[71]

The "complete revelation of incarnate divine goodness in history" is Jesus, but he is, in the final analysis, not the source of our ethics, because it is not the practice of his life but its philosophical implications that serve as such a foundation, and these implications are generally expressed in pagan, not Christian, symbols. "Adjustment to the conditions of continued existence within the world," and a reminder not to neglect "the problems of pragmatic existence in our longing for union with the resurrected Lord," which would cause us to "fail in our responsibilities toward one another and toward our world," govern Christian ethics.[72] In Yoder's terms, the question for a radically Christian ethic remains, in Walsh's conception, "What would happen if everybody did it?" whereas a more fitting question might be "What if nobody else acted like a Christian, but we did?" The latter, Yoder suggests, is the form that moral reasoning takes "wherever committed Christians accept realistically their minority status," while the former must, under such circumstances, appear "ludicrous" and "preposterous" to them.[73]

A pertinent description of such a Yoderian possibility is offered in James McClendon's "living as if," which can be contrasted with the realist alternative that Niebuhr has posed most cogently in our century. The "living as if" of McClendon's ecclesiastical eschatology clarifies some of the questions that Niebuhr's realism and Walsh's somewhat contravening demands seem to pose. The community that is established under a non-millenarian eschatology and that retains a balance of the real, yet with a peaceable (pre-Constantinian) ethic in mind, implies a clear vision of the transforming power of God. It is a prophetic stance that is not, however, a "metastatic" expectation of the magical transformation of the here and now.[74] It implies a unique view of Christian faith:

> Authentic Christian faith is prophetic faith; it sees the present in correct perspective only when it construes the present by means of the

prefiguring past (God's past) while at the same time construing it by means of the prophetic future (God's future). "This is that" declares the present relevance of what God has previously done, while "then is now" does not abolish the future but declares the present relevance of what God will assuredly do. . . . Moreover, these two, typical past and prophetic future, are not alternative visions between which to choose; they are and must remain, one vision, one faith, one hope.[75]

For McClendon, the prophetic future is given, not in a set of doctrines or dogmas, but in a set of "pictures" that include "the last judgment," "Jesus Christ returning," "Resurrection," "death, hell, and heaven," "the rule of God," "new heavens and a new earth," "the thief who comes by night," and so on. Depending upon their specific content, we might, in Voegelinian language, call these pictures "symbols" or "myths." McClendon prefers "pictures," because the term reveals the regulating role such items play:

> The futuristic pictures that characterize religious belief, such as life after death and the last judgment, are not objects of belief on the basis of ordinary sorts of evidence; and they are *not* the result of better or worse reasoning based on such ordinary evidence, either. . . . What distinguishes those who believe in the last judgment from those who do not is not different chains of reasoning, but radically different *pictures* of how in general the world goes.[76]

These pictures serve to make connections between the shape of the present and the shape of God's fulfillment such that that fulfillment enters in a concrete way into the present.[77] The ultimate fulfillment, however, is not to be sought in chronological, mundane history; its link to the present is manifested in the day-to-day life of Christians singly and in community:

> In a word, what history is about is the formation of a new race of human beings, a race made of all races, a people made of all peoples. Inasmuch as Jesus is crucified and risen, the making of that new community on earth, one governed by "the politics of the Lamb," is human history's last task. This people is meant under its Lord to rule the world! But it is not to rule it as Caesars and presidents have attempted to rule (and have supposed that they were ruling)—by fire and sword, by rockets and bombs, by the power of death. That is mere

triumphalism. The Lamb who creates this people provides for them a new kind of politics. Sometimes this kind works by indirect means, as when in the Netherlands or Great Britain or the United States "free churches have helped to create free societies." At other times, it works more directly, as when a Mohandas Gandhi ("an unimmersed follower of the Jesus of the Gospels") or a Martin Luther King, Jr., shows once more that suffering for a righteous cause can overturn principalities and powers. To be sure, this politics can fail as well, and sometimes in the short run it does fail. Yet in the heavenly hymn the final outcome is certain, for there the Lamb has already passed his power to his people. According to Revelation 5:9f, the sacrificial work of the earthly Jesus has already formed this "royal" people; we exist; the new politics has begun.[78]

But how does this vision answer Niebuhrian realism and Voegelinian charges of millenarian revolution? In response to Niebuhr, it simply denies that the Christian qua Christian is responsible for the way history or the world goes. Indeed, it charges that such an attempt to be responsible is itself tantamount to replacing the rule of God in history with the rule of idols, be they monarchs, states, clans, or tribes. If God reveals Himself in the pictures of the visions Paul and others had, including the vision of the Resurrected, as a God of peace, then Christians are to connect the mundane world to that vision by reflecting peaceableness. It does not, therefore, demand resignation, but activity under a new banner. Such a move is clearly "revolutionary," because it denies the standard premises of Christendom, not to mention the world, but it is not *a priori* unreasonable, and it begins not in the magic of revolution but in hopeful faithfulness to the pictures of the Vision:

> We do not, ultimately, love our neighbor because Jesus told us to. We love our neighbor because God is like that. It is not because Jesus told us to that we love even beyond the limits of reason and justice, even to the point of refusing to kill and being willing to suffer—but because God is like that too.[79]

A stance of "living as if" in this mode requires both a reconsideration of the concrete meaning of the theophany of Christ, and the "experiences of faith" that are the "original sources of order in the soul."[80]

The background claim of this chapter has been that Walsh and

Douglass share with Voegelin (and Niebuhr) a too-meager understanding of the politics of Jesus, but that Walsh and Douglass do point to "experiences of faith" in Paul's writings that regulate his eschatology into a stream that moves in the direction of McClendon's "living as if." Let me, in conclusion, consider each of these claims in order.

ESCHATOLOGY AND REALISM (B)

As he considered the politics of Jesus, it is clear that Voegelin did consider cursorily the pragmatic historical implications of Jesus' life, but he derived only transcendental, not practical ethical, meaning from it. The death of Jesus is a "sacrificial death," paralleled by the death of Socrates, and the meaning of it is "representative, because it authenticates the truth of reality."[81] And the truth of reality is to be found in those experiences of the soul that are found equally in the philosophy of Socrates-Plato-Aristotle, and in the theophanic experience of Jesus and his apostles. Beyond a fuller articulation of transcendent experience, however, Voegelin remains silent on the practical instantiation of these experiences. I turn from this silence to another possibility that also seriously engages both the theophanic experience and its practical-political engagements.

In a series of books and articles, Yoder has uncovered an image of the life of Jesus that is both consistent with the canonical Christian writings and uncompromising in its assertion of a radically new ethic that results from the theophanic eruption of Jesus' proclamation against the ethic of his surrounding culture and the wider pagan world. We have seen pieces of this image in the course of the present exposition. It is at the level of ethics or the politics of Jesus, argues Yoder, that the meaning of Jesus' life is first and foremost to be sought. And at that level, we find a radical ethic of peace. This ethic has been appropriated with varying expressions by a long tradition of Christian thinkers from Augustine to Francis of Assisi to Tolstoy. And indeed, Voegelin does admit this as a possibility, but one that he rejects as impractical or utopian.[82] A key reason for this rejection is Voegelin's explicit denial that God acts in history in a material way. God "is in" the Beyond, and theophany is not a reordering in any material way of the order of existence as we find it. The life of Jesus cannot, therefore, imply a radical ethic of peace, since this would be a metastatic activity. But, as Yoder's comment on the proper perspective for ethical questioning implies, this is only the case if pacifism is calculated in terms of *effectiveness* rather than obedience.

In Yoder's reading, Jesus' life embodies a radical ethic of pacifism, of which his death—resulting from the confrontation between the ethics of Jesus' new Kingdom and the Jerusalem authorities—is the political outcome, and the pre-Constantinian churches its post-Resurrection manifestations. Yoder's analysis covers a great deal of ground, and it cannot be cursorily summarized here. I may say, however, that a serious consideration of Yoder's argument that Jesus' life and ministry are of "direct significance for social ethics" and, indeed, "normative for a contemporary Christian social ethic,"[83] implies a reconsideration for modern, post-Christendom Christians of such matters as the Christian's relation to political power and violence. It also calls for a reassessment and perhaps a reappropriation of such Christian doctrines and symbols as the Atonement,[84] the Kingdom of Heaven, the Crucifixion, and discipleship.[85] It is Yoder's firmly argued contention, moreover, that his reading of the meaning of Jesus' life is a reflection of how that life was understood cosmologically and ethically in the early church and in the writings of Paul.[86]

The core of that understanding includes an assumption of disempowered minority status as the locus for ethical reasoning, a rejection of violence, regardless of mundane consequence, a presumption that one's membership in the "heavenly" kingdom does not preclude certain forms of participation in earthly affairs and claims for justice and the like directed at earthly rulers (but that the claims of the former at all times have priority over those of the latter), and an anticipation that the claims of the two kingdoms will most likely clash at one or more points of contact.

This "political" interpretation of the life of Jesus must now be carried over to the content of Paul's vision as a regulating quality in his vision of the church and of the End. It is clear that Voegelin saw in Paul's writings, despite his purported eschatological near-"obsession," the vision of a healing force over the apocalyptic fantasies already emerging in Paul's time:

> The tension between order and disorder in the one reality dissociates in the phantasy of two realities following each other in time. This is

the disruption of consciousness that was to be healed, through the epiphany of Christ and Paul's vision of the Resurrected, but the assurance that there is indeed more to history than empire: The emergence of the truth is the historical even that constitutes meaning in history; the transfiguration is in progress in untransfigured history.[87]

This transfiguration, however, occurs through the faithful witness of the church to its calling. The church is for Paul the "administration" (*oikonomia*) of the gospel, a body of believers that expresses in its communal life the "as if" of the "then is now" and the "this is that." As I argued in chapter 4, the church is a necessarily political entity, because it is a concrete entity occupying a concrete space in the world, making specific claims about the rule of God over the secular powers and with specific replies to their truth-claims. Because, as I also noted, the role of the church is not to transform the world by means of political power but to witness to it by the power of the Spirit, Christians can agree with Voegelin that "the disorder in reality does not disappear even when the theophany in the person of Christ restabilizes the order of existence and becomes socially effective through the organization of the Church."[88] Nevertheless , Voegelin advocates caution:

> Though the faith that responds to the theophany immunizes the soul to a high degree against the trauma of continuing disorder, the breaking point is never too far off. The phantasy of two realities has remained constant in Western history from antiquity to the present.[89]

Voegelin sees in Paul a "wavering between the acceptance of the one reality in which the Incarnation occurs and indulgence in the metastatic expectation of a second reality to come in the time of the living." On the present reading, however, Paul's eschatology is not "metastatic," but "*as if.*" Clearly, there are in Paul's letters the eschatological "pictures" that McClendon notes, but these are regulated by other aspects of the theophany Paul experiences. Along with the experience of "salvation," which is itself entwined in eschatological symbolism, these experiences include most especially the experiences of freedom and love.

"Freedom" is for Paul linked to the more immediate experience of being unfree. The experience of reality includes for Paul the experience of the inner compulsion to satisfy appetites badly, of human imperfecti-

bility, of the inability to perform morally as well as one knows one
should, of being bound to forces, spiritual, intellectual, and physical, beyond human mastery. For Paul, the life of Jesus is the first exemplar of a
life of freedom from such bonds (Rom. 5:12ff; 8:3; 2 Cor. 5:21). Jesus'
death was, therefore, an injustice, but one through which, by love, he
founded a new community composed of his faithful disciples.[90] This
community, in all its imperfections is to continue the life of Jesus by
imitation (1 Cor. 4:16; 11:1; 1 Thess. 1:6; 2:14; Eph. 5:1).

In this view of Paul, then, the "transfiguration of history" has, indeed, begun, and the "human carrier" or "institutional carrier" is neither king nor empire but the Church. Grounded in the experience of
the "vision of the Resurrected," the church does, indeed, bear witness
to the theophany of Jesus, "placing the vision in the perspective of God's
way with the cosmos and man," perhaps with somewhat less attention
to the "perspective of the Metaxy" than Voegelin would like, because
of its attention to the prophetic aspects of the vision.[91] It does so with an
eschatology that accepts both the "now" and the "then," and with a
knowledge of a decided advance in the believer's insight into the meaning of existence by the peaceable example of Jesus that he or she is to
emulate. This insight removes the Niebuhrian requirement for realistic
responsibility to make history go as we would like by compromising the
peaceable insight with foreign overlays:

> Let it be remembered that the failure of the Constantinian vision to
> produce a reliably Christianized world is not the result of its having
> been criticized by the radicals or undermined by the sectarians. Con-
> stantine and the leaders of his kind of church had control, after all; that
> was the point of their ethical approach. If then this strategy of being
> the church identified with the political structure could ever work, if
> the commitment to be the soul of the total society by baptizing all its
> infants and counseling its statesmen was ever a viable vision, and could
> work, it has been given a good try! . . .
>
> This recognition that the caretaker function of the church in so-
> ciety will no longer work and is not needed does not in itself provide
> an argument for pacifism, although it does undermine the reasons
> which originally led to pacifism's being rejected. . . . Through the
> breakdown of Christendom, Christians find themselves again in
> the position of a voluntary minority. For our grasp of the mission of
> the church, it may now be more possible to admit the relevance of the

testimony of the pre-Constantinian church, predominantly pacifist from the New Testament times until after the age of Tertullian. In that age, the logic of thinking from a minority stance, in which saving society is not a conceivable imperative, was clear.[92]

Clearly, such an exposition can do little to assuage the fears of a gnostic revolt against reality until we make clear what the shape of this new community was to be. For Paul, whatever code, creed, and cult the Christian church might embody is an instantiation of the love demonstrated in the example of Jesus. Thus, to return to Tillich's observation, all "religiosity" is subordinate to Christ. From a modern, post-Christendom perspective, however, this conclusion can only be tenable if Christians recognize their minority status and give up their all-too traditional (triumphalist) aspirations for political power on the one hand, and if they recognize and reject either the pull toward this-worldly transformation of all things by force or romantic resignation on the other. Christians neither wrest control of history from the One who will bring it to completion, nor do they resign in the face of the evil—perhaps inexplicable in the "now"—that will one day ("then") be no more. The church is the concrete institutional "society" that prefigures the "then," but in Paul's vision there exists no intra-mundane transformation beyond this institutional representation of God's peaceable reign among men. In this way the church is truly a "proleptic eschaton."[93]

CONCLUSION

This chapter began with two suggestions. The first, offered by Murray Jardine and others, is that we reconsider Christianity with regard to the possibility it holds out for civilizational ordering. My brief analysis of this problem in the context of Voegelin's work leaves some doubt about such a possibility of assuming any intimate link between the existential representatives of political power and the members of Jesus' "Kingdom," at least if our "Christianity" is to have a content consistent with its own internal claims about the authoritativeness of Jesus. The internal contradictions of Constantinian forms of Christianity, which include many current American conceptions of state-church relations,[94] make one dubious.

The second suggestion, based on the historical-intellectual analyses of Mitchell and Waterman, is that Christianity has continued to be a source of political identity into the modern era. Following Voegelin, however, it seems clear in a general way that such attempts all involve "compromises" with the original witness to the Christian vision. These accommodations, powerful as they may be, remain unsatisfying because of their unfulfilled and unfulfillable demand to combine in a consistent way radically different languages of experience that point to radically different stances concerning the practical response to their experienced realities. These dissatisfactions lead to a desire for resolution that can be either civilizationally fruitful or disastrous.[95]

At the same time, it may be possible for the philosophical language of Voegelin and the ethics-language of, say, Yoder to link up. Even though the radical ethic that Yoder opens to view proposes a specific perspective for encountering the world, it contains a strategy of both assimilation and dialogue with that world, based on a cosmology of openness to the divine ground whose nature of love and peace is revealed in the theophany of Christ. This cosmology can encounter other "linguistic worlds" without resort to closure, using instead the language of such worlds and addressing their questions to demonstrate its own pre-eminence.[96] Voegelin's penetrating and magisterial theoretical account of order in history is not mistaken: it lacks only a closer consideration of the nature of the transcendent, divine ground that manifests itself historically in the theophany of Jesus as this was experienced in the lives of the apostles and replicated among believers in various times and places. Which way this question goes will determine what kind of authority Christ is and what kind of freedom of the spirit is available to us.

NOTES

1. See especially David Walsh, *After Ideology: Recovering the Spiritual Foundations of Freedom* (San Francisco: HarperCollins Publishers, 1990).

2. Murray Jardine, "Eric Voegelin's Interpretation(s) of Modernity: A Reconsideration of the Spiritual and Political Implications of Voegelin's Therapeutic Analysis," *Review of Politics* 4 (fall 1995) 581–605.

3. Joshua Mitchell, *Not By Reason Alone: Religion, History, and Identity in Early Modern Political Thought* (Chicago: University of Chicago Press, 1993);

A. M. C. Waterman, *Revolution, Economics and Religion: Christian Political Economy, 1798–1833* (Cambridge: Cambridge University Press, 1991).

4. John Milbank, *Theology and Social Theory: Beyond Secular Reason* (London: Blackwell Publishers, 1990), 389; Mitchell, *Reason Alone, passim,* but esp. 11–18.

5. David Walsh, "Voegelin's Response to the Disorder of the Age," in *The Review of Politics,* 46 (April 1984): 282.

6. Walsh, "Voegelin's Response," 283.

7. Bruce Douglass, "A Diminished Gospel: A Critique of Voegelin's Interpretation of Christianity," in *Eric Voegelin's Search for Order in History,* in ed. Stephen A. McKnight (Baton Rouge: Louisiana State University Press, 1978), 146 (his emphasis).

8. Douglass, "Diminished Gospel," 146.

9. Jardine, "Interpretation(s)," 584.

10. Jardine, "Interpretation(s)," 585.

11. Jardine, "Interpretation(s)," 585.

12. For a brief overview of Voegelin's analysis of modernity as essentially gnostic, see especially *Science, Politics, and Gnosticism* (Chicago: Henry Regnery, 1958), *passim,* and his *Autobiographical Reflections,* ed. Ellis Sandoz (Baton Rouge: Louisiana State University Press, 1989), 65–68.

13. Jardine, "Interpretation(s)," 596.

14. Jardine, "Interpretation(s)," 596, 597.

15. Peter von Sivers has made some interesting critical observations on Voegelin's "Eurocentrism." See his "Introduction," in Eric Voegelin, *The Middle Ages to Aquinas,* vol. 2 of *History of Political Ideas,* ed. Peter von Sivers (Columbia: The University of Missouri Press, 1997), 14–17.

16. Jardine, "Interpretation(s)," 605.

17. Paul Tillich, *Perspectives on 19th and 20th Century Protestant Theology,* ed. Carl E. Braaten (New York: Harper and Row, 1967), 106.

18. Tillich, *Perspectives on Protestant Theology,* 106–7.

19. Eric Voegelin, *The New Science of Politics* (Chicago: University of Chicago Press, 1952), 1–31.

20. Eric Voegelin, letter to Leo Strauss, December 9, 1942, in *Faith and Political Philosophy: The Correspondence Between Leo Strauss and Eric Voegelin, 1934–1964,* trans. and ed. Peter Emberley and Barry Cooper (University Park: Pennsylvania State University Press, 1993), 8–9.

21. Eric Voegelin, *Revolution and the New Science,* ed. Barry Cooper, vol. 6 of *History of Political Ideas* (Columbia: University of Missouri Press, 1998), 214–15.

22. Eric Voegelin, "The Growth of the Race Idea," *The Review of Politics* 2 (1940): 289–91; *Revolution and the New Science,* 31–34; 71–81; Eric Voegelin, *Renaissance and Reformation,* ed. David Morse and William Thompson, vol. 4 of *History of Political Ideas* (Columbia: University of Missouri Press, 1998), 131–32.

23. Eric Voegelin, *The Later Middle Ages,* ed. David Walsh, vol. 3 of *History of Political Ideas* (Columbia: University of Missouri Press, 1998), 107–8; cf. Voegelin, *Science, Politics, and Gnosticism,* 108–9.

24. Voegelin, *Revolution and the New Science,* 59; cf. *New Science,* 3–22.

25. Voegelin, *Revolution and the New Science,* 149.

26. Voegelin, *Revolution and the New Science,* 56.

27. John Howard Yoder, *The Priestly Kingdom: The Gospel as Social Ethics* (Notre Dame, Ind.: University of Notre Dame Press, 1984), 135.

28. Roland Bainton, *Christian Attitudes Toward War and Peace: A Historical Survey and Critical Re-evaluation* (Nashville, Tenn.: Abingdon Press, 1960), 53.

29. A brief history of the period may be found in Kenneth Scott Latourette, *Beginnings to 1500,* vol. 1 of *A History of Christianity* (San Francisco: Harper and Row, 1975), 91–108. Latourette also speaks of Christianity's accommodations to paganism and the Graeco-Roman civilization as "compromises," but with regret, not praise.

30. What follows is a close summary of John Howard Yoder's historical analysis in *Priestly Kingdom,* 135–47.

31. This division is already clearly visible in St. Ambrose, "Duties of the Clergy." See *St. Ambrose: Select Works and Letters,* trans. H. de Romestin, vol. 10 of *A Select Library of Nicene and Post-Nicene Fathers,* ed. Philip Schaff and Henry Wace (Grand Rapids, Mich.: Wm. B. Eerdmans, 1955), 1–89.

32. Aurelius Augustine, *Letters of St. Augustine, Bishop of Hippo,* trans. J. G. Cunningham, vol. 6 of *The Works of Aurelius Augustine, Bishop of Hippo,* ed. Marcus Dods (Edinburgh, 1872), Letter 93, 400–412.

33. Yoder, *Priestly Kingdom,* 140.

34. Eric Voegelin, "The Gospel and Culture," in *Published Essays, 1966–1985,* ed. Ellis Sandoz, vol. 12 of *The Collected Works of Eric Voegelin* (Baton Rouge: Louisiana State University Press, 1990), 173.

35. Thomas Altizer, "A New History and a New But Ancient God? A Review Essay," review of Eric Voegelin, *The Ecumenic Age,* vol. 4 of *Order and History* (Baton Rouge: Louisiana State University Press, 1974), in *Journal of the American Academy of Religion* 43 (1975): 759.

36. Voegelin, *Ecumenic Age,* 241.

37. Voegelin, "Gospel and Culture," 188; Voegelin, *Ecumenic Age,* 241.

38. Voegelin, "Gospel and Culture," 192.

39. Voegelin, *Ecumenic Age,* 248, 249.

40. Douglass, "Diminished Gospel," (his emphasis), 153; Walsh, *After Ideology,* 128–29.

41. Voegelin, *Science, Politics, and Gnosticism,* 108–114.

42. Walsh, "Voegelin's Response," 284.

43. Walsh, "Voegelin's Response," 284.

44. Voegelin, "Gospel and Culture," 190.
45. Voegelin, "Gospel and Culture," 190.
46. Voegelin, "Gospel and Culture," 193. The term is from *Col.* 2:9.
47. Voegelin, *Ecumenic Age,* 258.
48. Voegelin, *Ecumenic Age,* 256.
49. "The symbol 'Christ' changes its meaning in the transition from the open field of theophany to the realm of dogmatic construction. If the question of the 'historicity' of Christ is raised with the 'Christ' of dogma in mind, difficulties will inevitably arise. For the 'Christ' of Nicaea and Chalcedon is not the reality of theophanic history that confronts us in the Pauline vision of the Resurrected; and to invent a special kind of 'history,' disregarding the theophanic reality on which the dogma is based, in order to endow the Christ of the dogma with 'historicity,' would make no sense. The trinitarian and christological dogma can be made intelligible only in terms of its own history, as a protective device that will shield the oneness of the Unknown God against confusion with the experiences of divine presence in the myths of the intracosmic gods, in mythospeculation, and in the noetic and pneumatic luminosity of consciousness." Voegelin, *Ecumenic Age,* 259–60. For Paul's easy elision from this experience to a "therefore" of ethics, see *1 Thess.* 1:13–14, 1:6–7; *Gal.* 5:13–26; or *Rom.* 8:1ff.
50. Voegelin, "Gospel and Culture," 199. A particularly useful illustration of this counter-argument may be found in Voegelin's analysis of the philosophy and theology of John Locke in *Revolution and the New Science,* 172–79.
51. Voegelin, *Ecumenic Age,* 269.
52. Voegelin, *Ecumenic Age,* 269.
53. Walsh, "Voegelin's Response," 278.
54. Milbank, *Theology,* 380ff.
55. Walsh, "Voegelin's Response," 275–76.
56. Walsh, "Voegelin's Response," 276.
57. Walsh, "Voegelin's Response," 277.
58. Hannah Arendt, *On Revolution* (New York: Penguin, 1965), 20, 38, 87–88; Augustine, *The City of God,* XV.1, v.
59. Niccolo Machiavelli, *The Prince,* chpt. xv, in *Machiavelli: The Prince and Other Works,* trans. and ed. Allan H. Gilbert (New York: Hendricks House, 1964), 141; Reinhold Niebuhr, *Christian Realism and Political Problems* (New York: Charles Scribner's Sons, 1953), 119–46, 184–203; Reinhold Niebuhr, *Beyond Tragedy: Essays on the Christian Interpretation of History* (New York: Charles Scribner's Sons, 1937), 155–69; Reinhold Niebuhr, *Moral Man and Immoral Society* (New York: Charles Scribner's Sons, 1932), xii–xiii, xx–xxv.
60. For an example, see Augustine, *Enarrationes in Psalmos* 136, cited in *The Political Writings of St. Augustine,* ed. Henry Paolucci (South Bend, Ind.: Regnery/Gateway, 1962), 317.

61. Albert Schweitzer, *The Quest of the Historical Jesus: A Critical Study of Its Progress from Reimarus to Wrede* (New York: Macmillan, 1948).

62. Ernst Benz, *Evolution and Christian Hope: Man's Concept of the Future From the Early Fathers to Teilhard de Chardin,* trans. Heinz G. Frank (New York: Doubleday, 1968), 20–21.

63. Benz, *Evolution,* 25.

64. Benz, *Evolution,* 26–34.

65. Gerhart Niemeyer, "Are There 'Intelligible Parts' of History?" in *The Philosophy of Order: Essays on History, Consciousness and Politics,* ed. Peter J. Opitz and Gregor Sebba (Stuttgart: Klett-Cotta, 1981), 312.

66. Neimeyer, "Intelligible Parts," 313.

67. Niemeyer, "Intelligible Parts," 313; Augustine, *City of God,* V.xxiv; VIII.ix.

68. Walsh, *After Ideology,* 154.

69. Walsh, *After Ideology,* 169.

70. Walsh, *After Ideology,* 183; for a picture of what this restoration would look like, see 191–278.

71. Walsh, *After Ideology,* 202.

72. Walsh, *After Ideology,* 221–22.

73. Yoder, *Priestly Kingdom,* 139.

74. Voegelin, *Autobiographical Reflections,* 68–69; Eric Voegelin, *Israel and Revelation,* vol. 1 of *Order and History* (Baton Rouge: Louisiana State University Press, 1956), 446–58.

75. James Wm. McClendon, Jr., *Doctrine,* vol. 2 of *Systematic Theology* (Nashville, Tenn.: Abingdon Press, 1994), 69.

76. McClendon, *Doctrine,* 77 (his emphasis).

77. McClendon, *Doctrine,* 77.

78. McClendon, *Doctrine,* 98–99.

79. John Howard Yoder, *The Original Revolution: Essays on Christian Pacifism* (Scottdale: Herald Press, 1971), 52.

80. Eric Voegelin, *From Enlightenment to Revolution,* ed. John H. Hallowell (Durham, N.C.: Duke University Press, 1975), 275n7.

81. Voegelin, "Gospel and Culture," 186.

82. Voegelin, "People of God," 979.

83. Yoder, *Politics of Jesus,* 23.

84. For example, see J. Denny Weaver, "Atonement for the NonConstantinian Church," in *Modern Theology* 6 (July 1990): 309–23.

85. Yoder, *Politics of Jesus,* 97, 132–34.

86. Yoder, *Politics of Jesus,* 163–232. Although the vast majority of Christian ethicists have been concerned with the Christian gospel, they have ultimately looked elsewhere for their sources of social ethics. The traditional arguments of

Christian theology, being permeated by pagan philosophy, deny that Jesus displays any social or political ethical norm that Christians can take seriously. In this case, the life of Jesus as a source for ethics is irrelevant, and we must look elsewhere (Yoder, *Politics of Jesus,* 11–23, 99–114). It may, indeed, be the case that Christians take with them a "very moderate amount of freight" from the example of Jesus as they cross the bridge from "sectarian" community to civilizational force (as they address the concerns of the world in the world's terms, as Voegelin argues they must to remain effective), but "the substance of ethics must be reconstructed" from other material, such as natural law, utilitarianism, or even emotivism (Yoder, *Politics of Jesus,* 19–20, 140, 116; Yoder, *Original Revolution,* 138). If this be so, then "it cannnot have been [Jesus'] intention—or at least we cannot take it to have been his achievement—to provide any precise guidance in the field of ethics. His apocalypticism and his radical monotheism may teach us to be modest; his personalism may teach us to cherish the values of face-to-face relationships, but as to the stuff of our decision-making, we shall have to have other sources of help." Yoder, *Politics of Jesus,* 19.

87. Voegelin, *Ecumenic Age,* 302.

88. Voegelin, *Ecumenic Age,* 302–3.

89. Voegelin, *Ecumenic Age,* 303.

90. For an exposition of the founding experiences undergirding Paul's idea of Christian community, see Robert Banks, *Paul's Idea of Community: The Early House Churches in Their Historical Setting* (Grand Rapids, Mich.: Wm. B. Eerdmans, 1980), 23–25.

91. Voegelin, *Ecumenic Age,* 248–49.

92. Yoder, *Original Revolution,* 128–29.

93. Niemeyer, "Intelligible Parts," 311.

94. Cf. Yoder, *Priestly Kingdom,* 172–95.

95. Von Sivers, "Introduction," 10–14.

96. Yoder, *Priestly Kingdom,* 48–54.

CONCLUSION

In quest of reality(?) Existence is not a fact(?) These seem bizarre formulations when we first hear them, but Eric Voegelin proceeds to convince us that they reflect a truth of the human condition that we might not at first imagine. We have seen the elusiveness of reality, of existence, in every chapter of this introduction to his thought and to his quest for reality. This quest turns out not to be merely an arcane philosophical enterprise that we can as well leave to the mystics and theologians. Deformation of reality leads to bad things, as Voegelin once charitably reminded a friend.[1] When "bad things" includes the totalitarian regimes of our century, deformation and recovery of reality are no longer a philosopher's parlor games but the serious business of politics.

And yet, what *is* the serious business of politics for Voegelin? What of Voegelin's "actual" politics? One may be inclined to ask: was he Social Democrat or Christian Conservative? Democrat or Republican? In the introductory chapter, I noted McAllister's review of Voegelin's (and Leo Strauss's) links to American conservatism, and I noted the general difficulties in locating Voegelin's everyday practical politics. His occasional seeming alliances with "conservative" causes were of secondary importance to his scholarly activities, and perhaps even to his conception of political responsibility as a citizen either of Austria or of the United States of America. Voegelin has been criticized in this vein, for example, for being insufficiently attentive to the problem of American racism, especially white racism toward African Americans. Voegelin's silence on this particular matter may have been strategic—an émigré scholar living in the Deep South in the 1940s would have to have been circumspect in his remarks. The silence may also have been intellectual—the two race books and the 1940 synopsis said all that Voegelin had to say on the

179

matter.[2] In either case, however, Voegelin's silence seems to side-step an important political problem. There is a good deal more, one might argue, to say about racism in America from a political or sociological perspective. Where, then, do we locate Voegelin on the political map with respect to other practical political problems of his time? Was he equally silent about them?

First, let us recall the basic principle that such an effort at "locating" becomes all too easily an episode of partisan ideological debate. Voegelin was a frequent target of such categorization, being identified as "a Communist, a Fascist, a National Socialist, an old Liberal, a new Liberal, a Jew, a Catholic, a Protestant, a Platonist, a neo-Augustinian, a Thomist, and . . . a Hegelian." He considered the advocates of such activity to be "objects of inquiry" who could never be "partners in discussion."[3] They were excellent representatives "of the intellectual destruction and corruption that characterize the contemporary academic world."[4] Thus, labeling Voegelin as belonging to a particular ideological camp can serve no edifying purpose. It merely helps to distort the very science of politics he sought to re-establish.

Second, a philosophically informed reticence to participate in ideological partisanship does not totally prevent political participation. Neither does it foreclose engagement in debate. "There are intellectual situations," Voegelin declared, "where everybody is so wrong that it is enough to maintain the opposite in order to be at least partially right."[5] Such an episode occurred in a specifically political vein in the Austrian politics of the 1920s and 1930s. Voegelin recalled it as a time for careful political judgment, which seemed beyond the ken of left- and right-wing ideologists alike:

> There was an Austrian government that firmly resisted any advance
> of National Socialism but was endangered in its effectiveness by the
> opposition, because the Social Democratic party, due to its Marxist
> ideology, did not want to admit that a small country like the Austrian
> Republic had to accommodate itself to the political pressures of the
> time. The Austrian veering toward Mussolini as a protection against
> the worse evil of Hitler apparently was beyond the comprehension of
> ardent Marxists, who could do nothing but yell "Fascism."[6]

Beyond these kinds of analyses, Voegelin's own direct participation in electoral and government politics was limited to voting, but this activity, too, involved practical political judgments that were informed at least in part by Voegelin's theoretical concerns as well as by strategic judgments:

> For two reasons I veered more in the direction of the Christian Socialist government. In the first place, the Christian Socialist politicians represented the traditions of European culture, whereas the Marxists at least overtly did not. . . . [Second,] What struck me most at the time was the stupidity of ideologists as represented by the leaders of the Social Democratic party. While I agreed with them regarding economic and social politics, the silliness of their apocalyptic dream in the face of the impending Hitlerian apocalypse was simply too much to stomach.[7]

Similarly, Voegelin had carefully considered the Austrian situation in the late 1930s, and he had calculated the risks of remaining in Vienna as a known opponent of the National Socialists:

> A profound emotional shock came in the critical moments of the destruction of Austria. I would have left Vienna long before 1938 if I had not assumed that Austria was safe in its defense against National Socialism. On the basis of my historically founded political knowledge, I considered it impossible that the Western democracies would permit the annexation of Austria by Hitler, because the event obviously would be the first of a series that would culminate in a world war. . . . It came as a great surprise to me that the Western powers did nothing.[8]

His misjudgment meant that he had to make hurried and dangerous preparations to leave Austria before his arrest, which would have been inevitable as soon as the politically important figures had been imprisoned.

Third, this experience, others like it, and Voegelin's own analysis of liberalism seem to have reinforced a skepticism regarding liberal democracy that we see articulated again in 1952 in the conclusion to *The New Science of Politics* and in his analyses of the Western crisis. As with the Austrian Christian Socialists, so Western liberal democracy generally seemed a carrier, as it were, of the Western tradition of civilization. For this reason it was, in specific historical instances, a regime to be supported:

Western society as a whole, thus, is a deeply stratified civilization in which the American and English democracies represent the oldest, most firmly consolidated stratum of civilizational tradition, while the German area represents its most progressively modern stratum. In this situation there is a glimmer of hope, for the American and English democracies which most solidly in their institutions represent the truth of the soul are, at the same time, existentially the strongest powers. But it will require all our efforts to kindle this glimmer into a flame by repressing Gnostic corruption and restoring the forces of civilization. At present the fate is in the balance.[9]

For at least two reasons, however, Voegelin's support for liberal democracy could not be unqualified. First, liberal democracy is an "institutional vessel" that does not guarantee its own contents:

His [a specific supporter of liberal democracy's] faith is unshaken that the combination of consent by the people and individual rights will always be the institutional vessel for the right spirit. In spite of the fact that evil spirits have grown lustily in these vessels in several instances and ultimately broken them, as in the case of the Weimar Republic, the problem of the spirit has not been dissociated in his faith from the problem of the institutions. Against such faith there is no argument; we can but hope that ultimately it will be justified by history. Our respect for the faith, however, should not prevent us from analyzing the assumptions on which it rests.[10]

Second, when Voegelin did analyze these underlying assumptions, he concluded that liberalism is less a coherent political doctrine, and still less a coherent philosophical school of thought, than it is a series of movements that are phases of a larger series of Western political and ideological movements in the modern era. Liberalism can be described in terms of a set of general attitudes toward political rule, economics, religion, and science, but these broadly characterized programmatic attitudes, as part of the European revolutionary movements since the Reformation, have become philosophically untenable in all but their weakest expression. Accordingly, any allegiance to the liberal perspective—which includes a broad range of possibilities—must be strongly attenuated, even while we recognize the recent historical role some Western liberal democracies have played in preserving Western civilization against the onslaught of ideological revolutionaries: "In the light of these considerations we can say that, on the one hand, liberalism decidely has a voice in the political situation of our time; on the other hand, however, today the ideas of autonomous, immanent reason and of the autonomous subject of economics are scarcely alive and fruitful; thus, the classical liberalism of the secularist and bourgeois-capitalist stamp may be pronounced dead."[11]

Whatever one may say of Voegelin's "conservative" leanings, they consist of neither a neo-classical liberal reaction to the welfare state as in the American conservatism of the 1950s to the 1990s, nor of a wistful longing for the *ancien régimes* of pre-Reformation Europe. Although Voegelin clearly considered the life of the spirit that is encapsulated in the achievements of the High Middle Ages to be a kind of high-water mark of European civilization, he eschewed a nostalgic desire for a return to that period or any other.[12] Such a longing would belong to the class of utopian political aspirations that Voegelin rejected. The longing induced by the texts of his dead friends, however, points to a life of the spirit whose political embodment remains elusive, even if its analytical possibilities for a science of politics are manifest in Voegelin's texts. McAllister and Ranieri both capture this political elusiveness in their separate recognition that Voegelin's political analyses are sufficiently unprogrammatic in political intent that his "politics" in any prescriptive sense evades ideological categorization.[13]

In a further observation concerning Voegelin's practical politics, I note that political developments of the kind he experienced in the Anschluss of 1938 play a role throughout his *Autobiographical Reflections*. The political affairs of the day impinge on the scholarly enterprise in numerous ways—scholars are denied opportunities for teaching positions, are removed, must flee, or are otherwise affected by the political situation.[14] Conversely, political events also stimulate scholarly research. Ideological diatribe in the public square may stimulate inquiry into the nature of ideologies, their content, logic, and form, while the occasion of a civil war may stimulate an inquiry into the theoretical basis of the state that is established in its aftermath.[15]

Beyond these episodic practical considerations, Voegelin generally had little to say publicly or in published works about specific policy questions. Although he gave a variety of public lectures outside of the university setting, he did not embrace the role of public intellectual, preferring to write as a scientist of politics. His general silence does not mean, of course, that such remarks were absent from his personal life or from his teaching activities. There are at least two ways in which Voegelin's scholarly and pedagogical activity must be understood not as an isolated, apolitical activity, but as a scientific enterprise whose critical content makes it a kind of citizen participation.

First, recall that intellectual corruption is not only a social and spiritual phenomenon, but also a political one. For example, Voegelin recalled that Karl Kraus' "Die Fackel" (The Torch) was "read by everybody among the younger people whom I knew," and that it "was the intellectual and moraliste background that gave all of us a critical understanding of politics and especially of the function of the press in the disintegration of German and Austrian society, preparing the way for National Socialism."[16] Thus, a "concern with language was part of the resistance against ideologies, which destroy language inasmuch as the ideological thinker has lost contact with reality and develops symbols for expressing not reality but his state of alienation from it."[17] From this vantage point, Voegelin was not, as a matter of principle, removed from social commentary. His extended reflections on the German society of the 1920s and 1930s and its corruptive effects on postwar German society, and again his critique of the German university of the 1960s, are only two examples of his distinct willingness to engage in the issues of the day from the perspective of political corruption and its political effects. Nevertheless, as a scientist of politics he engaged these issues at a higher level of abstraction and with a consistent view to much more theoretically complex reference points than would be expected in the everyday "social commentary" of a public intellectual.[18]

A second form of political activity took place in Voegelin's activities as a teacher. Although Voegelin was "politically an entirely unimportant figure," one young Marxist student in the 1930s was (agreeably) clear and regretful that "when we come to power, we have to kill you."[19] Nevertheless, Voegelin recalled amiable relations with the "young radicals" of the working-class left who attended his seminar in the 1930s at the Volkshochschule in Vienna. The "wild debates" that moved from the classroom to coffee-house discussions in the late evenings continued for many years with the most cordial of relations. Indeed, Voegelin helped some of the young socialists flee Austria after the German occupation. At the same time, relations with the middle-class National Socialist students at the University were much more tense. Voegelin's removal from his University teaching position followed immediately upon the National Socialists' ascent to power, and the attempt to arrest him followed not long afterwards. In both cases, it is clear that Voegelin's role as a teacher had political overtones. For him political science was always a form of resistance to the ideological radicalism espoused by his students of both the left and the right. His untenable situation after the Anschluss is evidence of this claim, and were this not the case more generally, totalitarian and dictatorial regimes would not be intent on silencing and even murdering scholars and intellectuals like him.

Voegelin's science of politics sounds a cautionary note that certainly gives the appearance of a kind of "conservatism," indicated perhaps by a sober reservation regarding any sort of transformatory claim for the political enterprise. While every society may be a cosmion, a little world of meaning,[20] that meaning has transgressed the boundaries of the humanly viable under the divine presence when it assumes a gnostic, ideological, transformatory, libidinous, or magical mode. Voegelin's science was a scholarly enterprise of analyzing and ultimately rejecting this move, and it was carried on for the most part at a more abstract level than the ordinary discourse of practical politics would permit. The everyday common sense of Karl Kraus and the common sense embedded in European civilization that might be retained in a particular political party platform are certainly important barriers to political utopias and murderous disorder. Alongside such barriers and others like them, a proper science of politics serves the political function of recovering and sustaining the order of existence among its students and practitioners, even if this function takes place at an abstract level.

The theory of consciousness that Voegelin developed as a part of his political science was an effort to grapple with the core of our lived experience. It points to the mystery of existence, and to the potential for deforming that mystery and thereby our very existence. A theory of consciousness is the product of an act of reflecting in an all-inclusive way on the comprehensive reality in which we participate and of which we are a part. It is an activity in the quest for that comprehensive reality within which we must orient ourselves and within which we have our existence. In the same way, further reflection on the activity of philosophy shows it to be both an activity of revealing the comprehensive reality as we reflect on it and articulate our reflections, and also an activity of resistance to disorder within the comprehensive reality. Politically, those regimes representing spiritual disorder, decay, and untruth in existence find themselves at odds with the representatives of the truth of the soul, and this conflict can lead to bad ends.

The quest for reality, if it is to be serious about politics, must include an account of human motivation in a theory of human consciousness. This need becomes especially apparent when the regimes a philosopher encounters can only be described as murderous. What motivates such murder? What creates an oppressive closure to the open-ended nature of existence so that some men seek to make the world over in their own image, as though the world of men were an artifact to be manipulated at will? The experiences of alienation, loss of faith in reality experienced, closure to divine transcendence, and desire to give the experience of alienation a concrete worldly significance lead to the aberrations of ideological politics when the forces of order are no longer sufficient to maintain a hedge against the wishful politics of alienation and magic.

One might, in an introduction to Voegelin's thought, examine his extensive analysis of the Israelite and Greek experiences of order, or, preceding them, the long history of mankind in cosmological empires, or, after them, the history of ecumenical empires and the "orthodox" empires of Islam and Western European Christendom that eventually followed.[21] But one must make choices. For an understanding of Voegelin's interpretation of modern Western politics, his treatment of the role of Christianity in the advent of modernity and in the modern state in the West is perhaps most crucial. Certainly, Voegelin's conception of the role of Christianity in the modern European polity provides revealing insights into his conception of the relationship of the life of the spirit and the everyday exigencies of fashioning political order in the concrete instance. It requires a balance for Voegelin in which neither the needs of the spirit living in the truth of reality, nor the concrete demands of people living together, are forgotten.[22]

In the continuing quest for reality in the modern era, we end where we began, with a question: What is freedom of the spirit, and how can it be made available to us? In the liberal societies of postmodern, postindustrial Europe and North America, such questions, having been sundered from the "secular" political realm, can hardly find public expression, let alone a public answer. For Voegelin, however, politics remains an activity of spiritual substance. When the life of the spirit is removed from considerations in the political realm, it is a loss, not a gain. Hence the impoverished politics of the administrative state, that universal and homogenous behemoth of the left and right Hegelians.[23] In that shadow, we may give Voegelin the final word:

The life of Reason in the classic sense is existence in tension between Life and Death. The concept of the tension will sharpen the awareness for this In-Between character of existence. . . . Man experiences himself as tending beyond his human imperfection toward the perfection of the divine ground that moves him. The spiritual man . . . as he is moved in his quest of the ground, moves somewhere between knowledge and ignorance. . . . Because of the divine presence that gives the unrest its direction, the unfolding of noetic consciousness is experienced as a process of immortalizing. With their discovery of man as the *zoon noun echon,* the classic philosophers have discovered man to be more than a *thnetos,* a mortal: he is an unfinished being, moving from the imperfection of death in this life to the perfection of life in death.[24]

NOTES

1. Gregor Sebba, "Prelude and Variations on the Theme of Eric Voegelin," in *Eric Voegelin's Thought: A Critical Appraisal,* ed. Ellis Sandoz (Durham, N.C.: Duke University Press, 1982), 8–9.

2. Manfred Henningsen, "Voegelin's Overcoming of Race as *Ersatzpolitik*" (paper delivered at the annual meeting of the American Political Science Association, Boston, September 1998), 4–5.

3. Eric Voegelin, *Autobiographical Reflections,* ed. Ellis Sandoz (Baton Rouge: Louisiana State University Press, 1989), 46.

4. Voegelin, *Autobiographical Reflections,* 46.

5. Voegelin, *Autobiographical Reflections,* 46.

6. Voegelin, *Autobiographical Reflections,* 40.

7. Voegelin, *Autobiographical Reflections,* 40–41.

8. Voegelin, *Autobiographical Reflections,* 42.

9. Eric Voegelin, *The New Science of Politics* (Chicago: University of Chicago Press, 1952), 7.

10. Eric Voegelin, "Nietzsche, the Crisis, and the War," in *Journal of Politics* 6 (1944): 188.

11. Eric Voegelin, "Liberalism and Its History," trans. Mary and Keith Algozin, in *The Review of Politics* 36 (1974): 520.

12. Eric Voegelin, *Science, Politics, and Gnosticism* (Chicago: Henry Regnery, 1968), 15, 21.

13. Ted V. McAllister, *Revolt Against Modernity: Leo Strauss, Eric Voegelin, and the Search for a Postliberal Order* (Lawrence: University Press of Kansas, 1996), 260–79; John J. Ranieri, *Eric Voegelin and the Good Society* (Columbia: University of Missouri Press, 1995), 245–56.

14. Voegelin, *Autobiographical Reflections*, 6–7; 42–43.

15. Voegelin, *Autobiographical Reflections*, 24–5.

16. Voegelin, *Autobiographical Reflections*, 17.

17. Voegelin, *Autobiographical Reflections*, 17–18.

18. Eric Voegelin, "Hitler und die Deutschen," (unpublished transcript, 1964); Eric Voegelin, "The German University and the Order of German Society: A Reconsideration of the Nazi Era," in *Published Essays, 1966–1985,* ed. Ellis Sandoz, vol. 12 of *The Collected Works of Eric Voegelin* (Baton Rouge: Louisiana State University Press, 1990), 1–35. Other exceptions may include the following: Eric Voegelin, "Necessary Moral Bases for Communication in a Democracy," in *Problems of Communication in a Pluralistic Society,* ed. Reynolds C. Seitz et al. (Milwaukee, Wis.: Marquette University Press, 1956), 53–68; Eric Voegelin, "Some Problems of German Hegemony," in *Journal of Politics* 3 (1940): 154–68.

19. Voegelin, *Autobiographical Reflections*, 43, 86.

20. Voegelin, *New Science of Politics*, 27.

21. For this formulation, see Voegelin, *Autobiographical Reflections*, 82; see also Eric Voegelin, *The Middle Ages to Aquinas,* ed. Peter von Sivers, vol. 2 of *The History of Political Ideas* (Columbia: University of Missouri Press, 1997), 15 and 188n.14.

22. "If philosophical existence is existence in awareness of man's humanity as constituted by his tension toward the divine ground, and if this awareness is in the practice of existence realized by the Platonic *periagoge*—the turning toward the ground—then alienation is the turning away from the ground toward a self that is imagined to be human without being constituted by its relation to the divine presence. . . . Turning toward, and turning away from, the ground become the fundamental categories descriptive of the states of order and disorder in human existence." Voegelin, *Autobiographical Reflections*, 100–101.

23. Francis Fukuyama, *The End of History and the Last Man* (New York: Avon Books, 1992); Barry Cooper, *The End of History: An Essay in Modern Hegelianism* (Toronto: University of Toronto Press, 1984), 244–327; Alasdair MacIntyre, *After Virtue* (Notre Dame, Ind.: University of Notre Dame Press, 1982), 30–35, 70–72, 75–78.

24. Eric Voegelin, "Reason, The Classic Experience," in *Published Essays, 1966–1985,* ed. Ellis Sandoz, 279.

INDEX

Albigensians, 101

alienation, 14, 67, 69; ideology and, 186

Ambrose, St., 142n22

Aquinas, St. Thomas, 21, 24, 61n46, 83–4, 129, 138, 142n20

Aristotle, 21, 24, 80, 83, 150, 158, 162, 167; catharsis, treatment of, 87; in Christianity, 135, 137, 155; consciousness, treatment of, 13; noesis, treatment of, 82; political science of, 151, 156; Voegelin's interpretation of, 71; wonder, experience of, 107

Augustine, St. Aurelius, 24, 142n20, 146, 174, 161; history, philosophy of, 161–2; peace, ethic of, 167

Bach, Johann Sebastian, 142n20

Bakunin, Mikhail, 67

Becker, Carl, 109

Billington, James, 109

Bonhoeffer, Dietrich, 143n42

Bosch, Hieronymus, 119n52, 112

Camus, Albert, 13

Christendom, 140; and textual interpretation, 131; Voegelin's view of, 131

Cicero, 35

Cohn, Norman, 109, 113

"common sense" tradition, 80, 82, 185

Commons, John R., 81

Comte, Auguste, 111, 115

consciousness: and ideas, 93–4; participating, 2, 33–38; philosophy of, 15–6, 17, 21–22, 29–31, 185; pneumopathology and, 14; structure of, 15, 36–40

conversatism, 19, 20

Constantinianism, 98, 126, 139, 140; characteristics of, 153–4; and eschatology, 159–60; and ethics, 153, 163

Copernicus, Nicolaus, 9

corruption: characterization of, 127–8; German intellectual, 126, 128–30, 150, 184; intellectual, 8, 126, 127–30, 139, 155, 184; political, 127–128

Cromwell, Oliver, 113

d'Alembert, Jean le Rond, 112

Diderot, Denis, 112

Doderer, Heimito von, 119n43

Dostoyevsky, Fyodor, 13

Edward, Jonathan, 81

189

ABOUT THE AUTHOR

THOMAS HEILKE is associate professor of political science at the University of Kansas. He is the author of numerous articles, including two on Eric Voegelin's political thought, and of several books, including *Voegelin on the Idea of Race: An Analysis of Modern European Racism* and *Nietzsche's Tragic Regime: Culture, Aesthetics, and Political Education*. He lives in Lawrence, Kansas, with his wife, Tara, and their two children.